Spiritspeak

Sharing Some Very
Good News

Nelson P. Miller

Spiritspeak—sharing some very good news.

Miller, Nelson P.

Published by:

Crown Management LLC – September 2018

1527 Pineridge Drive
Grand Haven, MI 49417
USA

ISBN-13: 978-1-7322387-8-7

All Rights Reserved
© 2018 Nelson P. Miller
c/o 111 Commerce Avenue S.W.
Grand Rapids, MI 49503
(616) 560-0632
millern57@gmail.com

For those who wish freedom—forever.

Contents

Foreword	1

1 Creation   5
Beginning. Purpose. Participation. Perfection. Demonstration. Light. Darkness. People.

2 Creator   23
Transcendent. Sovereign. Word. Father. Spirit. Reconciler. Rescuer. Restorer. Giver. Love. Supreme.

3 Coming   47
Ancestry. Incarnation. Presentation. Announcement. Maturation. Nature.

4 Immersion   57
Messenger. Message. Immersing. Essence. Passage. Persistence. Effect. Tempting.

5 Mission   76
Announcing. Teaching. Revealing. Healing. Liberating. Raising. Attracting. Students. Feeding. Prayer.

6 Character   104
Sacred. Human. Liberator. Master. Celebrant. Guide. Transfigured.

7 Rejection   120
Opposed. Divided. Derided. Suffering. Plotting. Anointing. Betrayal. Garden.

8 Execution   141
Arrest. Trial. Sentence. Crucifixion. Death. Burial.

9 Restoration   157
Resurrection. Appearances. Witnesses. Ascension. Alighting. Empowering. Persecution. Martyrs.

10 Return   181
Recovery. Fulfillment. Succession. End. Timing. Way. Power. Rescue. Torment. Judgment. Fury. Victory. New. Eternity. Destiny.

Conclusion   210

Foreword

I am a lawyer, law professor, and dean—not the sort of professional to whom you'd first think of turning for some very good news. Lawyers usually deal with crises like divorces, bankruptcies, and criminal charges, or with business, government, and regulation—not so much with history, morality, and spirituality. Yet lawyers train to organize evidence into coherent patterns and to tell true and deeply meaningful accounts out of those patterns. As a trial lawyer and law professor, and having published dozens of books, I've been doing exactly that for quite some time: telling important, rich, and complex true stories. I've also been studying good news, bad news, and the best news very closely for quite some time, while writing quite a bit about it.

In those studies, and writings, I came to realize that the most-popular form and format of the best news, that which we know popularly as the *good news*, can make for difficult reading. The good news usually appears in the form of four parallel accounts that overlap in part but are also distinct from one another—much like witnesses testifying at trial, each with their own recollection of and perspective on the same events. The traditional format then follows the four parallel accounts with a brief, breathless history of how the good news first spread. The traditional format then presents correspondence by several different writers to many different audiences, setting out doctrine drawn from the four parallel accounts, direct witnesses of the historical events, and ancient writings that preceded them. The traditional format concludes with a long, fantastical prediction of future events, written either in an allegorical style or predicting an exotic end, or some of both. I am an inveterate and sophisticated reader, and yet the traditional format challenges me. It might also challenge you.

The religious terms and ancient names and places that the traditional account contains, and the meaning-making history of those things, further complicate the reading. The writings assume at least some knowledge of various religious terms and ancient figures and places, of which the modern reader has zero knowledge unless already a well-trained student of the writings. The writings' meaning depends in large part on knowing the terms, figures, and places, and their history. And so as one reads the traditional account, one constantly asks, *About what, whom, and where are they writing?* These questions lead to the bigger question, *What does it all mean?* I have tried to explain even a small slice of the writings to a sophisticated reader unfamiliar with the forms, figures, and places, and gotten exactly nowhere with my explanation.

And so I figured my time had come to reorganize the four parallel accounts, brief history, correspondence, and concluding prediction into this single organized account. Organization is the first feature of this account. It traces the good news through only *one* time, not four times. It also sorts into pertinent places in that single account, the doctrine that the correspondence articulates. So, you can read a bit of the good-news account, and then read an interlude of doctrine that the writers drew from it, then resume the account, and then read a little more doctrine, until you finish the full account. I hope that this organization makes for a more-readable account. It took some substantial effort—in fact, two prior books getting it all organized.

The other substantial interpretation that I gave the traditional format was to remove religious terms and ancient names and places. I hesitated to do so and admit great risk in doing so. The terms, figures, and places mean incredibly much. But until one appreciates the basic good-news account, those terms, figures, and places can *hide* more meaning than they *reveal*. I didn't especially write this interpretation for the novice reader. Like any writer, I wrote it for myself and readers like me who have some knowledge of the religious terms and ancient names and places. I just found that those terms, names, and places may be hiding things from me and other readers. I needed a fresh good-news account, one that some of my friends may also appreciate.

You may justly question what business anyone, no less a lawyer and law professor, has reorganizing traditional accounts to retell the good news. You may well be right. A witness's role, though, may be to do exactly that, to interpret what one hears, sees, and reads, indeed to keep interpreting and reinterpreting as long as breath allows. No one need rewrite the whole account, as I have done here. Doing so is a frankly ridiculous proposition, one that I neither planned nor dreamed but yet came about. I hope that this writing is in at least some small respect the Spirit's work rather than my mindless musing or aimless ambition. Your interpretation of the same good news—because it never changes—may instead be in practical service, pragmatic counsel, or other more-useful manner. I still hope you find some small inspiration in this interpretation of some very, very good news, indeed the best possible news. Please forgive me all offense you find in the effort.

> The wind blows wherever. When you hear it, you don't know its source or direction. Same thing with everyone whom the Spirit carries. *John 3:8*

Spiritspeak

1 Creation

Beginning

Find this truth extraordinary, your utmost revelation, your moment-to-moment joy, that perfect love between a perfect Father and perfect Son is the universe's heart, soul, mind, and Spirit, the very reason for the universe's existence. Would you want to live in any lesser world? Start at the beginning because until you realize how everything truly started—yes, *everything*—you won't get *anything* else right. A Father, *the* Father spoke everything into being, just as he continues to speak things into being. Nothing, nothing at all existed until the Father said so.*Ro 4:17* He made everything that you see or sense, everything from the universe's vast expanse down to the soil beneath your feet.*Heb 1:10* But here's the thing: don't call it the *big bang*. The Father instead *spoke* everything into being through his Son the Word. And the Father did so that we would know how much the Son means to the Father—yes, *love* at the universe's heart and origin. The Father made everything for the Son because the Son is everything to the Father. The Father had a plan for everything before he began it. The Father would have made nothing without the Son because the Son is of and in the Father, and *the Father wanted you to know*.*Jn 1:3*

The Son is the beginning, yes, *everything's* beginning including *your* beginning, your fresh start, even when you expect death. The Father made the Son supreme in everything.*Col 1:18* You may find it unfathomable, but as the Father's Son, the Son is truly without father or mother or any other ancestry. The Son, like the Father, has neither beginning nor end.*Heb 7:1-17* And by the way, after the Father created the universe through his Son, the Father was done creating universes. He's not a *multiverse* god like some of you speculate. He made *one* universe, *your* universe. Forget your other imaginings. Focus on what you know and control.*Heb 4:3* What you think of the beginning of all things *matters*. Get it right.

> ***Get past worldly things.*** You face trouble from worldly affairs. But the Son gets you past them.*Jn 16:33* The Son is not worldly, not limited as the world is.*Jn 8:23* Don't follow worldly habits. Let your new mind transform you. Then you'll know what the Father wants.*Ro 12:2* To avoid being worldly, just love the Father. That means doing as he says including relying on the Son.*1Jn 5:4-5.* Try being like the Father's small child—that innocent. Don't try to be worldly. The world is incredibly corrupt.*Php 2:15* The Father rejects the worldly. He wants you innocent.*Ro 2:5-6* Keep the Father's Spirit, not a worldly outlook.*1Co 2:12* Live with the Spirit in mind rather than living worldly.*1Co 3:1* Don't commit yourself to worldly things. They're temporary. Don't get engrossed in worldly things. They're disappearing even as you pursue them.*1Co 7:29-31* To the extent possible, avoid worldly affairs. Focus instead on pleasing the Father.*1Co 7:32-34* Don't wage war as the worldly do.*2Co 10:3* Use the Son's good news instead. It demolishes things that hold people down.*2Co 10:4* The Father's Spirit shows what's worldly and corrupt. The Spirit shows that the world needs the Son.*Jn 16:8-11*

Purpose

This creation thing wasn't just for God to do something, as if to show off his power. The Father had a greater reason. The Father wanted us to know that he first loved his Son and only then created the world. The Father spoke everything into existence through his Son in part so that we would know how much the Father thinks of the Son, which is *everything*.*Jn 17:24* The Father wanted us to know that the Son had the Father's honor, power, and wisdom, and everything else, before the world even began.*Jn 17:4-5* In the Son, the Father created everything, both what you see on earth and everything else, too. Through the Son and for the Son, the Father created everything both visible and invisible, including forces, powers, systems, and authority.*Col 1:16* But the truth is more than that, deeper than that. The Son was already the invisible Father's image before the Father created everything through the Son. The extraordinary gift is that the Father wanted us to know him and so made everything through his Son who is his image, someone whom we can see, know, and even touch.*Col 1:15*

Thus the Son radiates the Father's honor, power, and wisdom, and everything else, just outright *radiates* it. Indeed, the Son exactly represents who the Father is. You look at the Son, you see the Father.*Heb 1:3* The Son is everything that you'd want to know about the Father, the ultimate Deity. The Son is the *living* Deity and, more so, the Deity having taken *human form*. Think of what that means for the ultimate and only Deity to *become like you*. Think of why he did so!*Col 2:9* The Father established the Son as above all things, the one true thing. He then brought the universe about *through the Son*. The Father much later revealed the Son *for your sake*, well after making the universe.*1Pe 1:20*

The Father said, with a word on which he can never go back, that the Son would have this exquisite role in bringing about the universe because the Father had made the Son perfect forever—yes, *perfect forever*. You can hardly imagine perfection and cannot at all imagine forever, things that only the Father truly knows.*Heb 7:28* Don't think that you live in a purposeless universe. Purpose pervades the universe, and especially your world. Admit it, know it. You see it, you sense it, and above all, you *depend* on it. So now, *act* like it. Act like your life and the lives of those about whom you care most depend on the Father's purpose *because they do*.

> **Don't be worldly.** An enemy corrupts the world, although the enemy has no power over the Son.*Jn 14:30-31* Worldly people hate those who rely on the Son but have no power over them.*Jn 17:14-16* Don't withdraw from the world. Just know that the Son asked the Father to protect you from the enemy.*Jn 17:15* Indeed, the Son sends you among those with worldly perspective.*Jn 17:18* All the worldly fall to the enemy.*1Jn 5:19* That's why the worldly hate you. You don't fall.*1Jn 3:13* The worldly reject you because they reject the Father.*1Jn 3:1* Worldly pursuits mean hating the Father, making him an enemy when he's not the enemy.*Jas 4:4* Live among the worldly as a foreigner and exile. Don't do as the worldly do, losing your only sense and purpose.*1Pe 2:11* Worldly people are lustful and greedy.*Col 3:5* Resist worldly influences.*Col 2:8* Don't belong to the world. Don't follow the world's rules.*Col 2:20* Don't pursue praise from worldly people.*1Th 2:6* To love worldly things is to abandon the good news.*2Ti 4:10* If you are jealous and you quarrel, then you are worldly.*1Co 3:3* The worldly are immoral and greedy—swindlers.*1Co 5:10* The worldly cannot accept the Spirit's good news because the worldly do not see or know the Spirit.*Jn 14:17* The worldly won't see the Son, but you will.*Jn 14:19*

Participation

Creation wasn't God just winding up the universe and letting it go like a mechanical clock, although that's exactly what many of you believe and teach. Because the Son was before everything, and the Father made everything through the Son, the Son continues to hold everything together. Everything would come unglued without the Son.*Col 1:17* Everything would utterly stop without the Son. Here is truth again: the Son keeps everything going *by speaking*, which is why again we know the Son as *the Word*.*Heb 1:3* You should have noticed in your perpetual thinking that the world is ripe with thought. Yet you may not have known that the Son's clear thought, his true word, or if you prefer his *perfect light*, that which everyone needs to see, keeps the world going.

The amazing thing, though, is that the Father planned from the universe's start that he would send the Son through whom he created it into the Son's own world. The filmmaker enters the film! The Son came just as the Father planned and announced, although few recognized him. Many of those who considered that the Son just might be who he and his Father said he indeed was, promptly rejected him—well, *killed* him, if you are ready for the full truth, although now we are getting ahead of ourselves.*Jn 1:9-11* The point is that the Father didn't quit once he created the universe through his Son. He just stopped making universes—he made only one—and then rested from that extraordinary work, just as he wants *you* to rest after a good week's work, so that you remember what he did.*Heb 4:4* Know, trust, and act like he remains utterly engaged in the world *because he does*.

Get the Father's rest. The Father rested after creating everything.*Heb 4:4* The Father offers rest for you.*Heb 4:9* The Father has a standing promise for you of rest.*Heb 4:1* Rely, and you enter the Father's rest.*Heb 4:3* You get both inner and outer rest.*Heb 4:10* Try hard to enter the Father's rest. Don't die for not trying.*Heb 4:11* Come to the Son when tired. He'll give you rest.*Matt 11:28* The Son is so gentle and humble that he gives your soul rest.*Matt 11:29* Those who reject the Father never enter his rest.*Heb 3:17-19* Acknowledge that the Father knows better, and he will set your guilty heart at rest.*1Jn 3:19-20*

Perfection

You also know the Father's *direction* with his creation, which is forward and up, toward perfection. Good thing that he did not make the universe to wind down, as many of you believe. Everything that the Father made has this sort of anticipation that the Father has more to do with us. You can *feel* it, that wonderful sense of waiting for the Father to finish this grand thing, a sense that you hold inside yourself but that cannot yet burst out to declare who you truly are.Ro 8:19 The Father has a good reason for waiting: he doesn't want to destroy what he and the Son created. No, he wants to *liberate* it. Look around you! Everywhere, you see decay and oppression. The Father doesn't want that ugliness, deadliness, and slavery. He wants to see you and everyone else who loves him, who desires his own splendid wishes, to be free, like the children of his who you are—children of the universe's maker!Ro 8:21

> **The Father decides—no one else.** The Father decides who and what to accept, and no one else.Ro 8:33 The Father accepts all freely through the Son's rescue.Ro 2:24 The Father presented the Son's death as a payment for you so that you could rely on the Son.Ro 2:25-26 Yes, the Father let his Son die for your wrongs, in *your* place. Then, he brought him right back to life so that you'd have life, too.Ro 4:25 The Son's death cleansed you of all wrong so that the Father could see you as clean, clear, good, just like his Son.Col 1:22 The Son made you without fault, when you know you are covered with faults. You can hardly even walk straight, no less talk straight and consistently do good. And you're dying!Jude 24-25 The Father brings you back from dead, dirty, done. His Spirit marks you as safe, guaranteed.Eph 1:13-14 The Son converted you from dead to living, from done to just beginning.Gal 3:14 The Father sealed you with his Spirit for the moment of bringing you back.Eph 4:30

Listen carefully: everything that the Father made through the Son has a *groan* to it, like the groan of a woman giving birth. Don't you moan and cry? Sure you do! Everyone does. You only groan, though, because you take the hint from the Father's Spirit that better things must come, things for which you wait eagerly. You are waiting for the Father to make you his child, aren't you? Or if that's too much for you, then just admit that your body is going to pot and you're hoping for its rescue. Better that you hope for your *soul's* rescue, but look forward instead to your *body's* rescue if you must.Ro 8:22-23 Yes, the Father made both your soul and your body, both the spiritual and material.Ro 9:21 The thing to remember, though, is that from the beginning the Father made this thing *for you*—for those of you who accept him. And don't begrudge him that. Why would he do everything for those who reject him? What sense would that make of the world? No, you'd much rather have a sensible world where your choices make a difference. If you want to live in a meaningless world, then go right ahead. No one's stopping you, but you'll regret it.*Matt 25:34* Live as a part of his profound movement toward perfection. He more than invites you to do so. He gave everything he had so that you could.

> ***Father and Son rule differently from worldly rule.*** The Son said that he and his Father rule unlike the worldly rule.*Jn 18:35-36* The Father rules for good things happening everywhere, producing benefits that you didn't even expect from your small effort.*Mk 4:26-29* The Father's rule produces good things even where bad things usually happen, good coming from bad, leaving only good where only bad was.*Matt 13:24-30* The Son just keeps making good happen in a bad world, where so many people pursue the bad.*Matt 13:36-38* But when it's all over, the Son will clean it all up so that only the good remains, shining under the Father's beneficent rule. What a day that will be!*Matt 13:40-43* The Father's rule produces great bounty for many from the smallest good thing.*Matt 13:31-32, Mk 4:30-32, Lk 13:18-19* Just mix in a little of the Father's rule, and everything changes for the better.*Matt 13:33, Lk 13:20-21* The Father's rule is so valuable that you should give up everything for it. You'll end up way ahead.*Matt 13:44* The Father's rule is so special that you should hunt it down, getting rid of everything else to do so.*Matt 13:45-46* The Father is great at sorting the good things from the bad so that the bad gets thrown away.*Matt 13:47-50* The Father doesn't make you earn it. He will treat you just as well whether you accept him early or late. Just join in.*Matt 20:1-16* Don't worry about being a late-comer. Who knows? The late-comers may get more than the early arrivals.*Mk 10:31, Lk 13:30* The religious leaders asked the Son exactly when the Father was taking over, but the Son said the timing was secret and that the Father's rule was already among them.*Lk 17:20-21* The Son added that you'll see it coming when things get especially bad for you. Just be sure to watch for it, keep talking to the Father, and don't sweat the small stuff.*Lk 21:29-36*

Demonstration

You have no reason to remain skeptical. The Father first announced his purpose to you and then *demonstrated* it to you through what he created. When the Father first brought his Son into the world, he had plain old shepherds, those hard-working auto mechanics and fast-food workers of that day, announce the Son's coming. And what they said was that the Father's own messengers, the ones whom the Father sent to tell the shepherds about the Son, would venerate, love, and adore the Son. Yes, paradise itself reveres the Son who is more than anyone or anything.*Heb 1:6* The Father had made the first human out of the earth's dust, material stuff. But when sending his Son to earth, the Father made a new human out of the spiritual stuff of paradise.*1Co 15:47* Once here on earth, the Son first showed that he controls everything by, of all things, turning big water jugs at a wedding banquet into jugs of the finest wine. The Son did this first-of-its-kind, I-can-do-anything miracle at his mother's request when his mother saw that the banquet host had run out of wine. The Son didn't make a cinematic show of it. He just did what was right on the spur of the moment, although an unprecedented wonder.*Jn 2:1-11*

That tiny wonder was only the beginning. The Son did wonder after wonder while here. After his weary students fished all night without catching a thing, the Son with one astonishing command filled their nets with two boatloads of fish.*Lk 5:4-7* When in a boat with his students, the Son with a word utterly calmed the wind and waves of a furious storm. The Son's instant mastery over powerful nature—*with a word! with a word!*—rightly terrified his students.*Matt 8:23-27, Mk 4:35-41, Lk 8:22-25* The Son did the same thing again later, calming the sea.*Mk 6:51* His next act sounds so preposterous that you make a joke about it today, but *the Son also walked on water.* And the walk wasn't short or easy. The Son crossed half of a churning lake, out to his students' boat.*Matt 14:22-25, Mk 6:45-51, Jn 6:16-20* Once again, the Son terrified his students with his utter mastery over what he and the Father created.*Matt 14:26, Mk 49-50, Jn 6:19-21*

> **Father and Son hold the power.** Look around you. What you see reflects the Father's power.*Ro 1:20* The Father's power brought the Son back to life. He'll use that same power to bring you back to life.*1Co 6:14* Rely not on your wisdom but the Father's power.*1Co 2:5* The Father's power protects you until the Son's final rescue.*1Pe 1:5* Yes, the power with which the Father brought his Son back to life is the same power for you. Father and Son have all power.*Eph 1:19-21* You suffer for the good news by the Father's power.*2Ti 1:8* The Father's power brings the good news to everyone who relies on the Son.*Ro 1:16* The good news is powerful.*1Th 1:5* The good news is the Father's power. Ordinary wisdom has none.*1Co 1:22-24* The Father's place is about power, not talk.*1Co 4:20* The Father has power to do immeasurably more than all you ask or imagine.*Eph 3:20-21* The Father's power is forever.*1Pe 5:11* The Father's power enables you to carry the good news.*Eph 3:7* The Spirit tells you about the Father's incomparably great

Spiritspeak

> power.*Eph 1:18-19* You are weak to show the Father's all-surpassing power.*2Co 4:7* The good news spreads widely and grows in power.*Acts 19:18-20*

Time that you stopped joking. You too should be terrified at his power—and elated, knowing who Father and Son are. The Son's students got the message. One of them, Peter, got right out of the boat and walked on water over to him. The Son can help you, too, walk on water. You, too, will master nature including your own decaying body, if you do as the Son's students did in revering him. They knew who the Son was. Who else could walk on water while helping you do so?*Matt 14:32-33* The students' boat also immediately reached the shore to which they had headed, when they had been rowing in a strong wind and rough seas for miles. No magician could do that.*Jn 6:21* Many who saw these things knew what was going on. The One who created everything was walking among you.*Jn 2:23-25* The Son kept stunning with wonder after wonder those who saw him, so that anyone with eyes knew that he controls everything that he wishes to control.*Jn 7:21* If you want hard evidence, then he gave you plenty of it. In the end, though, you must decide. Many of those who saw the hardest evidence outright rejected it. Don't be one of them.

> ***Learn from ancestors rather than follow them.*** The Father scattered your ancestors' bodies in the wilderness to keep you from doing the wrongs that they did.*1Co 10:5-6* Don't over-indulge like some of your ancestors did in revelry.*1Co 10:7* Don't commit sexual immorality as some of your ancestors did and died for making more of it than they made of the Father.*1Co 10:8* Don't test the Son as some of your ancestors did and died for it.*1Co 10:9* Don't grumble as some of your ancestors did and died for it.*1Co 10:10* These things happened to them as examples, warning for you. You now know better.*1Co 10:11* Your ancestors straying angered the Father who refused to let them rest with him.*Heb 3:10-11*

Light

The Father saturated his creation with light. You live in a world embedded with love, imbued with care, but also stained with hate and corrupted by evil. Anyone who denies human propensity for both enormous good and enormous evil is utterly blind. How many tens of millions must you protect and encourage before you see the possible good? And how many tens of millions must you kill before you see the evil? Light and dark, good and evil—that's your world. And in your world, the Son is your light, never any hint of your world's darkness. The Son lights what he and the Father created. Keep that simple truth straight, and things will go much better for you. Some of you want to attribute bad things to him, which makes no sense whatsoever, giving him qualities he never had.*Jn 9:5* The Son brought you life, not death. His life lights up *all* of you.*Jn 1:4* He *is* your life, if you'll have him. He is so much your life that when you recognize and accept it, you won't even die but will instead pass right through death back to living. *That's* the power that he holds over creation.*Jn 11:25* And this truth is no secret. The herald John who immersed the Son in the Jordan River told you that the Son is the light, so that no one could miss it.*Jn 1:6-8*

The Son gives true light not just to some but to *everyone*. Even though he made *all* of you, and *all* of you are his, some of you still refuse to recognize him, as if you were blind. And then some of you who do recognize him nonetheless obstinately refuse to welcome him, treating him like some doormat rather than your creator. Better watch out for that.*Jn 1:9-11* If you want to do things right, if you want to act consistent with the truth, then see what his light so plainly shows about who he is. Then share with others what you see so that they can see, too. They need to know that light comes from the Son who sees how they walk, just as you need to know it.*Jn 3:21*

> **Peace is yours.** The Son leaves peace with you. He gives his peace to you. His peace is different from the usual peace, not like an interlude but much more.*Jn 14:27* In the Son, you have peace.*Jn 16:33* The Father gives you abundant peace.*Jude 1-2* The Father wants you to have abundant peace.*1Pe 1:2* Peace to you from the Father.*Col 1:2* The Father is peaceful.*1Th 5:23* Father and Son give you peace.*2Jn 3* Peace to you from the Father and Son.*Gal 1:3* Father and Son want you to relax.*Php 1:2* Father and Son don't want you anxious.*1Co 1:3* They want you at peace, quiet, confident.*2Co 1:2* They want you easy going.*Ro 1:7* They want you to rely confidently on their assurance.*1Th 1:1* They urge peace on you, that nothing trouble you.*2Th 1:1-2* Father and Son wish you no trouble.*2Ti 1:2* Father and Son instead bring you peace.*1Ti 1:2* Peace comes from the Father's Spirit.*Gal 5:22-23* The Father offers you peace at all times and in every way.*2Th 3:16* Trust the Father, and you will experience peace.*Ro 15:13* The Father of peace is with you.*Ro 15:33* When you visit someone, offer them peace, and hope they offer peace back.*Lk 10:5-6* Unite with others in peace from Father and Son.*Tit 1:4* Your peace is in the Son, who destroys hostility.*Eph 2:14-15* The Son taught peace.*Eph 2:17* All relying on the Son have peace.*1Pe 5:14* Bring a message of peace from Father and

> Son.*Eph 1:1-2* Ask the Father for his peace. It's better than just knowing things.*Php 4:7* Knowing the Son brings peace.*2Pe 1:1-2* The Son's peace is inward, not outward. Sometimes, his peace looks divisive, but that's only outside, not inside.*Matt 10:34-37, Lk 12:51-53, Lk 14:25-26*

You think that you survive on what passes in and through you as you eat and drink, like you depended on created things rather than your Creator. But no, this light that the Father and Son bring is what feeds you, giving you endless life, not just hour-by-hour life that leaves you hungry again.*Jn 6:32-33* If you accept him, then the Son is your food, sustaining you in a way that food and drink could never do.*Jn 6:34* The Son is how you live. You would die without him.*Jn 6:48* The connections are profound but simple: the Son lives in the Father; we live in the Son; and the Son lives in us. Dwell on those connections, and *they'll* keep feeding you.*Jn 14:19-20* The Son's Spirit carries this life to you. Remember, your true life is not about feeding your body, these things that decay and disappear. Your true life is instead about receiving the Son's Spirit into your spirit. You are more than material, more than dust. You are spiritual, and be glad for it.*Jn 6:63*

> **Reconcile with one another.** The Son destroys barriers, the dividing walls of hostility. The freedom of his good news unites.*Eph 2:14-15* The Son intended to create one new peaceful humanity. He reconciled all to his Father, his death putting to death all hostility.*Eph 2:15-16* The Son brought peace to insider and outsider.*Eph 2:17* All have access to the Father by one Spirit.*Eph 2:18* The Son is not divided, so unite rather than divide.*1Co 1:11-15* Don't be angry with another who relies on the Son. Your contempt for another may consign you to hell's fire.*Matt 5:21-22* Instead, reconcile with any who have something against you. Make things right.*Matt 5:23-24* Settle quickly with an adversary before the judge makes you pay your last penny.*Matt 5:25-26, Lk 12:58-59*

Now, during this daylight that the Son supplies us, is the time to study, accept, and share this great news. Do it now while you can, not later when you can't.*Jn 9:4* The time to follow the Son's light is when he shines it, not later when the light disappears, when you'd be left to stumble around in darkness. The Father and Son will make you light, too, like the Son carries the Father's light.*Jn 12:36* The Father lives forever in light so brilliant that you cannot get near it. You cannot see the Father, not because he doesn't exist but because his light is so powerful that you cannot look at it.*1Ti 6:15-16* The Son, though—ah, the Son—now the Son you can see, hear, and even *touch*. Those who did see, hear, and touch the Son got positively giddy from the experience. They *had* to talk about not only the Son, this speaking Word of Life who was around at the start and will still be here when it's over, but also the Father.*1Jn 1:1-4* Their joy was so great that they *had* to tell everyone that Father and Son are pure light. They *insisted* that Father and Son had nothing to do with any bit of darkness.*1Jn 1:5* The Son revealed life and immortality, shining a light on them.*2Ti 1:10* The Son's shining a light is the only way to make things visible. Everything that the Son illuminates also *becomes* a light.*Eph 5:13* Live in the light, fulfilling the light while battling darkness with the full power that the Son's light gives you. Your world requires it.

Work at peace. Make every effort to do what leads to peace.*Ro 14:19* Make every effort to be at peace with the patient Father.*2Pe 3:14-16* Do good, and then expect peace.*Ro 2:10* Fear the Father, or you will not know peace.*Ro 2:17-18* Keep the Spirit's unity through peace.*Eph 4:3* Let the Son's peace rule your emotions. The Father called you to peace.*Col 3:15* Make every effort to live in peace with everyone.*Heb 12:14* Live peacefully with each other.*1Th 3:13* Wish to one another peace from Father and Son.*Phm 1-3* Teach others to be at peace.*Tit 3:1-2* Enjoy life. Seek peace.*1Pe 3:10-11* Practice what you learn. Then the Father's peace will be with you.*Php 4:9* The good news is one of peace. Share it.*Eph 6:14-15* Ask the Father that you may live at peace with authority.*1Ti 2:1-2* Live in peace, and the Father of love and peace will be with you.*2Co 13:11* Be good to those who share the good news with you.*Ro 16:3-4* Be nice to other members of the Father's body.*Ro 16:5* Greet one another kindly.*Ro 16:16* Greet one another warmly.*1Co 16:20* Accept and enjoy hospitality from one another.*Ro 16:23* Let others see your love.*2Co 8:24*

To put it another way, the Father's word created his place and your place, his place a perfect paradise, your place, earth, beautiful at times but nonetheless twisted, broken, dangerous, killing, and dying.*2Pe 3:5* Yet the Father shares bits of his paradise, hints, glimmers of his goodness and his place's perfection.*Jas 1:17* The Father even shares his celestial beings as messengers like flames of fire.*Heb 1:7* The Father's Spirit shares secrets with you into which even celestial beings long to look.*1Pe 1:12* Everyone in the Father's paradise bears his name.*Eph 3:14-15* Your Master has his own place.*Col 4:1* He lets you know what he thinks from his place.*Ro 1:18* He warns you from his place that you cannot escape.*Heb 12:25* Everyone hears the Father's voice and bends to his desire, both on earth and in his place.*Heb 12:26-27* Your role includes making the Father's wisdom evident to everyone in his place.*Eph 3:10-11* Everyone must hear of his good news.*Col 1:23* Indeed, set your mind on things in the Father's place, not

Spiritspeak

your place where things are broken, corrupted.*Col 3:2* Don't look down on anyone, not even children, because they have advocates with the Father.*Matt 18:10* Let little children pursue the Son because the Father's place belongs to ones like them. To get to the Father's place, you need to be like those little children.*Matt 19:13-15, Lk 18:15-17* You are not there yet, but you are headed in the right direction.*Jn 13:33, 36*

Unify. Work together. You have only one body.*Eph 4:4* Tell the truth to one another. You are one body.*Eph 4:25* Be peaceful as members of one body.*Col 3:15* Let teaching on the good way agree in all of the body.*1Co 4:17* Kick out of the body the person who insists on continuing in corruption. But don't judge them once you kick them out.*1Co 5:12-13* Come together as one body. No divisions among you.*1Co 11:17-18* Don't insult the body by humiliating its poorer members.*1Co 11:22* No one part of the body is inferior to another.*2Co 12:13* The body continues confidently through trials.*2Th 1:4* Let the body grow strong in peace. The Spirit helps.*Acts 9:31* Live in harmony with one another.*Ro 12:16* As much as possible, live at peace with everyone.*Ro 12:18* Strive together as one for the good news.*Php 1:27* Have the same mind, loving one another.*1Pe 3:8* Make every effort to stay together peacefully.*Eph 4:3* Plead with one another to think alike.*Php 4:2* Live peacefully with each other.*1Th 3:13* Think alike, and the Father will be with you.*2Co 13:11* Unite with the Son. Think alike.*Php 2:2* Accept one another. The Son accepted you.*Ro 15:7* Agree with one another so that no divisions exist among you.*1Co 1:10* Share the Son's attitude toward each other.*Ro 15:6-7* Keep meeting together. Encourage one another.*Heb 10:25* No divisions, or your meetings will do more harm than good.*1Co 11:17-18* Work hard and persevere in the body. But hold onto the Son.*Rev 2:2-6* Poor in the body is rich in Father and Son.*Rev 2:9-10* Keep the body true to the Son even when in a corrupt culture. Don't follow culture.*Rev 2:13-16* Do more and more in the body. Don't tolerate in the body those who mislead and corrupt.*Rev 2:19-24* Wake the body up. Finish the body's work.*Rev 3:1-3* Keep the body true to the Son's mission.*Rev 3:7-10* Don't let the body be lukewarm. Better hot or cold. Don't assume you're rich when you are instead wretched, pitiful, poor, blind, and naked.*Rev 3:15-18*

Darkness

The Son had a good reason for shining his light into the world that he and his Father created. He said that he didn't want anyone who followed him to be in the dark. Everyone who follows the Son sees.*Jn 12:46* Think of it: light shines only in darkness. Darkness never overcomes light. Light always prevails over darkness, which is why the Son shined his light to make his victory crystal clear to everyone who sees.*Jn 1:5* The conclusion is inescapable. Even though the Son shined his light in the world, people instead want their darkness. They want it dark so that they can keep doing the wrongs that they enjoy doing. They don't love light. They love darkness because they love wrong.*Jn 3:19* Don't underestimate people's hostility to the Son. These people *hate* the light. They know that the Son's light eventually shows their wrongs when they want to keep them hidden. They hate the Son's light because they don't want the light to expose their wrongs.*Jn 3:20* Wrongs happen in darkness, not in the light, surely not in the Son's light. No good happens in darkness. In darkness, the good things just don't get done.*Jn 9:4* The ancient seer Isaiah said that these people living in death's darkest shadow would see the dawn of the Son's great light. Isaiah said the Son's first light would be brilliant.*Matt 4:13-16*

> **Judge truth.** Watch out for those who pretend to be one of you but are not. They're out to destroy you.*Matt 7:15* Just look at the bad things that they produce, and you'll know they're bad. If they produce good, then you can rely on their teaching.*Matt 7:16-20* Sound teachers produce good things. Dishonest teachers produce bad things. What's inside comes out. Teaching proves itself.*Lk 6:43-45* Love truth or die.*2Th 2:10* The Father won't make you accept truth. You may choose your own destructive delusion.*2Th 2:11-12* Those who chatter idly become more and more idle. Avoid their teaching.*2Ti 2:17* Truth wins. Opponents don't get very far because everyone sees their folly.*2Ti 3:9* Care for sound teachers. The Father likes it when you do.*2Ti 4:14* The one who confuses you will pay.*Gal 5:9-10* The enemy's teachers pretend to be friends but get what they deserve.*2Co 11:15*

The Son said it: when you follow him, you never walk in darkness because he does not walk in darkness. He shines his light wherever he leads you.*Jn 8:12* You don't stumble walking in daytime. No, you stumble when you walk at night because you can't see anything. You have no light.*Jn 11:9-10* The Son warned everyone that they would have his light for just a little longer. Darkness would then overtake them.*Jn 12:34-35* The Son also warned that walking in darkness leads you nowhere. You don't even know where you are headed when you walk in the dark.*Jn 12:35* This wisdom has been around forever but is also fresh wisdom. Where the Son shines, darkness disappears. When you see the Son's light, you can shine it to show the right direction. He is always shining the true light that leads in the right direction.*1Jn 2:7-8*

Rely on the Son through challenges. Be happy when you must persevere because it matures and completes you.*Jas 1:2-4* Relying on the Son means relying. You don't get life forever by giving up at the first challenge.*Jas 1:12* The Father rewards those who persevere. Persevering invokes his compassion. How can he show compassion when you've faced no trouble?*Jas 5:11* You suffer only briefly. Don't let suffering steal your joy over living forever. Keep a perspective.*1Pe 1:6* Trials prove that you truly rely on the Son.*1Pe 1:7* Forget what's already happened. Think about what's coming.*Php 3:13-14* Don't lose what you've already gained.*Php 3:16* Just look around. Others persevere. So can you.*1Th 3:7-8* Talk up one another's perseverance. It'll help.*2Th 1:4* Think about the Son's perseverance.*2Th 3:5* Endure hardship.*2Ti 4:5* Endure.*1Ti 6:11* Suffering produces perseverance, perseverance character, and character hope. See?*Ro 5:3-4* Be patient when suffering. You'll come around.*Ro 12:12* The ancient writings show you endurance, don't they?*Ro 15:4* The Father helps you endure.*Ro 15:6* Think back to what you've already been through.*Heb 10:32* Suffer with others who suffer. What's coming for you is better than what you have.*Heb 10:34* The Father's got it. No one but he wins.*Heb 13:6*

Light and darkness have nothing in common. You simply can't put the two together. Only fools who don't know anything about reality think otherwise.*2Co 6:14* Don't bother trying to hide your mess. The Son's light reveals everything that you try to hide. Everything anyone tries to hide, everyone will soon know. See, people put lamps on stands to shine light into darkness. What good is hiding a light? Where the darkness is, or what the darkness hides, doesn't matter because it all comes to light.*Matt 10:26, Mk 4:21-22, Lk 8:16-17, Lk 11:33* The Father certainly sees everything going on with what he created. He sees it all, as plain as day, as if it all happened right in front of him, where he can decide what to do about it.*Heb 4:13* Need I say it again? Watch out. Every wrong comes to light, even the things that you speak in the dark, indeed even the things that you *whisper* in your most-private room. So just stop it.*Lk 12:2-3* Admit evil, and then battle it with the Son's powerful light.

Share truth. Always be ready to share the good news, with good energy. Receive it likewise.*Gal 4:16* Treat well those who help you learn the richness and depth of the good news.*Gal 4:19-20* Act like you know the good news. Don't be a hypocrite, knowing but not acting like it.*Gal 2:14* Many who spread lies defame the good news. Don't.*1Pe 2:2* A little confusion destroys the whole truth.*Gal 5:9* Just stop the secret and shameful ways. Surely don't distort the good news.*2Co 4:2* Cut the ground from under deceivers who pretend to rely on the Son.*2Co 11:12-13* The Father knows lying, and he knows liars.*2Co 11:31* Don't swear oaths. Just speak plain truth. The enemy fools around with the truth, making it into lies.*Matt 5:33-37* Do everything for the good news.*1Co 9:23* Work with others sharing the good news.*Php 2:22* Help those who share the good news.*Php 4:3*

People

You are part of what the Father and Son created. Yes, they *made* you. But they didn't just make you another part of what they created. They made you the *best* part, the first part, the highest part. Don't let anyone tell you that you are just a soulless animal, a chance collection of coalescing atoms, as so many of you teach and believe. You are instead different, better, not in your own nature, like it was to *your* credit that you have the Father's likeness, but instead because *he made you so*.*Jas 1:18* You forget this fact way too often. You sometimes admire the Father, as if that made you special, but you then turn right around and curse your own kind whom the Father made in his own likeness, the likeness of his Son. That two-faced attitude gets you nowhere.*Jas 3:9-12* Imagine how ridiculous having something that *you* made, like a breakfast waffle or drawing on a page, talk back to *you* would sound. So don't you, a mere person, talk back to the Father who made you. Oh, yes, he leaves you the power to do so. He's given you free will. Just use it properly, not for insults against the one who gave it to you.*Ro 9:19-20*

Honor Father and Son. The Son became human, dwelling among you. That way, you could see and honor the Son.*Jn 1:14* The Father put the Son over everyone.*Php 2:11* Be overjoyed at honoring Father and Son.*1Pe 4:13* Your purpose is to honor the Father.*1Pe 2:9-10* Laud the Father.*Jas 3:9* The Father rescued you through his Son so that you could honor him.*Eph 1:5-6* To be right with the Father, honor him.*Php 1:11* Honor forever to the Father.*Php 4:20* Your gatherings should honor the Father and Son, who do more than all you ask or imagine.*Eph 3:20-21* The good news is all about the Father's honor.*1Ti 1:11* The Father has honor forever.*1Ti 1:17* Honor to the Father forever.*2Ti 4:18* Speak well of the Father, all of you.*Ro 15:11* Give the Father honor forever.*Ro 11:36* Honor the Father for sparing you.*Ro 15:8-9* The Son honors the Father.*Ro 16:27* Honor to the Father forever.*Heb 13:21* Honor the Father in the Spirit and in truth. The Father is spirit, and so honor in the Spirit.*Jn 4:23-24* Doing good, as the Son's student, honors the Father.*Jn 15:8*

The good thing, the great message, is that you have that choice. You can take an entirely new attitude about the Father, an attitude that he and his Son offered to you after you proved that you had failed the whole creation thing. This new attitude is just like the one that the Son has for the Father and Father has for the Son. You'll be just like the Father, with the Father supplying all that you need to continue to be like the one who made you.*Col 3:10* From the start, you've been able to know what the Father is like from what he created. You've known how powerful and other-worldly he is from his having put *this* world together. You can't see him. But you can see what he made. And so you have no excuse for refusing to know him.*Ro 1:20* Once you do acknowledge and honor him, you are all bright and shiny, nothing hidden any more, nothing to regret, all good with the Father who could condemn you but refuses to do so, instead treating you like one of his children, his Son's own sibling.*Lk 16:8*

> **How do you react to the Son?** Some communities drive out those who rely on the Son. They don't want or feel that they need him.*Matt 8:33-34, Mk 5:14-17, Lk 8:34-37* Others sell out the Son.*Matt 26:14-16* Those who disown the Son, he disowns. Turnabout is fair play.*Lk 12:9, 2Ti 2:12* You've got to make a choice because if you're not with him, then you're against him. No standing on the sidelines.*Matt 12:30, Lk 11:23* Relying on the Son means walking it, not just talking it. You lie when you say you rely on him but do not live out the truth.*1Jn 1:6* Just don't desert the good news that you learned. No other good news exists.*Gal 1:6-7* Everyone needs the Son's rescue—everyone. You lie if you say otherwise—and make the Son a liar, too.*1Jn 1:8-10* Some who need the good news most, or know it best, still reject it.*Ro 10:16* Some who reject the good news, knowing it well, envy those who accept the good news, not knowing it so well. It's what you do about it, not how well you know it.*Ro 10:19* Rejecting the good news is like killing the Son all over again.*Heb 6:6* Careful: reject him, and he'll come right back to crush you. No getting around it.*1Pe 2:7-8* Once you start relying on him, keep it up. Don't let anyone cut you off.*Gal 5:7-8* Tell others the good news, and the Son will brag to the Father about you. Hide the good news, and the Son will reject you before the Father.*Matt 10:32-33, Lk 12:8-9*

The Son gave you an especially powerful way of thinking about yourself, indeed of acting, and it's simple. To be filled with the Father's light for which he made you, train your eye like the lamp that it is for you. Look at those things, and then think about those things that you *should* observe and ponder. That focus is how you stay healthy, filling yourself with light. Do the opposite, looking where you shouldn't, and everything will be dark for you.*Lk 11:34* The Son said to make light your priority, just like a lamp was shining on you—because it is.*Lk 11:35-36* The Father chose you out of nowhere. He wants to set you above and apart as royalty, as *his*. He called you out of muck and mire into his amazing light.*1Pe 2:9-10* See, the Father didn't just create light where everything was darkness, just for the sake of creating. His plan was to shine his light *right into us*, so that we could see and honor him when we encounter his image-bearing Son.*2Co 4:6*

> **Expect trials.** Relying on the Son isn't always a bed of roses. It certainly wasn't easy for the Son.*Matt 8:19-20* You'll face trials and suffering.*Matt 10:17, Mk 13:9* People will oppose you. But opposition is just opportunity to share the good news.*Matt 10:18, Mk 13:9, Lk 21:12-13* Strange as it seems, people can hate the good news, dividing even family members.*Matt 10:21-22, Lk 21:16-17* Family members may reject you over the Son. You may also need to reject old ways to rely on the Son.*Lk 14:25-26* Things could get bad, bringing even betrayals.*Mk 13:12* Stick with the Son through those trials. Do as he did. Prove your commitment to him. It's worth it.*Matt 10:38-39, Lk 14:26* Count the cost. Expect cost. It's worth it.*Lk 14:28-33* Give up everything necessary to rely on the Son.*Lk 14:33* They persecuted the Son, so they'll do the same to you.*Jn 15:20-21* They'll put you out of the traditional religious centers. They'll think that they're serving the Father. But they don't know him or the Son.*Jn 16:2-3*

That seeing and honoring the Father through the Son is how you get your name in his book, the good book, the one that gives you life forever. He has no formula. He hasn't made the way forward hard or mysterious. The Father just wants you to stand up for him.*Php 4:3* And at times, you have. While you used to stumble around in the dark, you now and then step into the Father's light. You just need to go the whole way and *live it*, no longer dabbling with light, one foot still in darkness. Now that you know the truth, *be good*. Do things the *right* way. Incredible as it may seem, when you do so, you make the Father happy about it. You *please* him. He *likes* it.*Eph 5:8-10* You can *shine*, even though everything around you is one big corrupt mess. You can be a *star*. You just need to hold onto these words like they mean everything to you, like your life depends on it—which it does.*Php 2:15-16*

Do you get it yet? The world is both light and dark. You live in a world that stark. You can't claim that you are in the light when you hate others who are in the light with you. No, then you are stumbling around in the dark. When you love others who are in the light with you, *that's* when you are solidly in the light. Then, you don't go bumbling about.*1Jn 2:9-11* Time to wake up. Time to stand up like you are no longer dead. The Son's light only shines on you when you do.*Eph 5:14* Dawn is coming whether you wake up or not. The light isn't going to wait for you. It will leave you behind if it must. Now is the time to get with it. Put aside your nonsense so that you stand squarely in the light. That's the way to survive, and not just to survive but to *thrive*.$_{Ro\ 13:12}$ Accept that you are for light, not for darkness. Choose light over darkness. Don't let darkness *own* you.$_{1Th\ 5:5}$ Let *light* own you.$_{1Th\ 3:8}$ And then happily thank the Father for qualifying you to live with him in his paradise of light with others who live in the light, too.$_{Col\ 1:12}$ The Son calls you the world's light. He wants you to shine that light so that others can see what good you are doing—and not to honor you but to honor the Father who made you. Stop hiding the good things you do.$_{Matt\ 5:14-16}$ People! Know your capacities in both directions, for good *and* evil. Then choose the good.

> **Your actions determine your fate with the Father.** You must receive the Son's cleansing and Spirit in new life to join the Father.$_{Jn\ 3:3-7}$ The rich don't easily join the Father because they pay too much attention to their riches.$_{Matt\ 19:22-24,\ Mk\ 10:23-25,\ Lk\ 18:24-25}$ Yet gaining the Father is still possible, even for the rich, because everything is possible with the Father.$_{Matt\ 19:25-26,\ Mk\ 10:26-27,\ Lk\ 18:26-27}$ Better to say you won't do the Father's work when you do then to say you will when you don't. Doing matters more than talking.$_{Matt\ 21:28-30}$ And changing from bad to good, even when you were doing a lot of bad, matters more than only doing a little bad, if you refuse to give up that little bad.$_{Matt\ 21:31-32}$ You'll suffer if you give the Father's followers a hard time. He's watching out for them and will set things right for them.$_{Matt\ 21:33-36,\ Mk\ 12:1-5,\ Lk\ 20:9-12}$ You'll especially suffer if you reject the Father's own son. Can you imagine?!$_{Matt\ 21:37-39,\ Mk\ 12:6-8,\ Lk\ 20:13-14}$ The religious officials get no pass. They, too, suffer when they reject the Son because they reject the Father when they reject the Son. The Father rewards those who do his work.$_{Matt\ 21:42-43,\ Mk\ 12:9-11,\ Lk\ 20:16-19}$ Just stand firm, nothing moving you, while always giving yourselves fully to the Father's work. Your effort isn't wasted.$_{1Co\ 15:58}$

2 Creator

Transcendent

To know the full truth of existence, though, of how things came into being, you must also know what you can about the One who made everything. While the Father is beyond everything, outside of everything, so that you could never know all about him, he has shown you what you may know. He is, for instance, both the beginning *and* the end, not only having started everything but also waiting to *finish* it. That insight alone should make an enormous difference to you. He was around before anything, he is around now, and he will be around forever, having all authority and power over everything. How is that for starters—and this from the student John who was so close to and beloved by the Son?*Rev 1:8* While the Father has these before-everything and after-everything qualities, though, he also nourishes you *right now* from life's very spring. He doesn't hold back. No, he gives *everything* to his children, who are the ultimate winners.*Rev 21:6-7*

> **Father and Son hold nothing against you.** The Father excuses you as if you were without fault.*Col 1:2* He does so because you rely on Father and Son.*1Th 1:1* Father and Son excuse you.*Php 1:2* Father and Son hold nothing against you.*2Th 1:1-2* Father and Son do not find fault with you.*1Co 1:3* Father and Son give you a complete pass.*Ro 1:7* Father and Son take no interest in your bad past.*Gal 1:3* With Father and Son, what's past is past.*1Ti 1:2* The Son has compassion on you.*1Co 16:23* The Son sees nothing of your faults.*Ro 16:20* The Son looks the other way from your brokenness.*2Co 13:14* Father and Son show you understanding you do not deserve.*2Co 1:2* The Son gives you a break that you did not earn.*1Th 5:28* The Son ensures that all of you have a chance, past or no past.*2Th 3:18* The Son does the same for all who rely on him.*Rev 22:21* May you face no judgment.*Col 4:18* May you feel whole again.*Heb 13:25* May you all be free from guilt.*1Ti 6:21* The Father's Spirit doesn't place blame.*Heb 10:29* The Father has compassion because of his nature, not your acts.*2Ti 1:9* You have done nothing to deserve his favor.*Ro 11:6* The

Spiritspeak

Father takes you as you are because of who he is.*Ro 2:24* The Father shows the same compassion for others along with you.*2Co 8:1* Temptations do not control you because you know the Father's kindness.*Ro 6:14* Do no wrong. The Father has given you a pass.*Ro 6:15* Kindness rules because of right relationship with the Father.*Ro 5:21* Stand steady in the Father's kindness.*1Pe 5:12* The Father's kindness helps you reject worldly passions, helps you live self-controlled.*Tit 2:12* The Father let you do wrong so that he could show you his unearned kindness.*Ro 11:32* Ask the Father for more, but his kindness is enough.*2Co 12:8* Don't stop short of the Father's generosity.*Heb 12:15* Let his compassion strengthen your resolve.*Heb 13:9*

Know, too, that the Father is so incredibly generous as to pursue you. You weren't even looking for him when he came to you. He showed himself to you without you even asking him to do so.*Ro 10:20* The Father who is your Rescuer doesn't want to lose as few as *one* of you. He wants to rescue every single one of you from the death to which you are headed. And good for you that he's doing so, rescuing you, simply by showing you the *truth*—no arduous procedure, no *earning* his rescue, but just expecting you to acknowledge the truth.*1Ti 2:3-4* Keep your head on straight. You were no one special. The Father chose you out of *nowhere* as if you were somebody special to him, which everyone is who will just acknowledge him as he asks. Is that too much to ask? You were stumbling around in the pitch black until he turned on a gorgeous light.*1Pe 2:9-10* You should be counting your blessings, thanking the Father from the bottom of your heart for what he did. He turned you from nothing to everything so that you could stand among the most-extraordinary people as one of them, indeed as one of *his*.*Col 1:12*

The Father excuses your wrongs. Those who rely on the Son can count on the Father excusing their wrongs.*Acts 10:43* The Father simply forgets what you've done wrong.*Heb 8:12* You must rely on the Son, though.*Col 1:14* The Father gave the Son that authority to wipe your slate clean.*Matt 9:6* The healing that the Son did showed he has that authority.*Mk 2:5-12, Lk 5:17-25* You must admit your wrongs. Don't lie, and don't make the Son a liar. You've got some wrongs to admit—probably lots of them.*1Jn 1:8-10* The Father won't hold them against you if you rely on the Son.*Col 2:14* The Son's death took care of it for you, giving you the Father's riches.*Eph 1:7-8* The Father restores you to right relationship with him, no matter what you've done.*Ro 4:6-7* The old way left too much cleaning up to do.*Heb 9:22* No, you need not worry about all the cleaning up.*Heb 10:18* The Father ignores everything. Just don't reject the Father's own Spirit who rescues you.*Matt 12:31, Mk 3:28-29* Reject the Spirit, and it's over for you.*Mk 3:29* You may have

> once rejected the Son before coming around to him, but just don't reject the Spirit once you do come around.*Matt 12:32, Lk 12:10* The more you've done wrong, the more you love the Son. The more you love the Son, the more ready he is to clean you up for his Father's embrace.*Lk 7:36-48*

Don't assume the Father to be stingy or hard toward you. All the Father did instead was to open his arms to you and keep holding them out, practically begging you to come to him. The very people whom he most chose, pursued, and protected were the stingy, hard, and difficult ones. They were the ones who rejected him despite his pursuit. See how willing the Father is?*Ro 10:21* Claiming that he owes you something never does any good. The Father has nothing to repay you because everything started with him. With everying from him, through him, and for him, how could he owe you anything?*Ro 11:35-36* But above all, here's the thing that you must know about the Father who created you and everything else, this glorious transcendent Being: you cannot possibly please him unless you accept that he exists. And look, accepting that he exists requires your confidence, not much confidence, but at least a little confidence. Because the Father transcends all he made, including you, he requires your tiniest confidence that he exists. Oh, and by the way, he also has enormous rewards for those who, acting on their tiniest confidence, begin to earnestly seek him.*Heb 11:6* So, go try it. Seek him.

> **Have Abraham's confidence.** The ancient patriarch Abraham let trust lead him to obey the Father. He went to the place he would later inherit, even though he had no idea where he was going.*Heb 11:8* His confidence led him to live in the promised land like a stranger in a foreign country.*Heb 11:9* His wife's confidence enabled her to bear a child when she was way too old, so that countless descendants could come from Abraham who was also way too old.*Heb 11:11-12* Abraham's trust led him to offer his only son to the Father.*Heb 11:17-18* Abraham trusted that the Father could raise the dead.*Heb 11:19* The Father uses your trust to reward you, just as he did with Abraham.*Gal 3:8-9* Abraham had nothing to boast but still got the Father's credit for his trust.*Ro 4:1-3* Abraham and his offspring received the Father's reward because they trusted.*Ro 4:13* Trust invokes the reward.*Ro 4:14-15* Reward comes to all who rely like Abraham.*Ro 4:16-17* Against all hope, when he was as good as dead, Abraham never wavered but instead had stronger confidence. He believed the Father's power and promise, and so received his full reward.*Ro 4:18-21*

Sovereign

Don't miss the Father's independence. While you are under various authorities of one kind or another, whether government, workplace, or family, for instance, you are not used to a fully independent *anything*. In your world, everywhere you see authority, you see its limitation. The Father, though, has no such limitation. Just the opposite: all authority flows from the Father, which is why you see earthly authority as limited. It *is* limited—by *him*! What the Father does is call you into his authority, into his presence where no other authority limits him._{1Th 2:12} Now, some will groan about ultimate authority in the Father, which does create certain challenges for you, although of the best kind. Yet the extraordinary thing about his invitation to serve under his ultimate, unbounded authority is not that his authority is absolute, unchallenged. The remarkable thing is that he counts you *worthy* of it._{2Th 1:5} The Father had no need to share his rule, his governance, his most-beneficent protection, and yet he did so—with *you* of all people. You should be absolutely jumping for joy over it._{Col 1:12}

What do you do then with the Father's inestimable invitation? The thing to do is to simply remain in view of the Father's ultimate rule, his overarching authority, welcoming it. Be glad for it!_{2Ti 4:1} Be glad, too, that the Father is bringing you safely under his rule where you are *his* with all the good that being *his* entails._{2Ti 4:18} We're not talking about him just giving you food and water. His rule isn't a welfare state or prison where you get three squares without any liberty or hope. No, his rule is about being right with everything, being entirely at peace, and, yes, jumping for joy, as his own Spirit fills you. His rule is about having a piece of *him*, indeed, having the *whole* of him. You're not joining a gang that supplies only brotherhood and a little protection. You're getting *everything*._{Ro 14:17} So again, just pull up a chair. Lean in and listen closely to the Father, knowing for sure that you're completely *in*._{Heb 10:22}

Help others accept the good news. Supply the confidence that others lack._{1Th 3:10} Working together helps you all trust._{Php 1:27} Let others give you confidence, too._{1Ti 3:2} Love others who rely on the Son._{Tit 3:15} Be happy that others rely on the Son._{1Th 3:9} Ask the Father to let you give others confidence._{1Th 3:10} Thank the Father that others are growing more and more confident._{2Th 1:3} Be a family in trusting the good news._{1Ti 1:2} The Father rescues women who continue in confidence._{1Ti 2:15} Be an example in relying on the Son._{1Ti 4:11} To not provide for one's own household is to reject the good news.*1Ti 5:8* Once you accept it, pursue it.*1Ti 6:11* Fight for it.*1Ti 6:12* Recall how others do.*2Ti 1:5* Pursue the good news along with others.*2Ti 2:22* The confidence of some, others will report everywhere.*Ro 1:8* You have only one good news.*Ro 2:29-30* The Father accepts a little confidence, just like he accepts a lot. So don't judge others.*Ro 14:2-3* You are no one to judge. The Father helps the weak stand.*Ro 14:4* Don't show off your confidence to make others feel bad. Help them gladly. You needed help, too.*2Co 1:24* Imitate others' confidence.*Heb 6:12*

Know another thing about the Father and his rule, the place to which he invites you, about which many have it so wrong. His realm is not a dark, gloomy, and stormy mountain burning with fire. His call to you is not like a harsh trumpet blast. His voice is not a bunch of frightening commands that you cannot bear, terrifying you so that you tremble with fear.*Heb 12:18-21* No, his realm, where he exercises utter authority, is instead a wondrous city full of joyful life, a paradise filled with millions of celebrating beings.*Heb 12:22* When you get there, you will have joined all others who love not only the Father but also his Son. The Father will have written your name across the city's skies, welcoming you as another full celebrant.*Heb 12:23* The Father had this plan for you since before he first created everything. The Father chose you to become perfect in his paradise, a saint in his sight.*Eph 1:4* The Father made this wondrous city for you and others about whom he suffers no embarrassment, when you call him your own. He is a Father whom you cannot embarrass, who takes nothing but full pride in you. Ever have a perfectly forgiving father like that?*Heb 11:16* The Father waits there for you, utterly ready to love and accept you in this paradise that he made for you before you even came to be.*Col 4:1*

Keep working for Father and Son. The Son said to stand with him when challenged. He'll give you your own authority under his authority, keeping you close to him.*Lk 22:28-30* The Son said that his Father gives special treatment to those who are poor materially but rich toward him.*Lk 6:20* Some thought that the Father was about to take everything over. But the Son showed that you have a lot to do before the Father takes over. Work at it because the Father rewards your hard work while punishing the lazy.*Lk 19:11-23* The more you work for the Father, the more the Father gives you. The less you do, the more he takes away. He casts aside those who do nothing for him.*Lk 19:24-27* You don't gain the Father's trust just by breathing.*1Co 15:50* When the Son's students asked which of them his Father would regard as the greatest, the Son said to forget it. The Father wants you like a little child, totally dependent on him, not on yourself. The greatest is the one who stoops lowest, like a child._{Matt 18:1-4, Lk 9:48} Until the Son came, people were trampling all over the Father's rule, but the Son set them all straight._{Matt 11:12} The Son treats everyone exactly as they deserve—no fooling around, no playing favorites._{Heb 1:8} Just do your best so that the Father opens his arms wide to you._{2Pe 1:10-11} And give a big welcome to others who are doing their best for the Father._{Col 4:10-11} And thank the Father that he welcomes you._{Heb 12:28-29} Indeed, jump for joy that the Father shares his rule with you. It's better than anything else you'll ever experience._{Col 1:12} The Father honors those who serve the Son._{Jn 12:26} The Son works constantly because his Father works constantly._{Jn 5:16-18} The Son came to serve._{Lk 22:27} The Father cuts off those who do not produce._{Jn 15:1-2} Keep relying on the Son, and you'll produce._{Jn 15:4-5} Serve the Son and you'll please the Father._{Ro 14:18} Enjoy serving the Father._{Ro 15:17}

Word

Another of the Father's qualities that you should recognize is his willingness to speak with you, a willingness that he need not have had but graciously extended to you. He is a Father of words, indeed of the Word. His word brings to you things that only the Father could possibly share, things that are a marvel and revelation to you, shocking and surprising you with their goodness._{Eph 3:3} He wants you to *know* things important to you, things that you can only know through his words. He has given you those words so that as you read and hear them, mysteries open up to you as they did for an ancient people so very long ago. The Father's Spirit revealed these mysteries to earnest students, sages, and seers who recorded them for you, giving you time-tested writings on which to rely._{Eph 3:4-5} By giving you his words, the Father let you come into the world again, in new birth, made all over again. But this time, you came as a spiritual being, ready to live fully as the Father made you, rather than trapped in your old dying flesh._{Jas 1:17-18}

Pursue right living. Pursue right relationship with the Father out of a pure heart._{2Ti 2:22} Be an example in right living._{1Ti 4:11} Offer yourself to the Father. He brought you from death to life. He made you right._{Ro 6:13} Obeying the Father leads to right living._{Ro 6:16} The Father captured you for right living._{Ro 6:18} The Father gives you what you need to live right. You have what it takes to escape the corruption that evil desires cause._{2Pe 1:3-4} Because the Father rewards you, you should be good, self-controlled, and loving. You should be living right._{2Pe 1:5-}

> 7 The Father will reward you for living right, longing for him._{2Ti 4:8} You should be full of goodness._{Ro 15:14} Be different, be *right*. Let people see how different you are, positively affecting everyone around you._{Matt 5:13, Lk 14:34-35}

What do you then do with the Father's wondrous word? Carry the Father's word like you would carry a sword. His word is every bit as good as a sword, indeed far better. Wield it to protect and advance. Make it work for you._{Eph 6:17} When someone shares the Father's word with you, accept it not as a human word but as it is, the *Father's* word. His word works in you like an engine, a battery, the living Spirit, when you accept it._{1Th 2:13} You should get used to accepting anything the Father's word authorizes. He shares things with you by telling you about them, his word carrying his gifts._{1Ti 4:5} You can hold down the message giver, but you cannot hold back the message. The Father's word always goes free, carrying freedom and the free along with it._{2Ti 2:9} Everything that the Father uttered within his word he did so that you may know. His word is for you, not to fill up a bookshelf. He intends that his word stop you, turn you in your tracks, and get you started again but right this time._{2Ti 3:16-17} And the Father makes you better at talking, not just aimless talking but the best communication, the smart communication, talk that recognizes the Father's Son in you, guiding you, making you the Father's child, too._{1Co 1:5-6} Don't miss that the Father is a talker and, wondrously, that his talk is for *you*.

> **The Father's word is your life.** The Father made everything by speaking. He spoke, and things existed._{Jn 1:3} Later, the Father's word became his Son, living with you—a living word! That living word was truth, too._{Jn 1:14} The Son said just what the Father showed him and what the Father said, so you'd know._{Jn 3:32-34} The Father's word works and wins._{Ro 9:6} The Father's word shares his secrets._{Eph 3:3} The Father's word lives, truly lives, showing you differences you'd otherwise not see, including your own condition, good or bad._{Heb 4:12} The Father's word made you spiritual, not just material._{Jas 1:17-18} Know the Father's word._{Eph 6:17} Accept the Father's word when others share it with you, so that it can work in you._{1Th 2:13} It's true only if consistent with the Father's word._{1Ti 4:5} The Father spoke the things that others recorded, to help you get your life together._{2Ti 3:16-17} The old rules were the Father's words, too._{Ro 2:2} The Father's words that others recorded guide and encourage you._{Ro 15:4} Speak the Father's words, too. Don't just know them._{2Co 4:13} The Father spoke his words for others, too._{1Co 14:36} Don't waste time with menial tasks when you could be sharing the Father's words._{Acts 6:1-6} If you work at it, then the Father's words will flourish and spread._{Acts 12:24} The Father's word builds you up so that the Father

can give you the bounty that he wishes.*Acts 20:32* When the Father speaks it, write it down and rely on it, because it's over and done.*Rev 21:5-6* Let the Son encourage you when weary.*Heb 12:3* Father and Son encourage you.*2Th 2:16-17* Draw hope from the Father's words.*Ro 15:4* The Father encourages you.*Ro 15:6-7* The Father sends others to comfort you.*2Co 7:6-7* You weep now, but later you'll laugh.*Lk 6:21*

Father

Does it surprise you that he who created everything and was before and outside of everything stands in a family relationship to you? He has revealed himself to you as *the Father*—a family role. Do you realize how endearing that concession, that the universe's creator treats you as *family*, should be? Don't miss your family relationship to the Father. The Father means so much to you that the Son said not to call anyone on earth *father*. Call only *him* Father. Don't get special things confused with common things, and don't let others think that you are confused. You have one Father over everything who counts for everything.*Matt 23:2* The one who made everything isn't some impersonal force or distant mad scientist. He is personal and close to you, your Father in the very best sense of that role. You are his sons and daughters, again in the very best sense.*2Co 6:18* You came through a family, and you'll leave through a family, to join paradise's family, all because you have the Father. Everyone is under the Father, and the smart ones honor him as Father. Be among those smart ones.*Eph 3:14-15*

You are the Father's body. When the Father sent his Son, he made earth the center of everything while elevating humanity above all but his own. You are now his body. Show it to the universe.*Eph 3:10-11* The Father's body includes all who rely on the Son.*1Co 1:2* Father and Son favor, comfort, and protect you and other members of the Father's body.*2Th 1:1-2* The Father favors the members of his body.*2Co 8:1* The Father's household, the body made of those who rely on the Son, is your foundation.*1Ti 3:15* The Father's body helps widows with real need.*1Ti 5:16* Members of the Father's body honor one another for sharing the good news.*2Co 8:18* As members of the Father's body, honor the Son.*2Co 8:23* The Son loved the Father's body so much that he gave himself up for that body, setting apart the body for the Father so that he could present the body to himself as radiant, without stain, wrinkle, or other blemish, but instead blameless.*Eph 5:25-27* The Son and the Father's body are a profound mystery.*Eph*

5:32 Imitate other members of the Father's body. The body suffers for the Father.*1Th 2:14* The Father established you, his body, with his Son's death.*Acts 20:28* The Son is the body's head.*Col 1:18* The Son rescues the body.*Eph 5:22-23* The whole body grows from the Son as head.*Col 2:19* The whole body grows in love. Each body part does its own work.*Eph 4:16* The Father made the Son the body's head.*Eph 1:22-23* You mature as the Father's body when the Son is the head.*Eph 4:15* The Son cares for the body as his own.*Eph 5:29-30* You are members of the Father's body.*Eph 3:6* The Son created in him one body.*Eph 2:15-16* You are all members of one body.*Eph 4:25* You build up the body.*Eph 4:11-12* Get along as one body.*Col 3:15* Each of you is a different body part.*Ro 12:5-6* Build up the body until you work together.*Eph 4:12-13* Keep one another's company in the Son's humble attitude.*Php 2:5-8* Treat one another as dear brothers and sisters.*Phm 15-16* If someone in your body does another wrong, then let the charge be to you and fix it.*Phm 18-19* Ask the Father to restore one another to the family.*Phm 22* Be like young children in humble innocence among one another.*1Th 2:7* Keep kind company with others who rely on the Son.*Gal 2:9* You many who rely on the Son are one body.*1Co 10:17* One body has many parts, as is true of the body of all you who rely on the Son.*1Co 12:12* The body has many parts, not just one.*1Co 12:14* You're all important to the body.*1Co 12:15-17* The Father placed each part in the body just as he wanted you to be.*1Co 12:18* The body needs different parts.*1Co 12:19* The one body has many parts.*1Co 12:20* No part can reject another part.*1Co 12:21* The weaker parts are indispensable. Honor them.*1Co 12:22-24* Have equal concern for each part.*1Co 12:25* If one part suffers, then every part suffers with it.*1Co 12:26* You are the Son's body, and each one of you is a part.*1Co 12:27*

The Father most shows his familial quality—his family relationship and role—in his relationship with the Son. You know the Father only through the Son. No one knows the Father except the Son and those to whom the Son chooses to reveal the Father. You thus know the Father only *because he is a Father*, without which you would not know him. His Father role is essential to your knowing him at all.*Matt 11:27* The Father wants his family close. Indeed, when the Son was finishing his work with you, he told his students that he was returning to the Father. While the students didn't want the Son to leave, the Son told them that they should be glad he was returning to the Father because the Father is greater than the Son. Don't be surprised. Aren't fathers greater than sons?*Jn 14:28* The point is that the Father named a Son, named *his* Son while echoing that he is the Son's Father. Everything you see was all about family—Father and Son.*Heb 1:5* Father named Son and claimed Son's fatherhood.*Heb 5:5-6*

> **Trust Father and Son.** Confidently hope for what you do not see, to the point of assurance.*Heb 11:1* Trust that the Father created everything you see.*Heb 11:3* You won't please the Father if you don't accept that he exists. And by the way, he rewards those who do.*Heb 11:6* The Father tests motives.*1Th 2:4* The Father will stick up for you.*1Th 2:5* The Father isn't giving up.*1Th 5:24* Confidence produces love.*1Ti 1:5* Right relationship with the Father takes confidence.*Gal 5:2-5* Your good deeds prove your confidence.*Jas 2:18* You can rely on the Father helping and protecting you.*2Th 3:3* The Father directs your motives into his love and the Son's perseverance.*2Th 3:5* Let truth nourish you.*1Ti 4:6* Fan into flame your trust in Father and Son.*2Ti 1:6* Live confidently in the good news of right relationship with the Father.*Ro 1:17* Hope confidently not for what you see and have but for what you don't yet have.*Ro 8:24-25* Draw near to the Father with full assurance.*Heb 10:22* A little confidence goes a long way. Then, nothing is impossible.*Matt 17:20-21* You can really make things happen, *big* things, with a little confidence.*Lk 17:5-6* You may ask the Son to give you more confidence, even if you already know that the Father can do anything.*Mk 9:23-24* Your work is to accept the good news that the Father sent the Son.*Jn 6:28-29*

Family also rules. The Father could have put anyone, like some celestial being, over everything. Instead, the Father in his choice of rulers put his Son in charge of it all. The Father left nothing over which the Son will not rule, including places that we do not yet see. Everything is a family affair, family business, Father putting Son in charge.*Heb 2:5-8* And the Father put the Son in charge to show that he is the great Father. No one but the Son could honor the Father in the same way.*Php 2:11* When the Father engaged the Son in the family business, the Father gave the Son reciprocal honor to what the Son was giving the Father. That's how family works.*2Pe 1:17*

> **The Son is your authority.** The Father gave the Son all authority.*Matt 28:18-20* The Son had his Father's authority to give his life and take it back again.*Jn 10:17-18* The Son speaks on the Father's authority.*Jn 14:10* The Son taught with authority.*Mk 1:21-22* Even the enemy submits to the Son's authority.*Mk 1:27* The Son has authority to excuse and heal.*Mk 2:5-12, Lk 5:17-25* The Father granted the Son authority over everyone so that he could give life forever to all whom the Father gave him.*Jn 17:2* The Father gave the Son authority.*Jude 24-25* The Son is the head of all authority.*Col 2:10* The Son will destroy all other authority before giving everything back to the Father.*1Co 15:24* Fear Father and Son who have authority to throw you into hell.*Lk 12:5*

Indeed, family does not stop there. Because you are part of the family, the Father gave his Son for you to show you that the Father also gives you everything, just as he gave everything to his Son. His Son merited the gift, while you did not. But because you are family, you receive the gift through the Son's merit.*Ro 8:32* The Son advocates for you with the Father, just like family.*1Jn 2:1-2* You are a family member, living with the Father as the Father's child, and the Father living with you as your Father, because you relate like family, like a sibling, to the Son.*1Jn 4:15* When you are like the Son, the Father gives you complete love, a family love in which no family member judges another. Isn't that family that you do not judge one another? The Father does not judge you when you remain in his family.*1Jn 4:17* And because you are his child, you can cry to him like a child cries to a father. The Father hears your cry as a father hears a child's cry—in the heart, with a passion to answer.*Ro 8:15* That the creator of everything treats himself as the Father and you as his child is one of creation's most-profound wonders. To see your life transformed, grasp it. Relate to your creator as the Father who he is.

> **Know the Father's authority.** The Father's authority is like a special invitation that many ignore and even reject openly and insultingly.*Matt 22:1-6* The Father will reject those people who feel that they don't need his special invitation. Then he'll invite the people who know that they do need him.*Matt 22:7-10* But those people still need to honor the Father, respecting his special invitation. He invites many but chooses few.*Matt 22:11-14* Many whom the Father invites will give what they think are good excuses for rejecting the invitation.*Lk 14:16-20* But the Father doesn't take excuses. He doesn't care who you are but just wants you to accept his invitation unconditionally.*Lk 14:21-24* The point is that the Father wants you under his authority rather than anyone else's authority.*1Th 2:12* Your job is to tell everyone that the Father's authority is right here by your side.*Matt 10:7* The Father will certainly bring you in when sharing his invitation is hard on you.*2Th 1:5* The Father will take you under his authority and rule—good for you!*2Ti 4:18* Just keep in sight of his authority. Don't let it go.*2Ti 4:1* Nothing can shake you loose from him unless you want to be out from under him.*Heb 12:28-29* The Father is generous with his light rule.*Col 1:12* The Father just wants you with his beloved Son.*Col 1:13* The Son will be right there with the Father to welcome you.*2Pe 1:10-11* Pursue the Father's rule.*Eph 5:5* The materially poor who are rich in thinking of the Father will gain his rule.*Jas 2:5* Those who keep themselves from corrupting desires will gain the Father's rule.*Eph 5:5* The Father's rule isn't about what you eat and drink but about being right with him, having his peace, and being glad that you have his Spirit.*Ro 14:17* The Father's authority is not talk but power.*1Co 4:20* You must be free from worldly desires to be under the Father's rule.*Gal 4:30-31*

Spirit

The creator of everything, the Father who treats you as family, has another quality that you should not miss. The Father is essence, Spirit. The Father relates to you through his essence, through his Spirit. The Father's essential Spirit is *love*, a love that the Father pours over you until that love soaks your heart. The Father is not a remote spirit but instead has sent his intimate Spirit to you, *given* his Spirit to you, to live right alongside you and in you.*Ro 5:5* You know that the Father's Spirit lives in you when you find yourself pursuing the things that the Spirit pursues rather than pursuing the things that your own flesh, your body, your appetites desire. The Father's Spirit is not absent, remote, unknowable. No, the Father's Spirit is instead someone whom you can sense, hear, and thus follow. When you pursue things that the Spirit pursues, following the Spirit as your guide and leader, you know that you are the Father's children, trusted and valued as family members.*Ro 8:14*

The Father's essence is a gentle Spirit. The Spirit does not frighten you like a ghost. The Spirit does not make you slaves like a tyrant would make you. Instead, the Spirit makes you the Father's child. The Spirit enables you to cry to your Father, giving you a child's plaintive and endearing voice rather than a devil's demanding voice.*Ro 8:15* The Spirit aligns with your spirit when you desire the Father to be your Father. The Spirit allows you to look and act like the Son, even to the point of suffering as the Son suffered for the Father, so that the Father can share with you the honor that he lavishes on the Son.*Ro 8:16-17* The Father searches your heart to see where you stand toward him. But the Father knows the Spirit's mind without any searching. And the Spirit stands up for you with the Father. The Father *wants* the Spirit to stand up for you, and so the Spirit gladly does so.*Ro 8:27* Be glad that the creator of everything is Spirit because Spirit comes to you, fills you, and guides you to the Father in whom you find everything.

> ***You, too, are spiritual.*** Your spirit goes beyond your mind, will, and emotions. Accept your spiritual nature, and then feed your spirit with the Father's words, not false and corrupt views from the enemy.*1Jn 4:1* Trust views that rely on the Son, not views that reject the Son. The enemy sends the views that reject the Son.*1Jn 4:2-3* When you rely on the Son, you show that you have gotten past the enemy's false perspective. The Father's Spirit in you, your

great helper, reveals and rejects the enemy's perspective.*1Jn 4:4* Those who don't rely on the Son accept the false worldly viewpoint, all material, no spirit, and no future.*1Jn 4:5* You may have the knack for distinguishing worldly viewpoints from the Son's spiritual standpoint, which is how things truly work.*1Co 12:8-10* Those who rely on the Son recognize others who also rely on the Son. Those who don't rely on the Son reject you. They rely on false worldly viewpoints, not the Spirit's truth about the Son.*1Jn 4:6* The Father deploys spiritual influences. You carry his Spirit when you share the good news.*Heb 1:7* The Father's spiritual influences help you. Trust and rely on them.*Heb 1:14* The Father's Spirit warns against following deceiving spirits drawn from the enemy's worldly viewpoint.*1Ti 4:1* Submit only to the Father's Spirit if you wish to truly live.*Heb 12:9* The Father's Spirit makes perfect those who receive him.*Heb 12:23*

Reconciler

The Father who created everything and who through the Son maintains everything is a peace-loving Father. He is not a tyrant or war monger. His great desire is to favor you, bless you, even though you have not merited your own flourishing. The Father simply extends favor to you both for himself and the Son.*Php 1:2* You get it all from the Father, not the harsh judgment that you deserve but instead the good things that you do not deserve and then the stability and assurance that go along with those good things. The Father shares all these things with you out of his love for you, a true and reliable love that has no condition other than your reciprocal love, formed from obedience.*2Jn 3* The Father and Son offer the same unmerited favor to each of you who love and honor them.*Gal 1:3* The Father loves you. He wants you to join his Son, to honor his Son, even while the Father showers you with such abundance. The Father is utterly willing to look the other way from your worst faults so that you may have his confidence, warmth, and security.*Jude 1-2*

The Father offers you all these things because he desires to settle once for all any score with you, to start anew with you, to resolve all questions in your favor, even where you do not deserve it. The Father only gives these extraordinary gifts of excuse through his Son. The Father wants you to accept his offer to reconcile and turn his offer into your own reconciliation service, making you a peacemaker, too.*2Co 5:18* The Father reconciled everything, made all things good with him again everywhere—yes, where you are on earth and where the Father is—to himself through the Son.*Col 1:20* And the Father had good reason. The Father reconciled the world to himself through the Son so that the Father could embrace the world again, your corrupted world. The Father could have ended the world for all its self-induced misery, destroyed the world and started over, but instead he resolved not to count your corruption against you. He just wants you now to carry his reconciliation message to others, the same reconciliation message that his Son carried to you.*2Co 5:19* The Father's great desire is for peace, everyone getting along, seeing you tranquil, content, and happy.*Col 1:2* Your peace is in the Father and in his Son. That's where you'll find it.*1Th 1:1* Just keep hearing the Father tell you of his peace and the peace that comes with loving his Son, and then you'll finally get it.*2Th 1:1-2* Indeed, that's the only way you'll get peace, from the Father and his Son.*2Ti 1:2* You are not going to find peace any other way. The Father is your reconciler.

Don't hold things against others. Don't hold things against others. The Father doesn't hold them against you.*Lk 6:36* The Father wants you to let things go.*Matt 9:13* Surely don't condemn the innocent. The Father wants you to let things go.*Matt 12:7* Honor the Father for not holding things against you. The Son submitted to human judgment so that the Father could let you go.*Ro 5:8-11* The Father decides on whom he has compassion.*Ro 9:14-15* Your rescue depends on the Father looking the other way, not your own effort.*Ro 9:16* The Father decides whom he will let go.*Ro 9:18* Let others go, or the Father will hold things against you.*Jas 2:12-13* The Father spares those who rely on the Son.*Php 2:27* The Father spares even the worst if they will just rely on the Son.*1Ti 1:13* The Father spares the worst to show just how special the Son's rescue is, including life forever.*1Ti 1:16* The Father spares households that look out for those who rely on the Son.*2Ti 1:16-18* The Father's willingness to let you off should make you want to do right.*Ro 12:1* The Father's willingness to let you off helps you teach others what to do.*2Co 4:1* Approach the Father confidently. He'll let you off.*Heb 4:16* The Father favors those who let others go.*Matt 5:7* Just ask the Son not to find fault with you, and he'll heal you.*Matt 20:29-34*

Rescuer

The Father doesn't just settle the score in your favor. He doesn't just reconcile with you on terms that you're going to love. The Father also *rescues* you. The Father draws you back from the precipice. He pulls you out of the worst situation: your death. Indeed, the Son said that his Father's will is that the Son lose *none* of you to the other side, to death. The Son said that the Father gave you to the Son so that he could release and free you from death's cold, hard grip. Now *that's* a rescue.*Jn 6:39* And that's just what the Father wants to do, to rescue you. He wants everyone who looks to his Son to live forever with the Son. The Son will just come right back to take you to paradise with him.*Jn. 6:40* Here's how the Father's rescue works: the only way to get from death to paradise with the Son is to let the Father draw you to the Son in these desperate last days. Listen for those whispers, and then heed them. Don't lose it all out of ignorance.*Jn 6:44* The Son kept repeating that none of you can come to him, come along with him, unless the Father makes it possible for you, which the Father has done and you just need now to do.*Jn 6:65* Only those of you who listen to and learn from the Father come to the Son. It's now all up to you.*Jn 6:45* You have one Rescuer, and the Father gave the Rescuer to you. Anywhere you look, he's the only one you'll ever find.*Acts 4:12*

The Father's rescue works because his power for you is the same as the great power he used to bring his Son alive right after his Son died. And the Father didn't just give his Son life again. The Father brought the Son right back to the Father's own side where the Father rules unquestioned, to put the Son in charge again of everything and everyone, not just now but forever.*Eph 1:19-21* The Father's rescue was to give you that great gift of living forever in his Son and only in his Son.*1Jn 5:11-13* The Father's rescue was permanent, good forever, not some passing fancy but instead right on through to, well, forever, to *no end.*2Th 2:16-17* You have every reason to honor the Father, to appreciate and thank him, for showing such incredible compassion.*2Co 1:3* The Father wants your rescue *now*, not later. Your best opportunity to catch on with him is right now.*2Co 6:2* The Father's rescue is huge, everything to you. Catch it.

> **The Son rescues you.** The Father so loved you that he gave his one and only Son that if you relied on the Son you would live forever.*Jn 3:16* The Son fulfilled the good news, just as the ancient writings predicted.*Mk 1:1* You know how to live forever: rely on the Son who is your only way, the true way to living forever. No one gets to do so without him.*Jn 14:4-6* The Son told the good news just as it is. All you have to do is rely on it. It's that easy.*Mk 1:14-15* The Son was after you, to rescue *you*.*Lk 19:10* The Son is your only rescue. He's it, no one else.*Acts 4:12* Thank the Father that the Son came to your rescue.*Tit 3:3-5* The good news has always been around, just hidden until the Son revealed it fully.*Col 1:26-27*

The good news was his, not something you or anyone else made up.*Gal 1:11-12* The Father had promised the good news, and then it was here.*Ro 1:2* The ancient writings were to get you ready for the good news.*1Pe 1:12* The Son is your rescue.*1Th 3:9* Don't mess it up, but if you do, then know the Son will still set the score straight with the Father.*1Jn 2:1-2* The Son can do it for others just as he does it for you.*1Ti 4:10* The good news should help you do as the Father wants.*Ro 16:26* The Father likes you. That's why he rescues you.*2Co 6:2* Doesn't matter who you are. You still get the good news.*Matt 11:4-5* Once everyone hears the good news, it's over.*Matt 24:14* The Son has the Father's permission to rescue.*Mk 2:5-12, Lk 5:17-25*

Restorer

The Father, though, does not just reconcile accounts with you and then rescue you. He also *restores* you, revivifies you, makes you new, better, and different in just the right way. The Father animates you with perfect new life because his power, honor, and authority, his *transcendence*, gave his dead Son, his sacrificed Son, new life.*Ro 6:3-4* Look, if the Father could do it for the Son, then the Father can just as well do it for you. You just need the same Spirit of the Father in you like the Son has his Father's Spirit in him. This living-in-the-Spirit you *can* do.*Ro 8:11* You can do it because your doing it was the Father's whole plan. The Father let the Son die at human hands and then brought him right back to life for the very reason to restore you with the Father, fully accepted rather than condemned in your own corruption. The Father made you acceptable again, so that *anyone* could accept you, even the perfect him.*Ro 4:25*

This restoration wasn't temporary or partial, either, like getting a pass from class but still facing the final exam. No, this restoration was to a new condition, *entirely* new, so new as to make you incorruptible. You should thank the Father on your knees for looking past everything you've done, when he gives you this entirely new life, like you were just born all over again. Your new birth is into a living, breathing dynamism, where every moment is better, always looking forward to the next. Yes, your new condition is to come back fully alive from the previously dead, never to die again, like the Son came right back to life, never to die again.*1Pe 1:3* The Father restores, fully restores, so that you can live in the perfect Son even when still dead in your old corrupted condition.*Col 2:13*

The Father wants you alive, not dead. You just rose up entirely alive with the Son when the Son walked from his fresh grave.*Col 3:1* Because the Father restores, the old you is long gone. You may not see all your new life yet, because your new life hides in the Son, but your new life is definitely there.*Col 3:3* Just wait for it, if you can't see it. It's coming. You'll see it when the Son gets here again, the Son who walked right out of his own grave.*1Th 1:10* The Father is a fixer, one whose fix is permanent and perfect.

> **The Son rescues you from death.** The Father let his Son die so that he could bring him right back for you.*Ro 4:25* The Son asked the Father to save him from death because he didn't want to separate from the Father. So the Father brought him right back to life.*Heb 5:7* The Son made himself nothing, obeying to the point of the worst possible death.*Php 2:6-8* The Son first healed, taught, and fed you, and then beat your worst enemy—death—for you.*1Co 15:26* The ancient writings said he would die but live after three days, just like he did.*1Co 15:3* The Father first fulfilled his promise then brought the Son right back to life for you.*Heb 13:20* The Son brings everyone together in new life, ending all fighting.*Eph 2:15-16* The Son became human because you are human. That's the only way he could die to break the enemy's power of death.*Heb 2:14* The Son took your curse for you, the payback you get from breaking the law all the time.*Gal 3:13* Your immersion for the Son was your burial. Now, you live a new life.*Ro 6:3-4* The Son's death and coming right back enabled the Father's Spirit to free you from payback and death.*Ro 8:2* You can be sad about your wrongs. Just let your sadness lead you to the Son rather than to death.*2Co 7:10* Now that the Son rescued you, stop messing around.*Heb 6:1-2* Don't worry about attacks on your body. Worry about losing not just your body but also you mind, will, and emotions, in hell.*Matt 10:28, Lk 12:4-5* The enemy gathers around those who are dying. Things just get worse and worse.*Lk 17:37* The Son can give life right back to the dead because the Father has life in himself that he gave to the Son to share.*Jn 5:25-26* All the dead will soon rise at the Son's call, some to live but others to face final condemnation.*Jn 5:28-29*

Giver

The Father is also a giver, generous beyond your comprehension. From when you first encountered the Father through his Son, and realized that you were better to follow than fight them, the Father put his mark on you. Except his mark is not some gang-symbol tattoo, nor a special piercing. No, he sealed you instead with his own Spirit. That's right: he had his Spirit bottle you up, surround you, guard you, and protect you so that no one important could mistake your allegiance. And when the Father did so, he ensured that you would receive everything that he has for you. Oh, you'll get his full gifts in due time, but until then, you're as good as rich, wealthy, guaranteed to receive what the Father has promised you.*Eph 1:13-14* And you know his greatest gift? His own Spirit is the Father's greatest gift because the Spirit cleans you up and makes you over for *him*, for the Father. You get everything new, including a new body. And the best thing of all is that you get all these gifts because you accepted the Father's gift of his Son.*Tit 5:6*

> ***Give generously.*** Giving is easy when you're rich. Try giving when you're poor. It counts for more.*Mk 12:41-43, Lk 20:41-44, 21:1-4* Sell stuff. Then give to the poor. That's how you pay it forward.*Lk 12:33* Yes, please the Father by giving. But you're only giving back to him what's always been his.*Ro 11:35-36* Give the poor person just as much attention as the rich person.*Jas 2:2-4* The poor accept the good news more readily than the rich.*Jas 2:5* The rich exploit, not the poor.*Jas 2:6-7* Joy with poverty can make for rich generosity.*2Co 8:2* Best to be poor while making many rich. Best to have nothing and yet possess everything.*2Co 6:8-10* Sell possessions, give to the poor, please the Father, and rely on the Son.*Matt 19:16-22* The rich find harder getting close to the Father.*Matt 19:22-24* Rescue, though impossible even for the rich, is possible from the Father.*Matt 19:25-26* Share with those who rely on the Son.*Php 4:15-16* Sharing with others pleases the Father.*Heb 13:16* Share in one another's struggles.*Php 4:14* Help the weak.*1Th 5:14* Share with the Father's friends. Practice hospitality.*Ro 12:13* Give as much as able, even beyond your ability, on your own.*2Co 8:3* Sharing is a privilege.*2Co 8:4* Exceed expectations. Give first to the Father and then to others.*2Co 8:5* Excel in giving.*2Co 8:7* The Father enriches you so that you can always be generous.*2Co 9:11* Give willingly, not under compulsion. The Father loves cheerful givers.*2Co 9:7* The point is not to relieve others while pressing you hard but that equality exists.*2Co 8:13* Give now so that others can return the gift later.*2Co 8:14* Give eagerly so that others boast about you and imitate you.*2Co 9:2-4* Give what you promise.*2Co 9:5* Give to those who ask.*Matt 5:42* Give, and you'll get more back.*Lk 6:37-38* Give without announcing it.*Matt 6:2-3* Welcome requests.*2Co 8:17*

Now, the Father sends instructions with this gift of his own Spirit. The Father is a generous giver, but he is also a *wise* giver. His instructions ensure that you get the Spirit's full benefit.*1Th 4:8* For instance, the Father's Spirit doesn't make you weak, defenseless, and timid. The Spirit instead gives you all the power that you would ever need. The Spirit also gives you love and, perhaps best of all, the ability to control yourself so that you can enjoy the other gifts as you should. The Spirit doesn't leave you some out-of-control fool.*2Ti 1:7* The Spirit also helps you influence others to join the Father's side. The Spirit gives you that effective power, genuine power that makes every difference in people's lives.*Ro 15:18-19* The Father's gift of his Spirit, to you and anyone else who loves the Father, is how you know the Father's many other gifts, too. The Spirit shows you those other gifts, things that you surely hadn't seen before but also of which you hadn't heard or even imagined. Have you really felt joy, true joy? And peace, deep peace, with full contentment? Have you even known how satisfying being entirely *good* can be?*1Co 2:9-10*

The amazing service that the Father's Spirit, his greatest gift to you, does for you is that the Spirit searches everything, even God's deep things, to reveal them to you. You don't just come up with these wonders on your own. The Spirit brings them to you.*1Co 2:10* That service is necessary because no one knows the Father's thoughts except the Father's Spirit, just as only your own spirit knows your own thoughts—and the Father's Spirit knows your thoughts.*1Co 2:11* The good thing is that you received the Father's Spirit when you followed the Son. You didn't receive the world's spirit, which would have done you no good. With the Father's Spirit, you can know the wonders with which the Father blessed you, gratis, without your having earned them.*1Co 2:12* Appreciate that the Father is a giver, and not a stingy giver but the most-generous giver of all.

> **This way works for you, too.** Those who die relying on the Son will also come right back to life.*2Ti 2:11* The Son's death made the Father take you back when you were still his enemy. The Son's coming right back to life gives you his permanent life.*Ro 5:10* With the Son having paid your sentence, the Father can look right past your faults.*Col 1:22* Get this: the Son even frees you from fearing death.*Heb 2:15* Because you decided to rely on his death, you get to come back to life like he did.*Ro 6:5* Because you died with him, so to speak, you also live with him.*Ro 6:8* If you rely on the Son, then even though your body dies corrupted, the Spirit gives you life because of the Son's incorruption.*Ro 8:10* If the Spirit who gave life right back to the Son lives in you, then the Spirit will do the same for you. Your body will live again.*Ro 8:11* You don't rely on the old rules anymore. Now, you're relying on the Son so that you can have his right-back life. Then you'll be working for the Father.*Ro 7:4* When you rely on the Son, everything is yours.*1Co 3:21-23* Love as the Son loved, and you go from death to life.*1Jn 3:11-14* Admit it: you've wanted to escape death. Who doesn't?*2Co 5:4* If you make your

old body your only devotion, then it's over for you. Rely on the Son.₂Co 5:6 Give up the old body to live with the Son.₂Co 5:8 You don't need to fear death when the Father knows you inside and out and values you more than dying things.Matt 10:29-31, Lk 12:6-7

Love

The Father has profound and wonderous qualities. But above all, the Father *is love*. You live in the Father and the Father in you when you love.1Jn 4:16 The Father knows those who love him.1Co 8:3 You love because the Father loved you.1Jn 4:19 The Father loves his people.Ro 1:7 Love comes from the Father. Loving shows you know your Father.1Jn 4:7 Those who do not love do not know the Father because *the Father is love*.1Jn 4:8 No one has seen the Father, but if you love one another, then the Father lives in you.1Jn 4:12 The Father teaches you to love each other.1Th 4:9-10 The Father directs you into his love.2Th 3:5 The Father pours his love into you through his Spirit.Ro 5:5 The Father's Spirit gives you love.2Ti 1:7 The Spirit produces love.Gal 5:22 The Father's love is with you.2Co 13:14 The Father loves whoever loves the Son. The Son loves and shows himself to those who love him.Jn 14:21 The Father loves those who rely on the Son because they loved the Son.Jn 16:27

Love one another. Love one another as the Son loved you.Jn 13:34 Love each other.Jn 15:17 Others should recognize that you rely on the Son by your love for one another.Jn 13:35 Do for others what you would have them do for you.Matt 7:12 Love the Father with all your mind, will, and emotion.Matt 22:34-38, Mk 12:28-30 Love your neighbor as yourself.Matt 22:39-40, Mk 12:31-32 The Father says to love him and your neighbor.Mk 12:34 Do as the Son says to show you love him.Jn 14:15 Those who do as the Son says are the ones who love him.Jn 14:21 Love one another as the Son loved you.Jn 15:12 Do everything in love.1Co 16:14 Spur one another on toward love.Heb 10:24 Love one another as brothers and sisters.Heb 13:1 Loving one another takes you from death to life.1Jn 3:11-14 Make your love obvious while letting it protect you.1Th 3:8 Confidence in the Son and clear conscience produce love.1Ti 1:5 Love as an example for others.1Ti 4:11 Thank the Father that your love for one another increases.2Th 1:3 Pursue love with others who pursue the Father.2Ti 2:22 Love is giving yourself up for others.Jn 15:13 Love is devoting yourself to another.Ro 12:10 Loving is reducing another's corruption.1Pe 4:8 Love like a mother loves her child.1Th 2:7-8 Love sincerely.Ro 12:9 Love strangers

> who rely on the Son, too.*3Jn 5-6* Love deeply, from the heart.*1Pe 1:22* Love builds up.*1Co 8:1* Love those whom you urge to rely on the Son.*2Co 11:11*

Loving the Father means loving his Son and those who rely on his Son.*1Jn 5:1-2* When the Father gave his Son's life for you, he gave you everything.*Ro 8:32* Nothing can separate you from the Son's love.*Ro 8:35-36* Nothing at all can separate you from the Father's love, either, his having given his Son's life for you.*Ro 8:38-39* The Father showed his love among you by sending his only Son so that you could live through him.*1Jn 4:9* Your loving the Father matters little compared to the Father loving you. And the Father loved you by giving his Son's life to rescue you. That rescue was from yourself.*1Jn 4:10* The Son loves his own, those who rely on him, to the end.*Jn 13:1* As the Father loved the Son, the Son loved you. So remain in his love.*Jn 15:9* You remain in the Son's love when you do as he says, just as he did as his Father said and so remains in his Father's love.*Jn 15:10*

> **Love even enemies.** Love enemies. Strange as it seems, do good to those who hate you. Ask the Father to help even those who mistreat you.*Lk 6:27-28* Let an enemy wrong you without wronging the enemy back.*Matt 5:38-39, Lk 6:29* Give your enemy more than your enemy demands.*Matt 5:40, Lk 6:29* Go the extra mile even for an enemy.*Matt 5:41* Love not just friends but enemies, too. Ask the Father to help them. The Father helped you.*Matt 5:43-45* You get no special reward for loving those who love you. Everyone does so.*Matt 5:46* Everyone greets their friends. Try greeting an enemy, too.*Matt 5:47* Even the corrupt who reject the Son do good to those who do good to them.*Lk 6:33* Even the corrupt lend to those whom they expect to repay.*Lk 6:34* Love enemies, doing good to them. Lend to them without expecting repayment. Then you'll get the Father's special reward. The Father loves the corrupt, too. He loves you.*Lk 6:35* Love truly, genuinely. To love is not to make a big noise about it.*1Co 13:1* To love is not to be brilliant.*1Co 13:2* To love is not to give away everything and suffer everything.*1Co 13:3* Love is instead patient and kind, without envying or boasting.*1Co 13:4* Love does not dishonor others, seek itself, easily anger, or keep records of wrongs.*1Co 13:5* Love does not delight in evil but instead rejoices in truth.*1Co 13:6* Love always protects, trusts, hopes, and perseveres.*1Co 13:7* Love never fails, even when predictions cease, speaking stops, and knowledge disappears.*1Co 13:8* Love is greater than confidence and hope.*1Co 13:13* Loving makes both you and the Son happy.*Jn 15:11*

Supreme

The Father has another attribute that you should always recall. No one and nothing is greater than the Father. He is supreme. He has power that not only creates and thus exceeds all other power but also power that continues forever, inexhaustible. Look at the night sky! Consider the vast universe! Although you don't see the Father, you can see how great is his power because *he created everything that you see*. You know a fine painter or craftsman from the work. Know the Father the same way._{Ro 1:20} People act as if they know more than he does, like they can lecture him and correct his ways. Presuming so is utterly absurd! No one knows the Father's mind enough to tell him what to do. He's a thousand steps ahead of you._{Ro 11:34} People think that he's not paying attention, like he's going to show up late. That's ridiculous! He has a sense of time that you'll never grasp. Time differs to him. A day to him is like a thousand years to you, and a thousand years to him like a day to you. Don't presume anything about him._{2Pe 3:8}

The Father will change his course if you change your course, that you can trust. What you do makes a difference to him. But who he is will never change. The Father does not change his attributes. He will always give the best and most-fitting gifts to those who love him and his Son. Nothing's going to change about that._{Jas 1:17} The Father has a depth, richness, intellect, insight, and stability to him so great as to fashion a rock-solid but still-spectacular universe. Don't underestimate him._{Ro 11:33} The Father can send his messengers anywhere, anytime. He makes those who serve him flames of fire, able to refine things into their essence, to get things done and done right._{Heb 1:7} The Father destroys what you call wisdom when not wise. He puts your smartest persons to utter shame with the things that they do not know. More so, though, the Father gave you and others who follow his Son the *cross* for power—a simple *cross*! Yet that cross produces in you a power that puts everything else to shame that others think is so great. In that way, the Father shares with you his great wisdom and intellect._{1Co 1:18-19}

Get the Father's true wisdom. If you want wisdom, then ask the Father. He gives you lots of it whether you have faults or not._{Jas 1:6} Think of the Father's words rather than just know them, and help others do likewise, so that you remain firmly established in truth._{2Pe 1:12-14} Think about true, noble, right, pure, lovely, admirable, excellent and praiseworthy things._{Php 4:8} Practice whatever you learn, receive, or hear from the wise, or see in them._{Php 4:9} The Son is your wisdom from the Father.*1Co 1:30* The Father makes you wise.*2Ti 2:7* The approved writings make you wise about the good news.*2Ti 3:14-15* Don't worry beforehand what to say because the Father will give you wisdom that your adversaries will not be able to resist or contradict.*Lk 21:14-15* Speak wisdom among the mature, but not the day's wisdom, which is nothing.*1Co 2:6* Declare the Father's wisdom, a hidden mystery from before time began.*1Co 2:7* Rulers did not understand it, or they would not have killed the Son.*1Co 2:8* Be wise in the way you interact with others. Make the most of every opportunity. Know how to answer everyone.*Col 4:5-6* Wisdom proves her children right.*Lk 7:35* Envy and ambition aren't wisdom.*Jas 3:14-16* Wisdom is pure, peace-loving, considerate, submissive, productive, impartial, and sincere.*Jas 3:17-18* Be wise about good but innocent about evil.*Ro 16:19* Be shrewd but innocent.*Matt 10:16* Those who think they know don't know as they should know.*1Co 8:2* Deeds prove wisdom right.*Matt 11:19* The Father hides the good news from the worldly wise.*Matt 11:25-26* The Father makes foolish the world's wisdom.*1Co 1:20* The Father's foolishness is wiser than human wisdom.*1Co 1:25* Speak what the Spirit teaches, not human wisdom.*1Co 2:13* Worldly wisdom is foolishness in the Father's sight.*1Co 3:19*

The Father also shows himself supreme in sticking with you when others would not. He isn't whimsical or arbitrary. You can *rely* on him because he is greater than any fad, fashion, or passing fancy.*1Th 5:24* The Father lavishes his love on you as the best father would on the best children.*1Jn 3:1-2* Because the Father is supreme and perfect, he could judge you and everything else deficient. Yet while he does judge all, he judges you right and perfect because he gave you his perfect Spirit.*Heb 12:23* Just think of the Father as pure light without any hint of darkness.*1Jn 1:5* More than that, think of the Father as he most is: hallowed, holy, honored, immense, dominant, potent, and perpetual. Think of him as your only Ruler, the Authority of all authorities, the Master of all masters. Only he is immortal, although he shares his immortality with you. Only he lives in light so brilliant that you can't get near it—but he lets you come near through his Son. No one has seen or can see the Father, but he lets you see him in his Son.*1Ti 6:15-16* Relate to the Father as you should. Hold him in absolute awe, as he consumes you with his love. Treat him with your greatest possible reverence.*Heb 12:28-29* Know who the Father truly is. It's not what you know but *who* you know, when you consider him. Nothing has greater consequence.

What Father and Son speak happens. Everything will disappear except what the Son says. His words are that important.*Matt 24:35, Mk 13:31, Lk 21:32-33* The Son's words carry the Spirit and your life.*Jn 6:63* What the Son said, the Father said first.*Jn 14:10* The words the Son's students heard from him were actually the Father's words.*Jn 14:24* The Son at first used figurative speech but later spoke plainly so that his students would get it.*Jn 16:25* The students finally did understand what the Son said, realizing then that the Son knew it all because the Father sent him.*Jn 16:29-30* The Son gave his students the words that the Father had given him, which the students accepted.*Jn 17:8* The ancient writings were all about the Son's offer of living forever, although those who read them didn't get it.*Jn 5:39-40* The ancient writings said that the Father sent the Son as his own.*Jn 10:34-36* The religious leaders who questioned the Son didn't know the ancient writings.*Matt 22:29* The religious leaders killed the Son because they couldn't take his word.*Jn 8:37* The Father's words show you that the ancient writings truly were about his Son's offer of living forever.*Eph 3:4-5* The Son did just what the ancient writings said he would do, which was to do as the Father told him.*Heb 10:7* You rely on the Son because you hear about him—that's it.*Ro 10:17* The Son's story eventually reaches everyone.*Ro 10:18* The Father's words are forever free, even if you might not always be free.*2Ti 2:9* The Father's words make you wise, which is to live forever through the Son.*2Ti 3:14-15* The ancient writings told it all, including the Son coming right back to life.*1Co 15:3* Better do as the Father's words say, or no one will listen to you.*1Co 14:37-38* Don't fake it. You understand what the Father is saying here.*2Co 1:13* Let people read you, too.*2Co 3:3*

3 Coming

Ancestry

When the Father sent his Son into the world, he wasn't going to have him appear out of nowhere as if in some magic show. The Father instead slowly formed a people who would identify the Son as descended from their royal line, even though the Son came from the Father.*Ro 1:3* The Father took fourteen long generations from Abraham who founded the people to the people's greatest king David, then fourteen more generations from David to a time of the people's exile, and then fourteen more generations to the Son. The generations and tracing of a royal line made sense out of the Son's coming, when otherwise his coming would have made no sense. You couldn't and wouldn't have comprehended it without this preparation.*Matt 1:1-17* If you prefer, then you can trace the Son's earthly ancestry back from the Son through well-known figures including David and Abraham, all the way to the first human Adam, whom the Father made.*Lk 3:23-38*

The Son, though, came from God the Father, not from an earthly father. You know how it happened, the historical account that you hear and celebrate at Christmas. The Father chose a young unmarried woman Mary, who was set to marry Joseph, to carry the Son into the world. Before Mary and Joseph married, the Father's Spirit carried the unborn Son to Mary.*Matt 1:18* Joseph at first assumed the worst about the pregnant Mary. But the Father's messenger appeared to Joseph in a dream saying to trust Mary as his wife because she had conceived only from the Spirit.*Matt 1:20* The Father's messenger told Joseph that Mary would give birth to the Father's Son whom Joseph was to name Jesus, or Yeshua or Joshua if you prefer, meaning *the Father rescues*. The Son would give people light to escape from their enslaving darkness. He would bring people *freedom*.*Matt 1:21* The ancient seer Micah had said that the Son would come from Bethlehem, not Galilee where Mary and Joseph lived. So when Caesar decreed a census of the entire Roman world, Mary and Joseph along with everyone else returned to their hometowns.*Lk 2:1-3* Joseph took the pregnant Mary from Nazareth in Galilee to Bethlehem in Judea because Joseph came from David's line. That's how the Son came from Bethlehem, just as the ancient writings had said hundreds of years earlier.*Lk 2:4-5* None would have accepted the Son if the Father had not so exquisitely and publicly prepared the way for him, heralded and anticipated for more than a millenium.

> ***Remain confident.*** The enemy tempts you to get you to lose your confidence.*1Th 3:5* Loving money will tempt you to lose your confidence.*1Ti 6:10* Those who follow the enemy have no confidence in the good news.*2Th 3:2* Confidence in the good news makes you right with the Father. Then, you don't worry about living forever or not. You know the Son handled it.*Ro 10:6-7* When you trust the good news, you know the Son took care of it.*Ro 10:8* Confidence in the good news relieves you from worry about the rules.*Ro 2:28* The good news respects the rules, though.*Ro 2:31* You don't have to know and follow the old rules. The good news takes care of you.*Matt 8:11-12* Hold on to your confidence. Keep a clean conscience, too. It helps your confidence in the good news.*1Ti 1:19* The Spirit warns against losing your trust.*1Ti 4:1* Just because some don't trust doesn't change the Father's trust. The Father remains confident even when no one else is.*Ro 2:3-4*

Incarnation

History turned, *hinged,* on the moment of the Son's coming. But the circumstances of the Son's coming were in themselves enormously significant. Mary indeed gave birth to the Son in Bethlehem, just as predicted hundreds of years earlier. The Son thus came not as a powerful ruler, a fully formed and unconquerable dictator. The Son instead came as a powerless, wet, bloody, helpless newborn infant, just like any of you. Mary wrapped him in cloths as any mother would do. Mary and Joseph hadn't even found a room for the birth, in the town full of census visitors. So she bore the Son in an animal shelter—an *animal shelter*—putting him in a manger. The Son came as humbly, innocent, and vulnerable, even *precarious,* as one could possibly come. The Father and Son had an utterly different way to rescue the world than the world itself would have pursued.*Lk 2:6-7*

Yet as humble as the Son's entry was, the Father wasn't going to let it pass unnoticed. The Father's messenger appeared in the night to shepherds who were watching flocks near Bethlehem. The Father didn't send his message to leaders, the influential, or the rich but instead to lowly shepherds, the night-workers, the social outcasts. The messenger's brilliance, shining into the night around them, terrified the shepherds.*Lk 2:8-9* The messenger first had to tell the shepherds not to be afraid of him. He then explained that he brought them good news, news over which they and everyone else should have great joy. The shocking good news was that the world's Rescuer, its ultimate Ruler, was now a newborn infant in nearby Bethlehem. The messenger told the shepherds to go find the humble cloth-wrapped Rescuer in a Bethlehem manger.*Lk 2:10-12*

At that moment of the messenger's stunning announcement, a great number of other celestial beings also appeared. They were all shouting honor to the Father. But they were also already promising peace on earth to those who would follow the Son.*Lk 2:13-14* What would you do? The shepherds did as they should, hurrying off for Bethlehem where, exactly as announced, they found Mary and Joseph with the baby in the manger.*Lk 2:15-16* The shepherds then spread their amazing word, honoring the Father while telling anyone who would listen that they had seen the newborn Rescuer, just what the messenger had told them. Mary saw these amazing things going on, treasuring and pondering everything in her heart.*Lk 2:17-20* Don't think that this event is all about Mary, either. Later, when the Son was going about doing his miracles, a woman said that the Father should bless Mary for birthing and nursing the Son, but the Son said instead that the Father blesses those who hear and obey the Father's word.*Lk 11:27-28* You get the message: celebrate *for you*, not for Mary, that the Son came.

The Son is your source for everything. The Son is full of compassion and truth.*Jn 1:14* Everything good you receive out of the Son's fullness.*Jn 1:16-17* The Son came to free the corrupt of guilt, not to congratulate the blameless.*Matt 9:11-13, Mk 2:15-17, Lk 5:29-32* The good news is that the Father thinks you're *it*.*Col 1:6* The Father had the Son's good news ready for you before time even began.*2Ti 1:9* The Son stood you up straight and brushed you off.*Ro 5:2* The Son gave it *all* to you.*Ro 5:17* The Father loved you so much that he brought you back from dead to living.*Eph 2:4-5* The Father put you right next to his Son, right next to *him*, so that you receive everything that the Son has.*Eph 2:6-7* The Son brought you what you did not deserve.*Ro 1:5* The Father's compassion rescued you. You did nothing, so don't brag about it.*Eph 2:8-9* Hold onto the Father's gift. Don't think

> you earned it. The Son gave it to you.*Gal 2:21* The Father gives you just as much rope as you need—no more, so don't test it.*Eph 4:7* Father and Son gave you good reason to expect to live forever.*2Th 2:16-17* The Father just pours his love all over you because of the Son.*1Ti 1:14*

Presentation

The people to whom the Son came had a way of doing things that they closely connected with their relationship with the Father. These rituals helped them honor the Father while setting themselves apart from other people who did not. Following ritual, Mary and Joseph had the baby Son circumcised. They then named him Jesus (Yeshua or Joshua, if you prefer), just as the Father's messenger had directed Mary to do before she bore the Son. The world now had its precious Rescuer. Everything was in order.*Lk 2:21* Joseph and Mary next took the Son to the capitol holy city Jerusalem. The Father had long before given the people a ritual for firstborn sons, in which parents offered a sacrifice to the Father to keep and cleanse their son. The ritual recalled that the Father had freed the people from their Egyptian captors at the cost of Egypt's firstborn sons. The ritual also foreshadowed that the Father would give his own Son to free people from their captive death. Mary and Joseph thus presented the infant Son at the holy city's religious center—again, with everything in order.*Lk 2:22-24*

Things, though, kept happening to make obvious that the Son was no ordinary baby. A sincere and moral man Simeon had long waited in the capitol holy city to see the One who would rescue the people. The Father's Spirit had shown Simeon that he would live to see the Rescuer.*Lk 2:25-26* Just as Mary and Joseph brought the Son into the religious center's courtyards, the Spirit moved Simeon to take the Son in his arms. Honoring the Father, Simeon said that he could now die in peace. Simeon told Mary and Joseph that he had now seen the Rescuer not only of the people whom the Father had chosen to receive the Son but *all* people.*Lk 2:27-32* Mary and Joseph marveled at Simeon's words. Simeon, though encouraging them, also warned Mary that the Son's coming would cause great upheaval and lots of opposition. The Son would expose what people truly thought. The Son's treatment would also trouble Mary's mind, will, and emotions.*Lk 2:33-35* An eighty-four-year-old widow Anna was also there, fasting and praying night and day at the religious center, anticipating something incredible.*Lk 2:36-37* And indeed, Anna approached Mary and Joseph at that very moment, thanking the Father while telling anyone who would listen that the Son was the people's rescuer.*Lk 2:38* The Father was gradually and dramatically making a record and building the case for all to see that the Son would rescue them.

> **The Son carries extraordinary power.** The Father gave the Son power before time.*Jude 24-25* The Son has power forever.*1Pe 4:11* The Father gave the Son his power.*Jude 24-25* The Son sustains all things by his powerful word.*Heb 1:3* The Father will show the Son in blazing fire with his powerful celestial beings.*2Th 1:7* The Son is over every other power.*Col 2:10* As an adult, power flowed from the Son to heal all who touched him.*Lk 6:19* The Son could feel power flowing out of him to heal those who touched him.*Lk 8:43-46* The Son taught in the Spirit's power.*Lk 4:14-15* Gather with the Son's power present.*1Co 5:4-5* The cross is the Father's power to you whom the Son rescues.*1Co 1:18-19* The Son lives by the Father's power.*2Co 13:4* The Son's death and coming back to life beat every corrupt power.*Col 2:15* Stick with that simple power, not fancy words.*1Co 1:17* Just know the power of the Son coming back to life. You, too, die obediently to come back to his life.*Php 3:10-11* The Son will by his complete power transform your body to be like his fabulous body.*Php 3:20-21* The Son is not weak but powerful in dealing with you.*2Co 13:1-3*

Announcement

The Son's coming, though, drew far wider notice than simply among shepherds and the sincerely devoted. His coming wasn't just a local thing. Eastern sages also knew the sacred writings about the Son. They, too, were watching for signs of his coming. From their studies of the anicent writings and observing the sky, they perceived a star announcing the Son's arrival. They were so sure that they followed the star hundreds of miles to the capitol holy city. There, they asked the city's leaders to honor the One who had just come as Rescuer of the Father's chosen people.*Matt 2:1-2* Naturally, their announcement roiled the capitol holy city, where all were well aware of the ancient writings' messianic prediction. The news was huge, *cataclysmic*, if true. The sages' announcement of course alarmed the city's viciously corrupt monarch who wanted no challenge to his iron rule. So he called together those from the religious establishment who might know anything specific about *where* the

Rescuer would come.*Matt 2:3* The establishment figures all knew that the ancient writings said that the Rescuer would arrive in Bethlehem. They told the wicked monarch, who began to plot what to do.*Matt 2:4-6*

Meanwhile, the star led the sages right to the place of the Rescuer's birth in Bethlehem.*Matt 2:9-10* The sages knew exactly what to do when they first saw the infant Rescuer with his mother Mary: they bowed in deep worship of him. Some even say that they *fell down*, prostrating themselves in humility before the Son. They also gave him treasures they brought with them including gold for his royalty, an aromatic oil for his divinity, and an aromatic resin symbolic of his coming sacrifice and burial. Now *that's* how you treat an encounter with the Son.*Matt 2:11* They knew that the Son's birth fulfilled what seers had recorded in the ancient writings. The virgin had indeed conceived to bear a son whom all would come to know as God With Us. The Father had come in the person and image of the Son.*Matt 1:22-23*

Horrifically, though, in one of the most-awful events that the ancient writings record, the wicked monarch wasn't done. The Father's messenger once again appeared to Joseph in a dream, warning him that the wicked monarch would try to kill the Son. So Joseph took Mary and the infant Son to Egypt for safety. They stayed in Egypt until the wicked monarch had died, fulfilling the ancient writings that the Father would call his Son out of Egypt.*Matt 2:13-15,19-21* The wicked monarch did kill all young boys in Bethlehem's vicinity, just after Joseph, Mary, and the Son had escaped. The ancient writings had indeed said that the vicinity's mothers would weep over their lost sons.*Matt 2:16:18* *Everything* went just as the writings had predicted. Even when Joseph brought the family back from Egypt, they went to Nazareth to avoid the dead wicked monarch's reigning son, this time fulfilling the prediction that the Rescuer would be a Nazarene.*Matt 2:22-23* Now you know these things. These things are not fairy tales. They are your own historical records that scholars say have unparalleled reliability for such antiquity. The Rescuer has well more than one billion followers who have read and trusted these things. You should have confidence.

Change when you need to do so. Feeling bad, wrong, guilty? Then change. Life forever leaves you no regrets.*2Co 7:10* Your conscience, that guilty sense that you have or want to avoid, makes you eager to change so that you can defend yourself.*2Co 7:11* The Father is kind to you to induce you to change.*Ro 2:4* You want rescue? Then turn from corruption.*2Ti 2:19* Tell others when you have done wrong. Admit it.*Jas 5:16-18* Don't be stubborn. The Father will remain angry at you.*Ro 2:5* Just stop the corruption. Hate your former mess.*Jas 4:8-9* Turn from those things in which others indulge.*2Co 12:21* Reject what you pursued before you knew the Father. Be like the Father whom you now know.*1Pe 1:14-16* Regret hurting one another, but don't regret causing sorrow with the truth.*2Co 7:8* Be happy not for bringing sorrow but when sorrow leads to change for the better.*2Co 7:9* Gently instruct opponents so that they come to their senses.*2Ti 2:25-26* Turn to the Father, and he'll wipe your slate clean.*Acts 3:19* The Son offers you life forever by turning you from wrongdoing.*Acts 3:26* Turn to the Father, relying on the Son.*Acts 20:21* Change because the Father's place is close to you.*Matt 4:17* Shame on those who refuse to change when they need to do so.*Matt 11:20-24* Teach others to change when they need to do so.*Mk 6:7-12* Better to do right than to talk right.*Matt 21:28-32* Change—or die.*Lk 13:1-3* Turn from wrongdoing, or perish.*Lk 13:4-5* Do some good now, while you have the chance. No guarantees for a tomorrow.*Lk 13:6-9* The Father's celestial beings celebrate when so few as one of you turns from wrongs. The Father pursues your change.*Lk 15:8-10* Stop doing those things that lead to your death.*Heb 6:1-2* The Father waits patiently for you to change so that you do not die.*2Pe 3:9*

Maturation

Even as his earthly parents raised him, the Son knew that he belonged to his Father from whom he had come. In raising the Son, Mary and Joseph followed every ritual that the ancient writings required of them. They raised the Son in Nazareth, where the Son grew strong.*Lk 2:39-40* The Father poured his wisdom into the growing Son. The Father's favor, poise, dignity, and decency were clearly in the Son, as one event especially showed.*Lk 2:40* Every year, Joseph and Mary returned to the capitol holy city with the Son, for the big festival celebrating how the Father freed the people from Egyptian slavery.*Lk 2:41* When the Son was twelve years old, though, he stayed behind at the holy city's religious center when his parents headed home. His parents thought that he was with them.*Lk 2:42-44*

When Mary and Joseph noticed that the Son was missing among their traveling party of relatives and friends, they returned to the capitol holy city. They searched three days for the Son, everywhere one might look for a twelve-year-old boy. Instead, though, they finally found him sitting in the religious center's courtyards listening to the teachers. And he was not only listening to them teach but was asking them hard questions._Lk 2:45-46_ These were the best teachers around, and yet the Son amazed everyone with what he knew and how he expressed it._Lk 2:47_ His parents, too, were astonished, although for a different reason. Mary asked the Son why he had let them anxiously search for him when he could at least have let them know where he was._Lk 2:48_ The Son replied that without even searching, they should have known exactly where he was—in *his Father's house.* The Son was referring to the holy city's great religious center that the people had made long ago. The ancient writings identified the religious center as the home of the one great God in the revolutionary monotheism that the people had carried into the world. Mary and Joseph didn't get it._Lk 2:49_

The Son wasn't being disobedient. He promptly returned with Mary and Joseph to Nazareth where he continued to obey them as he grew. The Son grew not only to adult stature but in wisdom. The Father showed the Son favor as he grew. But the Son was no religious recluse. The community's hard-working men also treated the Son with favor. For her part, Mary treasured in her heart every special thing going on with the Son as he grew._Lk 2:51-52_ This quiet life in Nazareth continued until the Son was about thirty years old. That's when his extraordinary public mission began in earnest._Lk 3:23_ This whole thing thus unfolded in an unprecedented mix of the natural and supernatural, divine and human, public and private, as exquisitely recorded in reliable records. The Father gave the Son the perfect entry—perfect that you would read, receive, and rely on it. Do so. Trust it.

> ***Obey Father and Son.*** If you love the Son, then do as he says._Jn 14:15_ Whoever do as the Son says love him._Jn 14:21_ The Father loves whoever obeys the Son. Father and Son reside with those who obey._Jn 14:23_ Those who don't obey the Son don't love him._Jn 14:24_ You are the Son's friend if you do as he says._Jn 15:14_ Do as you please, but some of it won't be good for you._1Co 10:23_ Obeying the Father helps you love him._1Jn 2:5_ Don't go back and forth. Just do as he says._2Co 1:17_ Be consistent rather than contradictory._2Co 1:18_ Do the good that others expect of you._1Ti 6:20_ Keep your head. Do your duty._2Ti 4:5_ Suffering for wrongdoing is nothing, but suffering for good commends you. The Son did._1Pe 2:20-21_ Obey the Father. The Son did._Jn 15:10_ The Son proved his obedience from what he suffered._Heb 5:8_ Obey the good news._Heb 4:2_ Doing as the Son says shows you know him, while failing to do as he says proves you don't know him._1Jn 2:3-4_ Please your commanding officer—the Son._2Ti 2:4_ The Father says to rely on his Son and then to love one another. Do both._1Jn 3:22_ When you do as

> the Father says, you live in him and he in you.*1Jn 3:24* Obeying, not just hearing, puts you in right relationship with the Father.*Ro 2:13*

Nature

Make no mistake who the Son was and is. Coming from the Father, the Son is without natural father or mother. You can't go back and say that the Son's lineage began here or there. The Son is instead without beginning or end because he was with the Father before anything began.*Heb 7:1-17* The Father named the world's Rescuer his own Son and at the same time said that he was the Rescuer's Father.*Heb 1:5* The Father said when he first brought his Son into the world that the Father's own messengers would worship the Son, and the messengers promptly did so.*Heb 1:6* Everything began with the Son. *Living*, truly living, began with the Son when he came to you, who until then were sure to die and remain dead. The Son is above and over everything.*Col 1:18*

You think that celestial beings are extraordinary? The Son is far superior to them because he came from the Father.*Heb 1:4-5* The Rescuer is the Father's Son, straight from the Father. The Father wasn't going to send any lesser being, but rather, the Son straight from himself.*Heb 4:14* The Father's Spirit, the *sacred* Spirit, the One who also comes from Father and Son, devoted to Father and Son, had everything to do with the Son's coming. The Father appointed, designated, and confirmed the Son through the Spirit.*Ro 1:4* The Father said that the Son is who the Father loves as the Son pleases the Father.*2Pe 1:17-18* The Son who appeared came as the kind and loving Rescuer, coming for you.*Tit 3:3-5*

The Son's coming served another profound role. The Son made the invisible Father visible, as the Father's very image. You no longer have to imagine seeing the Father but instead can see the Father in the Son.*Col 1:15* The Son simply *radiates* the Father's grandeur, his magnificence. No more guessing: the Son exactly represents the Father's very essence, his very being.*Heb 1:3* The Son is the Father's fullness, the Father's supernatural self, living in a human body that you can see, hear, and touch, showing you exactly who the Father is so that you don't have to dream or speculate. The Father wanted to make himself plain to you, and he did in the Son.*Col 2:9* This wonder was nothing distasteful for the Father, either. Rather, the Father loves having every bit of him, his entire spectacular self live and breathe in the Son.*Col 1:19* The Father's Son came as the one true, reliable Rescuer, everything that you could ever hope to see of that enervating wonder that makes this incredible universe work from start to finish and beyond. The Father's Son came so that we could not just know the Father but also be *in* the Father, to live in precious purity and truth.₁Jn 5:20 Know who came to you.

> **The work of the rules ended when the Son came.** The Father shares his Spirit with you and does wonders for you not because you keep rules but because you rely on the Son's good news.Gal 3:5 The Son's good news replaced the deadly old rule-keeping with the Spirit's life-giving freedom.Ro 8:2 The Son put an end to rule-keeping so that everyone who relies on him comes clean.Ro 10:4 The Father made the rules because things were a total mess. The rules were just until the Son came, though. The Son would restore true order.Gal 3:19 The rules showed how bad you all were. The rules showed that you utterly needed the Son to fix everything for you.Gal 3:21-22 The rules kept you locked up because you needed it. The Son's good news sets you free again.Gal 3:23-23 The rules didn't fix your problems. Rules can't fix desire. The Father's Spirit, influencing you who rely on the Son, fixes desires, turning desires to the Father.Ro 8:3-4

4 Immersion

Messenger

The Father did even more to prepare you to receive his Son than simply announce his coming. Important introductions, inductions, or *immersions* would take place, signifying several things. Here is how those immersions began. A virtuous religious leader Zechariah and his virtuous wife Elizabeth were doing everything that the Father had first commanded long ago. Yet they had no child and had grown old._{Lk 1:5-7} The religious custom was to choose a religious leader at random to enter the inner area of the religious center to communicate with the Father. The leader's role there was to burn incense representing the people's requests, while the people honored the Father outside. The random draw fell to Zechariah who thus entered the inner area, little knowing the encounter that would occur there._{Lk 1:8-10} When Zechariah entered, the Father's most-awesome messenger confronted him there. Fear naturally gripped the startled Zechariah, who likely expected to die._{Lk 1:11-12}

The messenger, though, told Zechariah not to fear. Instead, the messenger said that the Father was answering Zechariah's requests for a child. He was to expect his wife Elizabeth to bear them a son whom they were to name John._{Lk 1:13} The messenger added that their son John would delight them and many others because he would be great in the Father's sight. John would keep himself pure, never drinking wine. The Spirit would instead fill John even from before his birth, while Elizabeth still carried him._{Lk 1:14-15} And that was just the beginning. John would also call back to the Father many of the Father's people. John would be like the wonder-working seer Elijah of long ago, having Elijah's spirit and power. John's powerful words would turn parents' hearts to their children. He would turn those who were doing everything wrong to doing things right. Most of all, though, he would prepare the way for the Father's Son. The Son would have John as a special herald.*Lk 1:16-17*

Zechariah made just one mistake—but a big mistake. Rather than instantly accept the awesome messenger's word, Zechariah instead asked *how could he be sure* of what the messenger said. If the Father sends you a messenger, just believe the message. The messenger told Zechariah that the Father had indeed sent this good news. He also said, though, that Zechariah would now be mute until John's birth. Zechariah had failed to trust and would suffer the consequence.*Lk 1:18-20* When Zechariah emerged dumbstruck from the inner area, the people knew that he had seen a vision.*Lk 1:21* And indeed, everything happened just as the messenger said. Despite her old age, Elizabeth conceived John.*Lk 1:23-25* When Mary, pregnant with the Son, visited Elizabeth, John lept in Elizabeth's womb when he heard Mary's voice.*Lk 1:39-41* The Spirit filled Elizabeth who blessed Mary as the mother of her coming Rescuer.*Lk 1:41-45* Mary in turn blessed the Father in glorious song for the Father's favor, work, love, and care for his people.*Lk 1:46-55* The Son would have a special herald John.

Obey authority. Do right in everyone's eyes.*Ro 12:17* Obey human authority whom the Father empowers to punish wrong.*1Pe 2:13-14* Honor your ruler.*1Pe 2:17* Do as your employer requires, even when your employer is harsh.*1Pe 2:18* Respect your supervisor so that no one slanders the Father because of you.*1Ti 6:1* Serve even better supervisors who rely on the Son.*1Ti 6:2* Let others' obedience encourage you to care for one another.*2Co 7:15* Avoid those who don't follow instruction. They may feel shame and start to do right. If not, then warn them rather than treating them as an enemy.*2Th 3:14-15* Share the good news so that others may also obey Father and Son.*Ro 1:5* First, obey. Only then may you punish others who do not obey.*2Co 10:6* Subject yourself to governing authorities because the Father established them.*Ro 13:1* Anyone rebelling against the authority rebels against what the Father instituted.*Ro 13:2* Those in authority serve the Father for your good. Fear the ruler for good reason.*Ro 13:4* Pay your taxes because the authorities govern as the Father's servants.*Ro 13:6* Submit to the authorities not just to avoid punishment but also out of conscience.*Ro 13:5* Pay taxes. Give government what is government's. Give the Father what is the Father's.*Matt 22:18-22, Mk 12:13-17, Lk 20:20-26* Pay every debt.*Ro 13:8* Don't speak ill of your ruler.*Acts 23:5*

Message

The Father had a specific role for John, which was to prepare the way for the Father's Son. John was not the light but a witness to the Son's light. John was to tell about the Son's coming so that all who saw the Son coming would know what was happening.*Jn 1:6-8* And so here's how that message happened. When Elizabeth bore John, the people present assumed that they were going to name the child after his father Zechariah. But Elizabeth did as the great messenger had told her husband Zechariah and said instead that they would name the child John.*Lk 1:57-60* Zechariah was still mute, so he wrote on a tablet that indeed, they would name the child John. At that moment of Zechariah's obedience, Zechariah could suddenly speak again. All that he said honored the Father.*Lk 1:61-64* Indeed, the Spirit filled Zechariah to the point that he predicted that John would see what the Father was doing. Zechariah said that John would prepare the way for the Father's Son to rescue the people.*Lk 1:67-79* The whole event filled the people present with awe. News of John spread, while the people wondered just what he would be now that the Father was clearly touching him.*Lk 1:65-66*

John, always strong in spirit, indeed grew to be someone unusual. He lived on his own in the wilderness, alone in the wild, like an eccentric recluse, until the time came for him to speak publicly.*Lk 1:80* John ate no bread and drank no wine, keeping himself strong and pure. People nonetheless spoke of him like he was crazy, demon-possessed.*Lk 7:33* But John did exactly what the Father's messenger had predicted and what the ancient writings had also said about him. He stayed out in the wilderness, telling the crowds that came out to listen to him to set everything in order for the Son's coming. He heralded the new era of the Son.*Mk 1:2* John told everyone to clean up their act, to stop doing wrong and start doing right, because the Son was bringing a new rule in just the way that the ancient writings predicted.*Matt 3:1-3, Mk 1:3*

John made no pretense of looking like someone important. He had no desire to call attention to himself but instead to the coming Son. John wore a rough covering of camel skin held together by a plain leather belt. He ate locusts and honey, whatever came his way. And speaking of the Son, John kept saying that one more powerful than John was coming, one who was so much greater than John that John couldn't touch him.*Mk 1:6-7* John cried out that the Son was the one who, though coming after

John, would shoot right past John in significance. The Son would dwarf John because the Son was before John.$_{Jn\ 1:15}$ John told everyone without any regret that John was not their rescuer, and not an ancient seer reborn. He just kept repeating his wilderness call to set things straight for the coming Son.$_{Jn\ 1:19-23}$ John was the Son's predicted herald.

Later, the Son would say about John that no one on earth, no one naturally born outside the Son's own rule, is greater than John. John was the last and greatest of the old seers and sages. Yet the Son would also say that the least under the Son's own rule is greater than John—because they have the Son.$_{Matt\ 11:11,\ Lk\ 7:28}$ The Son also told the crowds who had gone into the wilderness to see John that they had not gone to see someone dressed in fancy clothes, the kind of thing that they could see every day in the city. No, they had gone into the wilderness to hear a sage, a seer, the Father's own messenger preparing everyone for the Son.$_{Matt\ 11:7-10,\ Lk\ 7:24-27}$ The Son explained that no one would believe the Son if he had said it himself but that John's saying it made it true for everyone. John wasn't saying it just to be right but to aid in your rescue. Believe John when he spoke about the Son.$_{Jn\ 5:31-32}$

The people loved listening to John because he told it like it was, telling the whole truth even when it embarrassed the religious leaders. But John was around only a short time.$_{Jn\ 5:35}$ The Son later said that the religious leaders who heard John simply refused to believe John. The religious leaders wouldn't change for anything.$_{Matt\ 21:32}$ The Son also later said that the ancient writings had predicted things right up until John came. The writings even described John.$_{Matt\ 11:14}$ In these ways, the Father prepared you from ancient times to accept his Son when he came. No one but the Father could have drawn all these things together so wondrously. John, though, had more to do than to herald the Son.

Honor the Son. The ancient seer Isaiah saw and predicted the Son's honor.$_{Jn\ 12:41}$ The Son did not seek honor, but the Father seeks it.$_{Jn\ 8:50}$ The Son doesn't honor the Son. The Father honors the Son.$_{Jn\ 8:54}$ The Son's obedience, to the point of death, honored the Father and allowed the Father to honor the Son.$_{Jn\ 12:27-29}$ The Father honored the Son and himself in allowing the Son's death and bringing him right back to life.$_{Jn\ 13:31-32}$ At the Son's immersion, the Father honored the Son.$_{2Pe\ 1:17}$ The Son's miracles revealed the Son's honor.$_{Jn\ 2:11}$ Whoever does not honor the Son does not honor the Father.$_{Jn\ 5:23}$ When the Father honored the Son, you received the Spirit.$_{Jn\ 7:37-39}$ The Father gave the Son majesty, power, and authority to present you to the Father.$_{Jude\ 24-25}$ The ancient seers searched to discover through the Son's Spirit when and how the Son would come, suffer, and receive his honor.*1Pe 1:10-11* The Son has honor forever.*Gal 1:5* Those who rely on the Son will honor him on his return.*2Th 1:10-11* You who rely on the Son should honor him.*Eph 1:11-13* Everyone should honor the Father through the Son, who has honor and power forever.*1Pe 4:11* The Father took up the Son to honor him.*1Ti 3:16* The Son had honor in his own town.*Matt 13:57-58* The Son does not seek honor from humans.*Jn 5:41* Those who reject the Son seek honor from one another without seeking the Father's honor.*Jn 5:44* The Spirit honors the Son because the Spirit receives from the Son what he reveals to you.*Jn 16:14* The Son brought the Father honor by finishing his work. The Father honored the Son with the honor the Son had with the Father before time.*Jn 17:4-5* The Son gave those who rely on him the honor that the Father gave him.*Jn 17:22-24*

Immersing

John had another role in addition to acting as the Son's herald. The Father told John that he was to *immerse* the people, *enjoin, initiate,* and *induct* them, into this message that they must change their ways to get away from their deadly corruption. The Father told John to share this message in the wilderness around the Jordan River. John was to draw the people out of the city, out of their culture, into a wild place where they would hear how to be free.*Lk 3:1-3* The ancient seer Isaiah had written long ago about John, whom the seer said was to call from the wilderness. John was to stand out in the wild declaring that the people must straighten up to get ready for the coming Son. The people must get ready for rescue, preparing the lifeboats as the ship goes down.*Lk 3:4-6* And so John took the people who came out to him in the wild country around the Jordan River, and he immersed them in the waters as this great sign of cleansing rescue. For all who saw what they needed, saw that they desperately needed help from their own corruption, John drowned their corruption in the passing waters, letting the waters carry off the filth.*Matt 3:4-6*

John was a huge success. Everyone both in the countryside and the capitol holy city made the trek out into the wild to see John in action. And they didn't just come for the spectacle. When they got there, they were fully ready to admit how broken, how wretched and pitiful they were. They were also ready for John to immerse them, to induct them into this new experience, this new life that was about to come. One by one, John soaked them so that they could imagine their corruption floating off in the passing waters, their demons drowned in the dunking.*Mk 1:5* John's words had a lot to do with their strong sense of conviction. He didn't hold back. John told the crowds who came out that they were *broods of vipers*. Anyone ever called you that?! He made them realize that they needed to run from the awful judgment that was about to come, while they still had the chance.*Lk 3:7* John told the crowds that they'd better start showing something for their lives. No more resting on their laurels, and no more claiming that their parents had done enough. If they didn't show something good coming from their own effort to change, then the Father was ready to cut them down like a fruitless tree, good for nothing but firewood.*Lk 3:8-9* John's words raised alarms with the crowds, as they should raise alarms with you. The crowd asked John what they should do. John was frank. He told them to stop hoarding and start sharing food and clothing with those who had none. He told tax collectors to stop overcharging. He told soldiers to stop extorting bribes with false accusations but instead be content with their pay. John knew the bad stuff that people do, and he just told them openly to stop it.*Lk 3:10-14*

The Father cleans you up. The Father makes you better in every way including speech and knowledge, confirming the good news.*1Co 1:5-6* Approach the Father sincerely, confidently, relying on the Son, scrubbed clean.*Heb 10:22* To clean you up, the Father first proved his Son perfect through his awful suffering.*Heb 2:10* The Father wants you cleaned up.*1Th 4:3* The Father invites you to a clean life.*1Th 4:7* The Father will clean you all the way through.*1Th 5:23* The Father isn't giving up. He will clean you.*1Th 5:24* The Spirit's cleansing work rescues you.*2Th 2:13* Being truly clean comes from relying on the Son. He did it all.*1Ti 3:16* Staying clear of wrongdoing, while being content with food and clothing, is great. You brought nothing into the world and take nothing out of it.*1Ti 6:6-8* Pursue right relationship with the Father and clean living.*1Ti 6:11* The Father invited you to a clean life.*2Ti 1:9* The Father rewards the pure in heart with seeing him.*Matt 5:8* The Father cleans you up by what he says, which is true.*Jn 17:17* What the Father says cleans you up among others.*Acts 20:32* The Son kept himself clean so that he could clean you up.*Jn 17:19* The Son made you perfect, like the Father.*Matt 5:48* The Father rewards those who want right relationship with him.*Matt 5:6, Lk 6:21* The Father gives right relationship when you rely on the Son.*Ro 2:22* The Father cleans you up when you rely on his Son.*1Co 1:2* The Son is your right relationship.*1Co 1:30* The Father showed you right relationship when he asked his Son to die for you.*Ro 2:25-26* The perfect Son's death cleaned you inwardly, clearing your conscience of acts leading to death. You now serve the living Father.*Heb 9:14* The Son's right relationship with the Father made right relationship for all.*Ro 5:17-18* The Son's obedience made you obedient.*Ro 5:19* The Son's right relationship with the Father gives you life forever.*Ro 5:21* You receive the Son's right relationship.*2Pe 1:1-2* The Father fills you with right relationship through the Son.*Php 1:11* Your whole spirit, soul, and body are blameless.*1Th 5:23*

At the same time that John immersed the people who admitted their need for immersion's symbolic cleansing, John condemned the religious officials who refused their own need for a cleansing immersion. The religious officials were relying on what their ancestors had done rather than what *they* should do. Ever tried that? It doesn't work. You don't get credit for your parent's purity, even if you have a saint for a parent. Your success depends on what *you* do.*Matt 3:7-8* The more that John condemned the officials, the more that they relied on their famous parents. John went so far as to say the Father may as well have given their famous parents *stones* for children, with these stone-stupid officials.*Matt3:9* John repeated his warning that the Father was ready to chop down anyone like the officials who refused to admit their own need for cleansing, to cut them up for firewood. They needed to quickly make a fruitful life, the kind of life that comes from admitting one's shortcomings. John was blunt to the point of offense, but they needed and deserved every bit of it.*Matt 3:10*

John's immersing the people in river water, though, was only the start of the profound new experience. John's water immersion symbolized the change that inductees were making. The final induction, the much-more powerful induction, would come when the Son doused the same people with the Father's Spirit. Spirit immersion would be more like fire immersion than water immersion because the Son was so much greater than John, leaving no real comparison.*Matt 3:11, Lk 3:16* John told everyone that he was just the first step. He said that the coming Son would immerse them, douse them, with the Father's Spirit.*Mk 1:8* And that's just what happened. After the Son came, died on the cross, and came back to life to appear to his students and hundreds of others, the Son told his students to wait in the capitol holy city. The Spirit would immerse them there, like a descending fire.*Acts 1:4-5* John explained the same thing to the suspicious religious officials who interrogated John.

He said that his water immersion was just an introduction for the Son who was already among them but whom they didn't yet know. They'd know the Son soon enough, and he would shock them.*Jn 1:24-28* John kept at his immersion mission, telling the people exactly what it meant, any way that he knew how to tell them. As John did so, he made sure that they understood that his message was good news, not condemnation for them but instead liberty.*Lk 3:18* John's introduction was a great start. Just wait for the far greater finish.

> **You were a wrongdoer.** You were a wrongdoer. The Son just cleaned you up so that to the Father you don't look like a wrongdoer.*1Co 6:9-11* Just wait to see Father and Son. The Son brought you back from all your wrongdoing. He made you eager to do good.*Tit 2:13-14* The Son paid for all of your wrongs, big and little, every one of them.*Col 1:14* The Son shared in your humanity. You are human, and so he became human so that by his death he would end death.*Heb 2:14* The Son freed you from paying for your wrongs with death.*Heb 2:15* The Son doesn't help celestial beings but *you*.*Heb 2:16* The Son had to become like you, fully human in every way, not a wrongdoer but taking on your wrongs, to pay for your wrongs.*Heb 2:17* The Son suffered when tempted, making him able to help you when wrongs tempt you.*Heb 2:18*

Essence

If John was to be the messenger, to *herald* the coming Son, then the moment would need to come for the final announcement, for the curtain to open. After the Son had grown to adulthood, when he was around age thirty, he traveled to where John was immersing the crowds in the Jordan River wilderness. The Son came for his own immersion.*Matt 3:13, Mk 1:9* John knew the moment immediately. Before the Son even reached him, when the Son was still approaching, John told the crowd that the Son had finally come. He told the crowd to look at the one who would fix for them everything that they'd ever done wrong. John also told the crowd that he was nothing next to the Son, to forget John and turn their full attention to the Son.*Jn 1:29-31* Appreciate the delicacy of the moment. Knowing who the Son was, John was ready to submit entirely to him, asking that the Son immerse John. But history records that the Son gently corrected John that John must immerse the Son. The Father had ordered things that way, and they would keep the Father's plan to perfection.*Matt 3:14-15*

And so John immersed the Son just as he had immersed all the people who came to him admitting their need for cleansing.*Lk 3:21* The Son needed no cleansing, though. The Son needed only the formal moment of induction into his own great movement, the greatest movement in history, the movement for which history came. The Son called to his Father at the moment of his immersion, and the Father answered. The Father opened the door that does not open, the door to the place of the Father's paradise. And out of that door the Father's Spirit, his essence, poured down on the Son. Those present said that the Father's essence came in the form not of a strange dragon, powerful horse, or radiant beam, but of a gentle dove, alighting on the Son's perfect form.*Lk 3:21-22* As the Son came up out of the water, the Father's door opened, and the Spirit dove, so ready for the great mission, fluttered out and down, entering the Son.*Matt 3:16, Mk 1:10* John himself said that he saw the Spirit come down from the Father right at that history-hinging moment. The Spirit, looking so like a dove, did not flutter off but remained on the Son. The Son now carried the Father's Spirit.*Jn 1:32* Indeed, the Son himself said so. He later told his students that when they immersed people, they should do it for the Father, for the Son, and for the Spirit.*Matt 28:18-20*

The extraordinary event left no mistake about what it meant. The Father's messenger who sent John to immerse people in water had told John that he would see the Father's Spirit descend on the Son. The messenger had also told John that the Son would then immerse people in the Spirit that descended. These things made perfect sense. The Father who is Spirit sent his Spirit to the Son to share with others in the way that the Father shared with the Son. John told everyone exactly that. The Father chose the Son to carry the Father's Spirit to the people.*Jn 1:33-34* But the people didn't have to rely on John's word alone. Right after the Spirit descended on the Son, the Father's own voice spoke from the open door, saying that the Son who had already so pleased the Father was indeed the Father's Son to love. The people heard from the Father, the Son, the Spirit, and John, all agreeing on what the Spirit's descent on the Son meant.*Matt 3:17, Mk 1:11, Lk 3:22* The Father himself confirmed from above that the Son was his to honor. The Father said it.*2Pe 1:17*

> **The Spirit points to the Son.** The Son asks his Father to send you his Spirit as a helper forever, if you listen to and rely on the Son.*Jn 14:15-16* The Advocate, this Spirit whom the Father sends, teaches and reminds you of everything that

the Son said.*Jn 14:25-26* The Son left for your good so that the Father would send you the Advocate—his Spirit.*Jn 16:7* The Advocate corrects what you always hear that's so wrong, those things that naturally condemn you.*Jn 16:8-11* The Advocate, the Spirit who goes out from the Father, tells you about the Son.*Jn 15:26* The Spirit honors the Son. The Spirit learns from the Son what he reveals to you.*Jn 16:14* The Spirit knows that all that belongs to the Father belongs to the Son.*Jn 16:15* The Father gave the Son his Spirit and power.*Acts 10:38* The Father gave you his Spirit, too, through whom you see that the Father sent his Son to rescue you.*1Jn 4:13-14* You must have the Spirit to know the Son.*Ro 8:9* If you rely on the Son, then even though you die in corruption, the Spirit brings you back to life in perfection.*Ro 8:10* If the Spirit who brought the Son back to life lives in you, then the Father will also bring you back to life.*Ro 8:11* The Spirit says that you are the Father's own, receiving what he has, if you suffer with his Son.*Ro 8:16-17* The Father knows what you think. The Father listens to the Spirit, too, as the Spirit advocates for you.*Ro 8:27* Know the Spirit's gifts.*1Co 12:1* You love the Son if you have the Spirit. You can only love the Son with the Spirit.*1Co 12:3* The Father used the Spirit to clean us up and rescue us. The Son's sacrifice poured the Spirit over us.*Tit 5:6* The Spirit proved the Son right.*1Ti 3:16* The Father is the Spirit. The Spirit frees you.*2Co 3:17* The Father's honor comes from the Spirit.*2Co 3:18*

Passage

John's immersing the Son was a passage from the old waiting, listening to the seers and sages predict a coming, to new life in the Son. The next day when the Son passed by, John repeated to the crowd to look at the Father's Son, the gentle one whom men would sacrifice.*Jn 1:35* When John much later was in prison for his condemnations of the officials, when John was hearing about the Son's public actions, John sent his students to confirm again that the Son was the Father's chosen one.*Matt 11:2-3, Lk 7:18-20* The Son replied to John's students about the wonders that everyone had seen, that the blind were seeing, lame walking, sick healed, deaf hearing, and dead living again. The poor were finally hearing some very good news.*Matt 11:4-5, Lk 7:21-22* The extraordinary events confused some people who thought that the Son was John or possibly the ancient seer Elijah or some other seer. But the Son's leading student Peter corrected them that the Son was the Father's chosen one. John was not the Rescuer but had instead introduced the Rescuer Son.*Mk 7:27-30*

The local governor later executed John, who had opposed the governor's marriage to his brother's wife. The execution confirmed the passage from the old waiting game to new life in the Son.*Matt 14:3-12, Mk 6:14-16* The governor had first had John arrested, bound, and imprisoned for opposing the governor's marriage to his brother's wife.*Mk 6:17-18, Lk 3:19-20* The governor's wife had nursed a grudge against John, hoping to kill him, but the governor had protected John out of fear. The governor knew that John was doing and saying the right things and that John was someone special.*Mk 6:19-20* John's preaching greatly puzzled and also entertained the governor, who liked to listen to John.*Mk 6:20* But the time soon came when the governor's wife was able to manipulate the governor into killing John. On the governor's birthday, his wife's daughter danced to please and seduce the governor. The governor offered the daughter anything up to half his kingdom. At her mother's urging, the daughter asked for John's head, and so the governor had John executed so as not to suffer embarrassment in front of his officials.*Mk 6:21-28*

The passage was now complete. John was dead, while the Son continued on with the work that John had forecast. John's students went to the governor's prison for John's body to lay the body in a proper tomb.*Mk 6:29* The governor soon had evidence that the passage John predicted was true. When the governor later heard of the Son's miraculous powers, the governor surmised incorrectly that the Son was John living again.*Matt 14:1-2, Mk 6:14* People confused the governor with varying reports that John lived again, that the ancient seer Elijah had reappeared, or one of the other seers of old had come back to life. All the governor knew was that he had beheaded John. The governor couldn't confirm who the Son was.*Lk 9:7-9* For his part, the Son told his students that John was the last seer whom the ancient seers had foretold would come to announce the Son. The Son also told his students that the Son would suffer just as the governor had killed John.*Matt 17:10-13, Mk 9:11-13*

Late in the Son's earthly service to the people, shortly before officials had him killed, the Son returned to the place that John had immersed the Son. Many people came to the Son there, saying that although John had never done anything special like the Son had done repeatedly, everything that John had said about the Son was true. The realization impressed the people, many of whom decided to follow the Son.*Jn 10:40-42* And so, the Son's immersion proved fully effective, although the Son knew that he still had an awful immersion to face—his torturous murder.*Lk 12:50* Effective transitions require a process. One doesn't just go from one thing to the next without a passage. Immersion's initiation was just as appropriate for the Son as for you.

> **The Son trusted. So can you.** The Son trusted his Father who appointed him.*Heb 3:2* The Son's trust put him over the Father's house, meaning over you, if you, too, trust.*Heb 3:6* Even if you don't rely on Father and Son, the Son will trust and rely on the Father because he cannot disown himself.*2Ti 2:13* Your trust is in the Son.*Ro 1:5* The Son is on your mind and in your motives because you trust.*Eph 3:16-17* The Son roots you in the good news.*Ro 16:25-26* Just keep trusting the Son.*Col 2:6* Remain confident in the Son. And appreciate it.*Col 2:7* Your trust put you in good stead with the Father.*Ro 5:2* You can rely on the Father for having connected you with his Son.*1Co 1:9* The Father makes you rely on the Son.*2Co 1:21* Rely only on the Son. No fooling around with others.*2Co 11:2* Examine yourself to be sure that you are trusting the Son. Don't fail your own examination.*2Co 13:5* Don't fail the test.*2Co 13:6* Keep up your confidence in the Son. He made it all the way. So can you.*Heb 4:14* Your mind, will, and emotions depend on your confidence in the Son. His success is your success.*Heb 6:19-20*

Persistence

Immersion as a rite of passage persisted, serving to introduce those who learn and accept the truth, to the new life that the truth affords. After the Son's death, the great moment came when the Father sent his essence, his beloved Spirit, to the crowd in the capitol holy city who listened to the student Peter tell about the Son. Peter and the Son's other students immersed those many in the crowd who accepted Peter's good news. The number immersed was about three thousand, but more kept coming in the following days. That's how it all got started.*Acts 2:39-41, 47* Another student Philip was telling everyone in another region about the Son's good news and their new access to the place where the Father rules. Many in that region, too, accepted the good news and, with it, accepted immersion into the Son's new life. One of those accepting immersion was a sorcerer whom Philip's signs and miracles astonished.*Acts 8:5-13*

> **Rule your body.** Govern your body so that it does not keep you from reward.*1Co 9:27* Your body is the Spirit's home.*1Co 6:19* Honor the Father with your

> body. You are the Father's, bought at expensive price.*1Co 6:20* Your old corrupt body died with the Son.*Ro 6:6-7* Give up your body to the Father.*Ro 12:1* Keep your body from wrongs. Don't listen to its corrupt desires.*Ro 6:12* Control your body. Make it honorable.*1Th 4:3-6* Don't live for the body's desires. If you do, then you'll die.*Ro 8:12-13*

The immersions kept coming in those early days after the Son's time on earth, just as the immersions have continued to the present day. Peter told the good news, this news of getting close to the Father again, once and for all, to a kind-hearted and thoughtful commander in Rome's army and to his family and friends. Try finding a kind Roman commander! But the Father sent his essence, his beloved Spirit, to the commander and those with him, anyway. Peter and his fellow students promptly immersed them into the Son's new life, confirming that they were now part of the Father's family.*Acts 10:44-48* Likewise, the Father opened a cloth seller's heart to hear the good news from the super-student Paul. Paul and his fellow students then immersed her and everyone in her house.*Acts 16:13-15* The good news' spread just wouldn't stop, especially with the unprecedented events that were happening around it. Officials imprisoned Paul and a fellow student for sharing the good news. But when an earthquake promptly set them free, the jailer and his household embraced the good news and accepted immersion along with it.*Acts 16:25-34*

You can see that opposition to the good news does nothing more than spread it more effectively and quickly, and spread immersion along with it. For another example, people who followed the old law and seers, in a region far from the capitol holy city, abused super-student Paul for his good-news message. But all the opposition did was to get Paul to go next door to tell others who would listen appreciatively. And they all accepted the truth and, with it, accepted immersion. They were *in*, right where they should be.*Acts 18:5-8* Read more about the good news' spread later, but for now, just know that immersions went on long after John and still play their role in initiation and induction today. Transitions still take place.

> **You share the Son's honor.** The Father invited you to share his Son's honor.*2Th 2:14* The Spirit says with your spirit that you are the Father's children who, if you suffer with the Son, share the Son's honor with him.*Ro 8:16-17* Your suffering does not compare with the honor the Father will show you.*Ro 8:18* Those whom the Father accepted, he also honored.*Ro 8:30* The Father shows his anger, while also delaying its full effect from those who reject him, to let you

know the riches of his honor.*Ro 9:22-23* The good news is your hope for honor.*Col 1:27* When the Son returns, you will share in his honor.*Col 3:4* The Father invites you into his honor.*1Th 2:12* Others who rely with you on the Son are your honor when the Son returns.*1Th 2:19-20* When you honor the Son, you receive his honor, not that you earned it but as a gift from Father and Son.*2Th 1:12* You whom the Son rescues receive honor forever.*2Ti 2:10*

Effect

Inductions, initiations, rites of passages—they have their critical effect. That was the way that all the people whom John immersed felt. They knew as the Son had said that the Father's way of starting with an immersion was right. The religious officials disagreed, but what did they know? They hadn't even tried it. John hadn't immersed them because they would have nothing to do with it. Those who tried it knew it worked as it should, marking once for all their passage into the Son's new life.*Lk 7:29-30* The effect didn't depend on John doing the immersion. When later, the Son's students began to immerse people in water as John had done, John was fine with their doing so, saying that *he* surely wasn't the Son. He was only sent to announce the Son. John was done—and happy about it. Everything now was up to the Son and his students. John *wanted* to be out of the picture because the picture was now all about the Son.*Jn 3:22-30*

So here's what happens with immersion. When you get immersed, as the Son accepted immersion, your bad stuff gets *buried*, not just glossed over but buried *deep*, permanently. That wondrous lifting and cleansing happens because your old self dies just as the Son died, not ending everything, but instead so that you have a new life free from the weight and stain of the old bad stuff. The Father brings you back just as he brought the Son back, and not to live your old worn-down, weighted-down life but to live a new weight-free, burden-free life. That's how immersion works—a big deal for you, not just a little bit of sprinkling.*Ro 6:3-4* Immersion buried you right alongside the Son but simultaneously raised you up right alongside the Son. Immersion doesn't do so magically, as if the power was in the water, but instead through the Father's power that your confidence in the Father's plan releases. Yes, you are a critical part of the working, but the Father's power through the Son's service and the Spirit's presence is what works.*Col 2:12*

> **You, too, should excuse others.** The Son's students also have the power to excuse wrongs.*Jn 20:23* Excuse as often as you must. Stop counting.*Matt 18:21-22* The Father excused you. You'd *better* excuse others, or the Father will treat you as you treat others.*Matt 18:23-35* No matter how many times someone wrongs you, if they apologize, then excuse them.*Lk 17:3-4* The Father treats you as you treat others. Excuse another's wrong, then the Father excuses you. Don't excuse, then the Father won't excuse.*Matt 6:14-15* Excuse each other, just as the Father excused you.*Eph 4:32* Put up with others. Drop your grievances. The Father dropped his against you.*Col 3:13* If you excuse others, then they will excuse you. Otherwise, the enemy will get you all.*2Co 2:10-11* Excuse those who abandon you.*2Ti 4:16* Yes, you may punish another for harm, but then excuse the harm. Otherwise, the punished one will fall apart, and you'll have done no good.*2Co 2:6-8* Ask the Father to excuse others.*Jas 5:13-15* Don't deal with those who hold grudges.*2Ti 3:2-5*

This process doesn't depend on your merit, as if the Father were picking winners and losers. Instead, everyone immersed with the Son succeeds because they take on the Son as if the Son were their clothing.*Gal 3:27* And immersion has nothing to do with physical cleaning, as if the Father wanted you looking good. Water immersion instead has everything to do with cleaning your conscience, cleaning up your *act*, so to speak, and not just cleaning it up for your neighbor but for your all-important *Father*.*1Pe 3:21* Who immersed you doesn't matter. Don't fight over it. John isn't around to dunk you any longer. No one is better at immersion than another because those who immerse you can't do what the Son did. They don't immerse you into *their* commitment, conviction, or religion. Your immersion is with *the Son*, the real thing, not some pretender. The Son brings all of you together.*1Co 1:11-15* Immersion points only one way, and that way is to the Son, not to any other person and not to any other conviction.*Eph 4:5*

> **Pursue honor.** The Father gives life forever to those who seek honor by persisting in good.*Ro 2:7* Do everything for the Father's honor.*1Co 10:31* Everyone who does good can expect honor.*Ro 2:10* Hope for honor from the Father. Your suffering for the Father honors you.*Ro 5:3* Your service to the Father honors you.*Ro 15:17* The honor you receive forever far outweighs your troubles that achieve that honor for you.*2Co 4:17* You must know the Father to receive his honor.*2Th 1:8-10* Even the old way had tremendous honor. How much more the new way.*2Co 3:7* Do as the Spirit says, and you'll receive far greater honor than by keeping rules.*2Co 3:8-9* What once gave honor no longer gives honor the way

> relying on the Son gives honor today.*2Co 3:10* What lasts forever gives the greater honor.*2Co 3:11* Keep looking to the Father's great honor.*2Co 3:18*

Remember, too, that immersion doesn't just have to do with water, the symbolic cleansing. Immersion also has to do with the fire-like dousing from the Father's essence, his beloved refining Spirit. Two early followers showed you immersion's dual role. A prominent follower Apollos taught with great enthusiasm and accuracy about the Son. But Appollos only knew about John's water immersion, the cleansing part. So, two other early followers explained to Apollos the Father's way more fully, this time including the Spirit's dousing.*Acts 18:24-28* The same thing happened when Paul found some followers in another region who had John's immersion but hadn't even heard of the Spirit's dousing. So Paul immersed them again in the Son's name. When he touched them, the Father's Spirit came on them so that they spoke in other languages and made predictions. First cleansing, then the Spirit's power!*Acts 19:1-7*

Immersion is all one Spirit. One and the same Spirit doused you all, whether you were one of the favorites or on the outside. You might have been your own boss or had someone else as a boss. Neither one matters. You are now all in this thing together, just as you should be. You all draw from the same Spirit.*1Co 12:13* And by the way, this immersion, this introduction or initiation? It all means *nothing* except that the Son came right back to life after death, new life with a new body, just as you will also get new life and a new body.*1Co 15:29* Desire and value your immersion. It's the start of all good things.

> **The Son came to rescue you from death you deserve.** The first man whom the Father made turned away from the Father, but the perfect Son wouldn't do so.*Ro 5:14* The Son first immersed himself in water in symbolic cleansing and later bled in real sacrifice, showing that he was the Father's great Rescuer.*1Jn 5:6-9* The Father's messenger told Joseph to name the Son *Jesus*, literally *He Rescues*, because that was what the Son would do, rescuing you.*Matt 1:21* You accept the Son's tremendous offer of freedom from death when you hear that others did so.*Jn 4:39-42* The Son's death and life again brings together everyone who accepts it, no matter who or where they are.*Jn 11:49-52* Only the Son can clean up your mess.*Jn 13:6-10* Everyone knows that the Son is how you get to live forever with the great creator Father.*Jn 14:4-6* When the Son was done opening your way, he rejoined his Father.*Heb 1:3* When the Son died to excuse you and save you from your past, he was finished, rejoining his Father to wait

for everyone to come under him.*Heb 10:12-13* Although the Son had his Father's substance in human form, the Son gave up everything to die as your rescuer.*Php 2:6-8* You choose, but whoever accepts the Son accepts what the Father says about him, while whoever rejects the Son makes the Father a liar.*1Jn 5:10* The truth is that the Father gave us life forever in his Son and only in his Son.*1Jn 5:11-13* The Son makes everything wrong with you right for you.*Matt 9:6, Lk 5:24* When you accept the Son, whom the Father certainly accepted although many reject, the Father makes you something special, so that you can give back to the Father what he can accept through his Son.*1Pe 2:4-5* The Father sent his Son so that you who rely on the Son will never be embarrassed.*1Pe 2:6* You know that the Son, whom the Father gave you for only a little while before taking him back where he belongs, died as a gift for everyone.*Heb 2:9* Better that you rely on the Son than keep sacrificing your brothers and sisters.*Heb 12:24*

Tempting

Introduction, immersion, though, isn't into a life of ease. Getting a conscience, that wonderful voice that leads you into all good things, means *listening* to the conscience, to the Spirit's voice. And sometimes the conscience requires resisting things that won't help you but will instead harm or destroy you. The Son's post-immersion experience is the perfect example. Right after John immersed the Son, the Father's Spirit led the Son into the wilderness. The Son's forty-day wilderness experience was to test him, to tempt him with the corruption that immersion had just rejected, and thus to confirm immersion's profound effects.*Matt 4:1, Mk 1:12-13* The Son had the Father's Spirit filling and strengthening him against temptations of the strongest sort. Forty days without food challenges everything.*Lk 4:1-2* Forty days without food certainly left the Son hungry, just as it would leave anyone hungry, if one were even able to somehow survive.*Matt 4:2, Lk 4:2* Imagine the Son's extended wilderness isolation with wild animals all around. Fortunately, the Father's guardians attended and cared for the Son.*Mk 1:13*

Your freedom is in the Son. If you do as the Son says, then truth sets you free.*Jn 8:31-32* When the Son sets you free, then you are indeed free.*Jn 8:36* The Father made you for freedom, not to indulge yourself but to serve one another humbly in love.*Gal 5:13* You do everything required of you when you love your neighbor as yourself.*Gal 5:14* Live free of wrongdoing.*1Pe 2:16* No one condemns you because the Son advocates for you with the Father.*Ro 8:34* Don't worry about anything.*Php 4:6* Have no needs. Let what you have satisfy you.*Php 4:11* You've had a lot and a little. Neither matters.*Php 4:12* You can do everything with the Son's help.*Php 4:13* The Father meets all your needs.*Php 4:19* Don't worry whether you work for another or not, but gain your freedom if you can.*1Co 7:21* You are always free with the Father because you obey the Son.*1Co 7:22* Don't slave for others when the Father paid everything to set you free.*1Co 7:23* The Father can rescue you from the worst imprisonment.*Acts 12:3-17*

Yet at the Son's most-difficult moment, at the end of the forty-day test, the adversary tempted the Son. Oh, yes, you have an adversary. That's the way things work, the adversary catching you at your weakest moment and with the strongest appeal. Here, the adversary reminded the Son that the Son could turn stones to bread to satisfy the Son's hunger.*Matt 4:3, Lk 4:3* But the Son had the right answer, taken right from the ancient writings. The Son told the adversary the truth that the Father's words feed the body, too, not just bread. You can live on the Father's words.*Matt 4:4, Lk 4:4* The adversary next tried a different approach. Having the Son stand on the religious center's highest point, the adversary said that if the Son truly was the Father's Son, then the Son should jump down. Quoting the ancient writing just like the Son had quoted those writings, the adversary said that the Father would have his guardians catch the Son on his way down so that the Son didn't get hurt.*Matt 4:6, Lk 4:9-11* Once again, though, the Son quoted the writings right back to the adversary, not to test the Father who is your ruler. One must use the writings in the spirit that the Father intended them. Anyone can twist words. Instead, follow their purpose and meaning.*Matt 4:7, Lk 4:12*

Work on yourself. Keep at it. Now that you rely on the Son, act like it. Grow up. Cut out your old ways.*Ro 6:1-2* The Son fixed everything for you. You don't have to go back to your old ways.*Ro 6:6-7* The Son did it. Now you can, too.*Ro 6:10* Act like the Son. You don't need your old ways anymore. You're living.*Ro 6:11* Just stop your old ways—no fooling around with them.*Ro 6:12* Don't give in even a little. A little leads to a lot.*Ro 6:13* Nothing holds sway over you anymore. The Son freed you.*Ro 6:14* Just because you've got the Son, though, don't take it as an excuse to go back to your old ways.*Ro 6:15* You're a slave of one or the other, the Son or your old ways. Better the Son and life than your old ways and death.*Ro 6:16* Yes, you are free. No, that doesn't mean to do anything you wish. You're free. Stay free.*1Co 6:12* Come back to your senses. Just stop messing around. Know your Father's desires rather than following your own.*1Co 15:34* Killing the Son was weakness, not power. The Son coming

> right back to life? Now *that's* power. And that's the power that turns you from wrong.₂Co 13:4

Finally, the adversary took the Son to a mountaintop for one last test, until later. From the mountaintop, the Son could see every splendor in the world, everything. The adversary offered it all to the Son if the Son would bow in obedience to the adversary. That's what the adversary does, offering you things that you do not at the moment have but also do not need, spurring your hunger and contention rather than giving you contentment.*Matt 4:8-9, Lk 4:5-7* This time, too, the Son had the right response, drawn directly from his Father's ancient words. The Son told the adversary to honor and serve only the Father who is the ultimate ruler.*Matt 4:10, Lk 4:8* The Son's perseverance worked, as perseverance always works against the adversary. The adversary left, while the Father's guardians came to attend to the Son.*Matt 4:11* The adversary wasn't finished but instead planned to watch for a better time.*Lk 4:13* That's what the adversary does: watch, plan, tempt, and test. But it's all to no avail when you rely on the Son and on the Father's Spirit. Expect temptation, but know that you'll win. You're immersed and protected.

> *Going your own way? Cursed.* If you reject the Son's words, then watch out. You'll be walking around blind.*Acts 13:6-12* If you're not relying on the Son, then you just don't see things. Your past clouds your sight.*2Pe 1:9* The greedy and lustful, those who don't restrain themselves, find themselves cursed, stupid, dumber than an animal.*1Pe 2:14-16* Storms drive along the unrestrained who never find satisfaction. They're headed for the pit.*1Pe 2:17* Don't let even a hint of unrestraint poison the well for you and your friends.*Eph 5:3* Banish obscenity, foolish talk, and coarse joking. Just thank the Father.*Eph 5:4* You'll never get to live with the Father and Son if you're pursuing every fleshly desire.*Eph 5:5* The Father gets angry about unrestraint.*Eph 5:6* Don't cozy up to wrongdoers.*Eph 5:7* You get nothing from chasing desires, only shame and death.*Ro 6:21-22*

5 Mission

Announcing

Life should have mission and purpose, shape and form. Who would have things any other way? The Son certainly had reason for coming, reason for living his earthly life with purpose, to leave a legacy and achieve a life goal. The Son's purpose was the Father's plan, a plan to which you are integral, at its heart. After his immersion and tempting, the Son got right to work. The Son began to proclaim, announce, and pronounce his purpose to anyone who would listen, just as you should make your own intentions clear. The Son said to turn around, turn from the wrong path to the right path, because the Father's door was now open. People now had the opportunity to stand under the Father's good rule, to live in the Father's paradise, to have the Father's benefit, protection, and counsel, even to inherit as the Father's child.*Matt 4:17* After the governor put John in prison, the Son went back to his home region to proclaim the Father's good news. People no longer had to wait or go to great lengths because the Father's rule was instead near. People need only turn around, listen, and accept the good news.*Mk 1:14-15*

The Son pursued his mission wherever it took him. The Son would speak in one village and then take his students to another village to speak there, too. He kept explaining that he came to do exactly that, which was to proclaim his good news.*Mk 1:38* Because of his persistent efforts, news about the Son spread quickly throughout his home region. Everyone heard of what he was saying and doing.*Mk 1:28* So many people chased after him that they had no room to hear him, not even standing in crowds outside trying to hear him in the indoor places that he spoke. The Son just kept telling them his good-news message, which again, was his mission.*Mk 2:1-2* When he finished in one place, he moved on to another. The Son just kept saying that he had to tell the good news about what he was doing, the news of how you'd all be able to get near to his Father once again. He had to reach every town that he could because that was why the Father sent him.*Lk 4:43-44* The Son traveled from one town and village to another, telling the good news of his Father opening the door, inviting everyone in again. The Son's main twelve students traveled with him, as did several women who helped to support the traveling band out of their own means.*Lk 8:1-3* The Son pronounced and proclaimed all through his home region.*Matt 11:1* He also told his main twelve students to go out on their own with the good news, just as he was doing.*Mk 3:13-14* The mission was to tell of the Father's open door, not to keep it a secret. And the open door was the Son.

> **Use your talent.** The Son said that whoever relies on him will do more than he did.*Jn 14:12* If your talent is predicting, then do so confidently.*Ro 12:6* If your talent is serving, then serve generously.*Ro 12:7* If your talent is teaching, then teach consistently.*Ro 12:7* If your talent is to encourage, then do a lot of it.*Ro 12:8* If your talent is giving, then give a lot.*Ro 12:8* If your talent is leading, then do so diligently.*Ro 12:8* If your talent is looking the other way, then do so cheerfully.*Ro 12:8* The Father accepts whatever is your talent.*1Co 12:5* The Father gives everyone different talents.*1Co 12:6* Use your talents to help others.*1Pe 4:10* Serve with the Father's strength so that everyone honors the Father.*1Pe 4:11* Don't envy another's talent.*Php 4:17* Treat gifts as pleasing the Father.*Php 4:18* The Father supplies many talents for his body.*1Co 12:28* Not all members do the same things.*1Co 12:29* Not all have the same talents.*1Co 12:30* Eagerly desire greater talent.*1Co 12:31*

Teaching

The Son's mission was straightforward and his message simple. Yet the good news was also so profound that simply telling it wouldn't have been sufficient. Instead, the Son also had to teach the message's meaning. The Son had to give the good news its fullness, interpret it to the people so that they truly understood. The Son did so much teaching that people, like Martha, one friend in a family of friends whom Jesus especially loved, called the Son *the Teacher*.*Jn 11:28* The Son's students also called the Son *the Teacher*. And the Son said that his students were right to call him that because *the Teacher* is who he is.*Jn 13:13* From the start, right after the Son received the Father's Spirit at his immersion and then returned to his home region, the Son taught in the local religious centers. When the Son taught, he taught with the Father's Spirit, giving his teaching power and authority.*Lk 4:14-15* The Son went everywhere in his home region, teaching in the religious centers, explaining exactly what his good news meant. He left nothing mysterious but instead spelled out everything.*Matt 4:23, Mk 1:39*

> **Sound teaching is critical.** Hesitate to teach. The Father evaluates teachers more strictly.*Jas 3:1* Share good things with your teacher.*Gal 6:6* Sound teachers back up their teaching with action.*2Co 10:11* Training as a speaker means nothing next to knowledge.*2Co 11:6* Follow a teacher's example, as the teacher follows the Son.*1Co 11:1* Imitate those whose good news you welcome, even as you imitate the Son.*1Th 1:6* You, too, may be a model to others who learn of your confidence in the Father.*1Th 1:7-8* Do not welcome those who teach incorrectly, or you will share their error. *2Jn 10-11* Speak to sensible people, letting them evaluate what you say.*1Co 10:15* Be able to teach.*2Ti 2:24* Aspire to be like your teacher, not above your teacher.*Matt 10:24-25, Lk 6:40* Teach others to do as the Son said.*Matt 28:18-20* Reason with those whom you teach.*Acts 18:19-21* Teach at all times. Teach patiently and carefully.*2Ti 4:2* Teach not with persuasion but the Spirit's power.*1Co 2:4* Teach openly everything the Son secretly taught you.*Matt 10:27* Teach only the good news.*Ro 10:15* Teach only to increase your students' confidence in living forever.*Tit 1:1-3* Don't teach out of envy or competition.*Php 1:15-16* Whatever your motive, teach only about the Son.*Php 1:18* Teach diligently with your whole self, always improving.*1Ti 4:13-15* The good news is sound teaching.*1Ti 1:11* Teach only soundly.*2Th 2:15* Teach from the writings.*Ro 15:4* Speak the Father's words.*1Pe 4:11* Speak the Son's truth as your conscience confirms.*Ro 9:1* Teach only right things, without letting anyone look down on you.*1Ti 4:11* Teach only sound things.*Tit 2:1* Demolish pretension. Keep everything consistent with what the Son says.*2Co 10:5* Listen to wise teachers to ensure you teach the good news.*Gal 2:2* Do your best. Gain the Father's approval for sound teaching.*2Ti 2:15* Teach using everyday examples.*Ro 6:19* Who teaches doesn't matter. What's taught matters. What's learned matters.*1Co 15:11* Teach the good news.*2Ti 4:5* Fully proclaim the good news.*Ro 15:19* Someone must teach if others are to rely on the Son.*Ro 10:14* Teach wherever a door opens.*2Co 2:12*

The Son taught like it *meant* something. The Son's teaching was so clear and consistent, so commanding, that it amazed the people. They'd never heard anything like it from the other teachers in the religious centers. The Son was different. Everything that he said carried its own authority.*Mk 1:21-22, Mk 6:1-2, Lk 4:31-32* The Son's teaching was so powerful and gained such a following that one of the members of the religious ruling council made a secret nighttime visit to speak with the Son, to learn more of what was going on. The ruling-council member wanted to keep secret that he knew that the Son taught with the Father's approval. The wonders that the Son did as he taught, which only one from the Father could possibly do, had convinced the ruling-council member, but he wasn't ready to see the Son overhaul the religious order.*Jn 3:1-2* The Son wasn't going to stop, though, certainly not just to obey the religious officials. Instead, the Son kept traveling through all the towns and villages, always teaching in their religious centers, always telling the same good news. No one, not even the religious leaders, were going to change the unstoppable message.*Matt 9:35*

> **Don't stop. Keep at it.** You have plenty to do. Do it, and things will go well for you right up to living forever.*Jn 4:35-36* Sometimes others do the hard work and you the easy.*Jn 4:37-38* Finish what the Father starts. Nothing else has any value.*Matt 15:13* Do what the Father assigns you, whether this or that.*1Co 3:5-6* Whatever you do that works is the Father's doing.*1Co 3:7* Work to please the Spirit, and the Spirit will help you live forever.*Gal 6:8* Be effective and productive by sharing the Father's qualities.*2Pe 1:8* Work even when you can't yet see the result.*1Co 15:37* Keep doing good. You'll get yours.*Gal 6:9* Do good wherever the opportunity arises but especially among those who rely on the Son.*Gal 6:10* Help those who share the good news. No one else will.*3Jn 7-8* Give to those who share the good news. You owe them for helping you.*Ro 15:26-27* The more you do, the more you receive.*2Co 9:6* You reap what you sow.*Gal 6:7* Sow desire, reap destruction.*Gal 6:8* Sow sparingly, reap sparingly.*2Co 9:6*

The Son's compassion for the crowds kept the Son teaching thoroughly and diligently. He saw how harassed and helpless the people were. Their religious leaders were doing nothing for them, leaving them unguided, clueless, guessing, when they needed *answers*. They needed a leader whom they could understand and trust, a leader who *cared* about them.*Matt 9:36, Mk 6:34* And so the Son kept teaching in every town of the region, no matter what the teaching required to reach the crowds.*Matt 11:1* For instance, the Son once sat in a boat to teach the people on the shore of a lake. With people all around him, the boat was the only place that he could get any room to speak and teach.*Matt 13:1-2, Mk 3:7-9, Mk 4:1, Lk 5:1-3* The Son even went to his hometown religious center to teach, where there, his teaching amazed the people.*Matt 13:53-54* The Son's teaching was nothing ordinary. The things that he said *astonished* the crowds, not with impertinence or foolishness but with *truth,* things that *resonated* with the people whom he taught.*Matt 22:33* The Son also took his teaching to the capitol holy city. Early each morning, the Son would go in to the city to teach at the religious center's courtyards and then head back out each evening to camp on a nearby mount.*Lk 21:37-38* The Son taught relentlessly, at a pace with which his students could not keep up.

> **Reject bad teaching.** Bad intentions produce bad teaching.*Lk 6:45* Guard against false teaching.*Matt 16:5-12, Lk 12:1* The concern is not what you eat. It's what you *hear and believe.*Matt 16:5-12* Dishonest teachers harbor bad thoughts.*Matt 9:4* Some teachers just try to make students follow them rather than pointing students to the Son.*Acts 20:30* If supervising teachers is your job, then have them teach the true good news rather than useless myths and speculation.*1Ti 1:3-5* To teach, you've got to know what you're talking about. Don't teach with meaningless talk.*1Ti 1:6-7* Learn from those whose actions prove what they say, not from hypocritical liars with no conscience.*1Ti 4:2* Ignore strange teachings. Stick with the sound things that you know.*Heb 13:9* Reject depraved teachers who oppose the truth. It's okay to judge here.*2Ti 3:8* People who teach against the Son's words do so for their own satisfaction. Watch out for smooth talk and flattery.*Ro 16:18* No one can catch the Son in his own words. Flattery often precedes an attack on the truth.*Mk 12:13-14*

The religious leaders didn't like that the Son was successful when they were not. They didn't like that the Son's teaching was attracting crowds when no one would even listen to them. Yet after several losing tries, the religious leaders realized that they could not say a word in reply to the Son's teaching. The Son was way too smart for them. So after a while, no leader dared to ask him any more challenging questions. They always ended up looking like the fools whom they were.*Matt 22:46* Even when the Son taught in the religious center's courtyards, his teaching amazed the sophisticated city people. His teaching seemed to come out of nowhere. They hadn't seen the Son studying with the religious scholars, so they asked him where he had learned without even having been taught.*Jn 7:15* The Son just said that his teaching was not his own. He credited his Father for his teaching. The Son wasn't going to take any of his Father's honor. He wanted his Father to have all honor. That kind of humility is what makes teaching true.*Jn 7:16-18* The Son urged his students to stay humble when they taught. He said not to call one another teacher because you have only one great Teacher. Just call one another brother or sister, because you are all equal when it comes to teaching.*Matt 23:8* Don't even call one another instructors because you have only one great Instructor.*Matt 23:10* See, the Son taught you everything that he learned from the Father. That's why the Son doesn't call you a servant but instead calls you friends. Servants don't know their master's business, but you do know the Son's business, like a friend would.*Jn 15:15* Just leave it at that. You know everything that the Son taught you, everything that you need to know. Just go teach it like the Son taught you.

Stop going your own deadly way. The Son has spoken, so you can't pretend not to know what to do. You used to, but no more.*Jn 15:22* Once the Son proved it to you with everything incredible that he did, he settled the thing. Those who reject him do so without reason, senselessly, just as predicted.*Jn 15:24-25* Once people started disobeying the Father, death had to follow. Corruption decays.*Ro 5:12* Everyone carries that corruption. No getting around it. You need the Father.*Ro 2:12* Everyone does wrong. Everyone.*Ro 2:23* One went his own way, and everyone followed. But the Son who did no wrong turned it all around.*Ro 5:14* The Son brought life rather than death.*Ro 5:15* Going your own way leads to death, but relying on the Son relieves you of that effect.*Ro 5:16* Death ruled from the moment humans went their own way. But now the Son gives you a chance again at life.*Ro 5:17* You all died for leaving the Father, but the Son brought you back to life.*Ro 5:18* One led you to death, and so one, the Son, led you back to life.*Ro 5:19* Doing wrong just doesn't pay.*1Jn 5:17* Without the Son, wrongdoing has you.*Ro 2:8-11* Stop doing wrong, or calamity will soon catch up with you.*Jn 5:14*

Revealing

The Son's teaching, though, has an unusual quality to it. The Son's teaching tests, examines, and evaluates the hearer, revealing the hearer's condition. The words representing the Son's teaching are living and active. They appraise you as you read and hear, probing your heart, telling you where you stand. You don't judge the Father or the Son, the quality, depth, and accuracy of their teaching. Rather, the Father's words, words the Son speaks, judge you, revealing *your* condition. That deeper quality explains why the Son taught so many things in stories laden with hidden meaning.*Matt 13:3, Mk 4:2* Indeed, everything that the Son taught included analogy, metaphor, parable, or fable. The meaning-laden stories delighted the crowds because they knew the Son's intended meaning. They felt how the stories tested and examined their own thinking, letting them reach their own right conclusions. Just to be sure, though, the Son explained the stories to his students when they were alone.*Mk 4:33-34*

> **The Father invites you apart.** The Father invited you to a different life.*1Th 4:7* The Father doesn't revoke his invitation.*Ro 11:29* The Father makes you up to it by granting your desire for goodness and good acts.*2Th 1:11* The Father invited you to share his Son's honor.*2Th 2:14* Father and Son choose confident leaders.*1Ti 1:1* The Son appoints teachers.*1Ti 1:12* The Father makes some special teachers.*1Ti 2:7* The Father invited you for his purpose.*2Ti 1:9* The Father knows who are his.*2Ti 2:19* The Father asks some of you to do new things.*Ro 1:1* The Son appoints some to pursue those who don't rely on him.*Ro 1:5* The Father invites a whole people to stand apart.*Ro 1:7* The Father invites some to do new things for his Son.*1Co 1:1* You were nothing special when the Father invited you apart.*1Co 1:26* Remain in the situation you were in when the Father invited you.*1Co 7:20* Remain in the same situation you were in when the Father invited you, but be responsible to the Father.*1Co 7:24* Live as the Father assigns and invites you.*1Co 7:17*

The students asked the Son why he taught in stories and didn't just make his meanings plain. The Son explained that he wanted those who wished to know about the Father and his rule, those like his students, to understand the meaning. But at the same time, the Son wanted those who had no interest in truth to recognize their ignorance. The stories did exactly that, giving the meaning to those who desired it but leaving meaning hidden from those who did not.*Matt 13:11, Mk 4:10-12, Lk 8:10* The Son said that the heart, the desire, must come first. You can't hit someone over the head with it. That approach doesn't work. Instead, whoever has a heart for truth, the Son gives more truth. But whoever does not have that heart loses whatever little truth they so far have. That's the way that true learning, meaningful learning, works.*Matt 13:12, Lk 8:18* The Son spoke in parables so that those who had no interest in him would hear his words but not understand them and would see him but not see who he was. The Son was only fulfilling the ancient seer Isaiah's prediction that the hard-hearted people would close their eyes and ears, even with the Son right beside them ready to teach and help.*Matt 13:14-15, Lk 8:10* In short, the Son treats well those who hear and accept it, and see and recognize it. From long ago, sages and saints had badly wanted to see and hear the Son but had no chance to do so. Those who did have the chance needed to respect and seize it but mostly didn't.*Matt 13:16-17*

> **No boasting.** Stop all bragging. It corrupts you.*1Co 5:6-7* The Father chose lowly and despised things, and even things that don't exist yet, to nullify worldly things, so that no one may boast before him.*1Co 1:28-29* Boast only about your service to the Father.*2Co 10:13* You may also boast about those who rely on the Son about whom they heard from you.*2Co 10:14* You may always boast about the good work that others do.*2Co 10:15-16* Brag about the Father.*1Co 1:31* Brag about the Son's willingness to die for you and how his doing so changed you.*Gal 6:14* Boast about the Father.*2Co 10:17* Don't boast as the worldly do.*2Co 11:18* If you must boast, then boast about your weakness.*2Co 11:30* Boast only about your weaknesses.*2Co 12:5* Just let others think of you based on what you do and say, not on your boasting.*2Co 12:6* Boast about your weaknesses so that you have the Son's power.*2Co 12:9*

The Son gave an example of how his stories worked. When he told a story about a sower of seeds, he meant that he is the sower and his words are the seeds. When the story said that some seeds fall on a hard path where birds steal the seeds before they root, he meant that some people have hard hearts and let evil take the place of his words.*Matt 13:19, Mk 4:14-15, Lk 8:4-12* When the story said that some seeds fall on rocky soil, with the shallow-rooted plant then dying in the heat, he meant that some people love his words but at the first sign of trouble leave his words behind.*Matt 13:20-21, Mk 4:16-17, Lk 8:13* When the story said that weeds and thorns choke out some new plants, he meant that some hear and receive his words but lose them to life's worries and wealth's deceitfulness.*Matt 13:22, Mk 4:18-19, Lk 8:14* When the story said that seeds falling on good soil produce a huge crop, he meant that those who hear and pursue the word show great bounty for doing so.*Matt 13:23, Mk 4:20, Lk 8:15* By using stories to teach, the Son fulfilled what the ancient seers had said that he would speak hidden things that people could easily unravel if they wished, but they must first desire to do so.*Matt 13:34-35*

> **Wrongdoing is natural to you. Stop it.** Rely on the Son. Don't expect him to rely on you. You're not reliable.*Jn 2:23-25* You are unspiritual, corrupt.*Ro 7:14* You don't even see the bad that you do. When you do see it, you don't know why you do it. You just know that bad is natural to you.*Ro 7:15-20* You may want to do good, but somehow you don't.*Ro 7:21* Corruption keeps you trapped.*Ro 7:23* You are a wreck. Your mind thinks of the Father, but your body pursues desires that lead to death. Good thing that you have the Son's rescue.*Ro 7:24-25* Before

> the Son rescued you, you were a disobedient fool, trapped by your own pleasures and passions, a real hater.*Tit 3:3-4* You were dead, doing what everyone else did.*Eph 2:1-2* You had no restraint. And when you stopped, your old friends turned on you, didn't they?*1Pe 4:3-4*

Healing

While the Son's mission was to share the good news, which also required lots of teaching, the Son spread the good news so quickly in part by healing people as he went from town to town. As the Son traveled throughout his home region, telling the good news and teaching, he healed every disease and sickness that he encountered. No wonder the message spread so quickly: the Son's healings were miraculous, instant recoveries from even the worst conditions, not just a little medication or therapy here or there.*Matt 4:23* For example, the Son instantly healed a man with a horrible skin disease, not a condition from which one saw any recovery, no less instant recovery. The man had asked if the Son was willing to heal him. Indignant, the Son said that of course he was *willing*. That's why the Son had come, to set things right for all who asked.*Matt 8:2-3, Mk 1:40-42, Lk 5:12-13*

> **Be happy about rescue.** Be happy about the Son's return.*Jn 16:21-22* The Son's return should fill you with joy.*Jn 17:13* Your confidence in your rescue should lead to huge joy.*1Pe 1:9* The Father's Spirit produces joy in you.*Gal 5:22* Take great joy in the Son's rescue.*Jude 24-25* Rejoice in the Father always.*Php 4:4* Be happy, all the time.*1Th 5:16* Be joyful in hope.*Ro 12:12* Be happy as you trust the Father.*Ro 15:13* You make others happy.*Ro 16:19* Rejoice even as you work at it.*2Co 13:11* The Son was happy.*Heb 1:9* Take joy in the Father!*Php 3:1* Sing and make happy music.*Eph 5:19-20* Be glad even for trials. Your reward will make you happy.*Matt 5:12* Be especially happy about others' confidence in the truth.*3Jn 3-4* Take deep joy in your common rescue.*Php 1:7-8* Take joy, too, when your children accept the truth. *2Jn 4* Others who rely on the Son are your joy.*1Th 2:19-20* Take joy in others' confidence.*1Th 3:9* Have unbounded joy in one another's confidence.*2Co 7:4*

The asking part, that people who wished healing should desire and ask for it, was significant. The Son wouldn't heal those who weren't interested in it. You've got to *want* it to get it, today just as then. Yet the Son found plenty of people who did want it and who knew that the

Son could provide everything. In one case, a Roman army commander asked the Son to heal the commander's servant who wasn't even there. The commander said that the Son's doing so should be no problem for the Son because the soldiers followed the commander's commands, so why wouldn't healing occur on the Son's command? The commander's confidence amazed the Son, who based on that confidence went ahead with the instant healing from a distance._{Matt 8:5-13, Lk 7:1-10} The Son also healed a royal official's son from a distance when the official begged the Son to do so. The son recovered at the exact time that the Son had told the official that his son would live._{Jn 4:46-54}

Wherever he went, the Son did instant, miraculous healings. In one instance, the Son first asked an invalid who had waited for many years for healing if the invalid wanted to get well. When the invalid said that he did want to get well, the Son simply told him to pick up his mat and walk, and the man promptly did._{Jn 5:1-9} On another occasion, the Son healed his leading student Peter's bedridden mother-in-law of a fever, simply by touching her hand, after which she got right up to serve the Son._{Matt 8:14-15, Mk 1:29-31, Lk 4:38-39} People brought the sick to the Son from all over the region, and he healed every one of them instantly. The ancient seer Isaiah had predicted that the Son would do so, saying that the Son would take up your infirmities and bear your diseases._{Matt 8:16-17} When the Son would heal, as he did a paralyzed man on a mat, the awed crowd would honor the Father for giving the Son such power. They knew the right source of the Son's power._{Matt 9:8, Lk 5:26}

The healings just kept coming and coming, each depending on the healed person's confidence that the Son could do as they asked. For another unusual example, the Son healed a woman who said to herself that a touch to the Son's cloak would be enough._{Matt 9:20-22, Mk 5:25-34, Lk 8:40-48} And the healings weren't just of fevers and other illnesses. The Son could give literal sight to the blind, as he did for two men after they confirmed that they knew that he could._{Matt 9:27-31} Everywhere he went, to every town and village, the Son healed every disease and sickness he encountered, where those suffering wanted to heal._{Matt 9:35} The Son healed a man's shriveled hand._{Mk 3:1-6} The Son just told another man with a shriveled hand to hold it out, and the Son promptly healed it as good as the other hand._{Matt 12:13, Lk 6:6-10} On and on the healings went. The Son healed a blind and mute man so that the man could both talk and see._{Matt 12:22}

Spiritspeak

> **Better to rely on the Son.** Some haven't heard the good news yet, while others just plain rejected it.*Heb 4:6* No one who tastes the good news' full power and goodness, its great gift, but then turns away, turns back to it again. Once you get it, you keep it.*Heb 6:4-6* Turn away from the good news, and you'll find yourself unable to think, see, or hear.*Ro 11:8* Those who don't have the good news have envy, deceit, and malice instead.*Ro 1:29* Those who don't have the good news have gossip, slander, insolence, and arrogance instead.*Ro 1:30* Those who don't have the good news have no understanding, love, or ability to forgive.*Ro 1:31* Those who don't have the good news don't see that wrongdoers die. They keep doing wrong and encourage others to join them.*Ro 1:32* Anyone on their own, without the good news, becomes worthless, corrupt.*Ro 2:12* Don't turn away from the Father and his wonderful life.*Heb 3:12* When you hear the good news, accept it. Don't rebel.*Heb 3:15* The Father doesn't want you shrinking back.*Heb 10:38* Shrinking back from the good news destroys you.*Heb 10:39* Whoever hates the Son, hates his Father as well.*Jn 15:23*

Sometimes, the Son's methods were unusual. He once healed a deaf and mute man by putting his fingers in the man's ears, touching the man's tongue, looking to up to his Father, and saying *open*.*Mk 7:31-35* The Son healed a blind man by spitting on the man's eyes, putting his hands on him, and when the man could only see what looked like trees walking around, putting his hands on the man's eyes again.*Mk 7:22-26, Jn 9:1-12* The Son also restored the sight of two blind men sitting by the roadside, after they called to the Son to give them a break.*Matt 20:29-34* A blind beggar did the same thing, shouting to the Son to give the beggar a break. When the crowd told the beggar that the Son was calling for him, the beggar got up and ran to the Son who told him that his confidence had restored his sight. And guess what? The formerly blind beggar could then see.*Mk 10:46-52, Lk 18:35-43* The Son also healed blind and disabled persons who came to him at the holy city's religious center.*Matt 21:14* The leading student Peter said that the Son healed everyone who trusted the Son because the Son had the Father's presence and power. Peter had it right. No one but the Father's Son could possibly do what the Son did.*Acts 10:38* And then, how could anyone resist the Son's message and teaching, when the Son was constantly doing such compassionate wonders?

> **Learning is a start, but arrive at the truth.** Some are always learning but never able to accept truth.*2Ti 3:7* Watch out for and keep away from those who put obstacles in your way that are contrary to the teaching that you learned.*Ro 16:17* Do not deceive yourselves. Stick with what you know. Don't accept the

world's so-called wisdom, which is really foolishness. You already know the Father's truth that makes you truly wise.*1Co 3:18* The world's wisdom is foolishness. The Father's truth catches the worldly in their craftiness.*1Co 3:19* The world's so-called wise thoughts are futile.*1Co 3:20* Come back to your senses. Return to what you know and *who* you know. Otherwise, shame on you.*1Co 15:34* Don't put up with fools or those who exploit you. Get the life that you know.*2Co 11:19-20* Stand up for one another. Discerning truth and doing good are hard enough.*Heb 3:13*

Liberating

The Son did more than heal physical illnesses. He also freed the mentally ill of the enemy's awful oppression. People would bring to the Son for healing, all those with mental illness, including some whom the enemy had completely taken over. In each instance, the Son would drive away the enemy, who knew whom the Son was.*Mk 1:32-34* The Son traveled throughout his home region, driving out the enemy's mentally disabling influences.*Mk 1:39* In a local religious center, a man whom the enemy had completely taken over cried out to the Son, asking whether the Son had come to destroy the enemy's influences.*Mk 1:23-24* The Son told the enemy to shut up and come out of the man, which the enemy did with a violent shake and shriek, amazing the people.*Mk 1:25-27, Lk 4:33-36* The Son cured all those whom the enemy's influence troubled.*Lk 6:18*

Some of these liberations were spectacular. The Son cast the enemy out of two violent men who were under the enemy's complete control. The enemy's influences asked the Son to send them into a herd of pigs. When the Son did, the herd rushed into a lake to drown.*Matt 8:28-34* Another record shows the Son casting the enemy, who said his influences were many, out of a violent man living among the tombs.*Mk 5:1-10, Lk 8:26-31* The enemy asked that the Son not torture him.*Mk 5:7, Lk 8:28* The Son sent the influences into a herd of about two-thousand pigs that then rushed drowning into the lake.*Mk 5:11-13, Lk 8:32-33* The Son drove the enemy out of a man who could not talk, after which the man spoke, amazing the crowd, the members of which had never seen anything like it.*Matt 9:32-34* The Son also told his students to drive out the enemy.*Matt 10:8* The Son gave them authority to do so.*Lk 9:1* Seventy-two students whom the Son sent out to work returned happy that even the enemy submitted to them.*Lk*

10:17 The Son replied that they should instead be happy that they were going to live forever.*Lk 10:20*

> **Get rid of wrongdoing.** Rid yourself of moral filth and the prevalent evil. Just accept what the Father planted in you that rescues you.*Jas 1:21* Ignore people who love themselves and pleasure rather than the Father. Ignore the boastful and proud, the abusive and ungrateful, those without love, the unforgiving and slanderous, those with no self-control.*2Ti 3:2-5* Let the Father's Son and Spirit clean it all up—*all* of it.*1Co 6:9-11* Your corruption makes the Father's perfection all the clearer.*Ro 2:5* Do the right things that the Son does. Don't do as the enemy does, those things that the Son came to destroy.*1Jn 3:7-8* Imitate good, not evil. The good are from the Father. Wrongdoers don't know him.*3Jn 11* Suffer in body as the Son suffered. Doing so keeps you from pursuing evil desires. You instead do what the Father wants.*1Pe 4:1-2* Do as much good now as you did wrong before.*Ro 6:19*

Some said that the Son used the enemy's means to liberate people of mental illness. The Son replied to look at him. Did *he* look like an enemy? Of course not.*Matt 10:25* The Son healed a blind and mute man whose mind the enemy had completely taken over.*Matt 12:22* The Son healed the enemy-controlled daughter of a local woman who had shown the Son that she knew he could do it.*Matt 15:21-28* The Son sent the enemy out of a bizarre-acting boy whose father brought him to the Son for liberating. The boy had seizures that often cast him into fire or water.*Matt 17:14-18, Mk 9:17-27, Lk 9:37-43* The Son told his students, who were unable to throw out the enemy, that they needed to ask the Father's help.*Mk 9:28-29* The students' repeated failure to rely on the Father to heal the more-difficult cases frustrated the Son.*Lk 9:41*

> **Father and Son appoint teachers.** The Father commissions teachers to share the good news.*Col 1:25* The Father appoints sound teachers.*1Ti 2:7* Teach as approved by the Father, to please him rather than people.*1Th 2:4* Teach by the Son's authority.*1Th 4:1-2* Claim competence not in yourself but from the Father.*2Co 3:5* The Father authorizes teaching, so keep at it.*2Co 4:1* Teach out of your reverence for the Father. Clear your conscience.*2Co 5:11* Be out of your mind for the Father but in your right mind for others.*2Co 5:13* You are the Son's representative, the Father appealing through you.*2Co 5:20* Others accept your teaching when they accept the Son's teaching.*Jn 15:20* Don't teach like you're the one. Teach that the Son is the one.*2Co 4:5* Fancy teaching only reduces the good news' attraction.*1Co 1:17* No fancy teaching. Just teach reliance on the Son.*1Co 2:1-3* Teach the Son's boundless riches. Keep it plain.*Eph 3:8-9* Teach only what the

Son taught. Keep the confidence of both Father and Son.*2Jn 9* Teach the good news from the Spirit.*Col 3:16* Thank the Son for authorizing your teaching and strengthening you.*1Ti 1:12*

The religious officials once told the Son to get out of the capitol holy city because the governor wanted to kill him. The Son instead said that he would press on liberating the mentally ill of the enemy. Besides, seers always died in the capitol holy city.*Lk 13:31* After the Son died and came right back to life, the students found themselves able to throw the enemy out of anyone suffering mental illness.*Acts 5:16* A leading student Philip, who took the good news far off, threw the enemy out of many who would let out a shriek.*Acts 8:5-8* A female slave who earned her master money by predicting the future followed the leading student Paul and others around, annoying them by shouting that they were the Father's servants. Finally, Paul turned around and threw the enemy's influence right out of her.*Acts 16:16-18* The Father did other extraordinary wonders through Paul, so that handkerchiefs and aprons that touched him had the same power to throw the enemy out of the mentally ill.*Acts 19:11-12* The Son liberated the mentally ill, not just the physically disabled.

Stop the wrongdoing. If you don't know the rules, then you go wrong and die. If you know the rules but break them, you must pay for rule-breaking.*Ro 2:12* Wrongs anger the Father.*Col 3:6* Wrongdoers angered the Father who let them die rather than join him peacefully.*Heb 3:17-19* You're warned: the Father doesn't let anyone get away with breaking the rules.*1Th 4:6* Wrongdoers pay.*Col 3:25* You were once a wrongdoer, angering the Father, and you knew it.*Col 1:21* Now that you're on the straight and narrow, let those with whom you used to do wrong go their own way, especially when they give you a hard time for reforming. They'll pay.*1Pe 4:5* Some wrongs are obvious. Other wrongs sneak up on you.*1Ti 5:24* Be slow to blame others for wrongs. But when you know they've done it, don't spare them. Better to deal with you than with the Son.*2Co 13:1-3* Quietly show your friends where they're going wrong.*Matt 18:15* If they continue, then have others confront them, too.*Matt 18:16* If they still continue, then go ahead and tell everyone. No more quiet advice. Maybe they'll reform.*Matt 18:17* Those who claim they've never done wrong can't see the wrongs they do.*Jn 9:40-41*

Raising

The Son, though, did even even greater works than to heal the sick and restore the mentally disabled. The Son had such life within him, was so fully the Father's own, so much in control of everything, that the Son could also bring the dead back to life. The Son reminded those who questioned his nature and role that with his coming, the blind could see, lame walk, diseased recover, and deaf able to hear. And then the Son raised the dead—brought the dead and gone right back to life.*Matt 11:4-5* In one example, the Son saw a procession carrying a widow's dead son on a bier. He'd had nothing to do with the procession but just felt great compassion when seeing the grieving widow. So he touched the bier, just touched it, and with that one little touch he brought the widow's dead son right back to life.*Lk 7:11-15* Astounded, the people promptly said that the Father was there. The Father had come to help his people. News of the miracle spread rapidly throughout the whole area.*Lk 7:16-17* Yes, healings had done a lot to spread the good news, but bringing a dead person back to life did more.

> **Accept the Son. You have the strongest evidence.** The Son's students failed to rely on the Son when they thought that a storm would drown them.*Matt 8:23-27, Mk 4:35-40, Lk 8:22-25* The students failed to heal a mentally disturbed boy whom the Son then healed. The students had too little confidence.*Matt 17:14-20, Mk 17-27* If you only have a little confidence, then you'll likely lose it.*Matt 25:29* The Son on his return may not find many with a lot of confidence.*Lk 18:8* Even after the Son did wonders, many still had no confidence in him, which is just what the ancient writings predicted.*Jn 12:37-40* People who do many wrongs obviously don't rely on the Son.*2Th 3:2*

The Son did that astounding miracle more than once. Another time, a leader of one of the local religious centers came to the Son saying that although his daughter was dead, the leader knew that the Son could bring her back to life. The leader told the Son that all the Son needed to do was to touch her, and the girl would live again. Others laughed at the thought that the Son could do anything for the dead girl. But the Son did just as the confident leader asked. He took the girl's hand, and the girl came back to life and stood right up—no more laughing matter. The Son showed the doubters that his power was real.*Matt 9:18-26, Mk 5:21-43, Lk 8:40-56* In an even more dramatic turn, the Son heard that one of his friends was sick. The Son didn't heal him right away, instead waiting until the friend had died, indeed waiting several days until the family entombed the dead friend. Then, with a crowd watching, the Son stood outside the tomb and called the dead friend right back to life. The friend came walking out still covered in grave clothes. The friend had been dead four days, stinking and stiff, but the Son brought him right back to life with the command to come out.$_{Jn\ 11:1-44}$ The miracle of bringing a four-day-dead person back to life set the crowds on fire. They now knew for certain who had come, the Father's own Son, and they told everyone about it. Do you also know?

> ***Know what coming right back to life is like.*** Know the power of suddenly living again after death, like the Son. That hope makes worthwhile the opposition you'll face for relying on the Son.$_{Php\ 3:10-11}$ Knowing you're coming right back to life should put you on your knees thanking the Father. He gives you a reason to live, truly *live*.$_{1Pe\ 1:3}$ The Father has given you a reason to trust him and rely on him. He did it for his Son so that he could do it for you. Shouldn't you speak well of him?$_{1Pe\ 1:21}$ The Son's coming right back to life rescues you because the Son now has the power to do as he wishes, which is to do the same for you.$_{1Pe\ 3:21-22}$ Either way, relying on the Son or not, you're his. He controls your outcome, which is exactly the point. He wants you to respect and rely on him.$_{Ro\ 14:7-8}$ Death came through a man's bad choice. Living forever came through the Son's best choice.$_{1Co\ 15:21}$ The Son turned death on its head. Death just turned you back to the Son, who was always your life.$_{1Co\ 15:22}$

Attracting

Naturally, the Son's good news and the teaching and healing that he did along with it attracted huge crowds. The same would happen today. When after his immersion the Son returned to his home region to teach in the local religious centers, glowing from the Spirit's presence and power, news spread of him like wildfire. Everyone had something good to say about him.$_{Lk\ 4:14-15}$ The crowds were nearly uncontrollable. One crowd gathered so quickly and pressed in so hard when the Son wasn't even teaching that the Son and his students could not eat.$_{Mk\ 3:20}$ Wherever he went, hillside, village, or even lakeside, large crowds gathered, expecting him to teach.$_{Mk\ 2:13}$ The Son would sit high up on a mountainside, and a large crowd would gather below for him to teach.$_{Matt\ 5:1-2}$ Then, when he came down from the mountainside after teaching, large crowds would follow him, waiting for him to do something miraculous or to stop and teach again.*Matt 8:1*

> **Show courage.** Let your courage astonish others, no matter your credentials.*Acts 4:13* Don't even let deadly threats discourage you.*Acts 14:19-20* Don't hesitate to teach publicly, everywhere, and anything that helps.*Acts 20:20* Teach boldly.*Acts 28:30-31* Boldly remind others of important points.*Ro 15:15* Teach authoritatively. Don't let them get you down.*Tit 2:15* Take honor from suffering as a teacher.*Eph 3:13* Teach with the Son's powerful energy. Contend strenuously to mature others' confidence in the Son.*Col 1:28* Contend hard not only for those whom you know but also those whom you have not met.*Col 2:1* Teach courageously, looking for results even when facing strong opposition.*1Th 2:1-2* Death works against your teaching so that life works in you. *2Co 4:12*

The Son didn't seek attention, didn't ask for the large crowds. Just the opposite: he would tell the people whom he healed not to say anything. They would tell everyone anyway. News then spread all the more, so that the crowds grew larger to hear his teaching and see his healing.*Lk 5:15* The Son wasn't just a local phenomenon, a local favorite, either. Large crowds gathered everywhere the Son went, whether in his home region around the lake, or across the lake's other side where the people weren't even of the same religion, or in the capitol holy city, or out in the wilderness. Everywhere the Son went, more people came.*Matt 4:25* People traveled long distances just to see and hear him. People even came all the way from the coastal region, and not just a few people but people in great numbers.*Lk 6:17-18*

When the people saw the Son's power, a power that healed instantly, the people wouldn't just sit and listen. They would press in around him, trying to touch him. They wanted his power to rub off on them, to heal anything wrong with them.*Lk 6:19* The more that the Son healed, the more who wanted healing. People with all kinds of diseases would push their way forward through the crowds to touch him for healing.*Mk 3:10* And sometimes, reaching the Son took more than just pressing through the crowd. In one instance, the crowd listening to the Son teach was so large that men bringing a paralyzed man to him for healing couldn't get through. So they took the paralyzed man up on the roof of the house where the Son was teaching. They then dug down through the roof to let the paralyzed man down in front of the Son, for the Son to heal him.*Mk 2:3-12, Lk 5:17-25* When the Son healed the man, the amazed people, who had never seen anything like it, praised the Father for the Son's work.*Mk 2:12*

Spiritspeak

> ***Turn others from wrongs.*** Turning others from errors rescues them from death.*Jas 5:19-20* Teach the good news to those who are still corrupted, dead, so that they can live.*1Pe 4:6* Teach those who don't know the Son.*Gal 2:7-8* Your obligation is also to the foolish.*Ro 1:14-15* Help others to be self-controlled.*Tit 2:1-3* Urge others to be self-controlled.*Tit 2:4-5* Older men should set a good example for young men to be self-controlled.*Tit 2:6-7* Teach so that none are open to blame.*1Ti 5:7* But don't bother teaching when they're not listening. You'll do no good.*Matt 7:6*

Word spread so much that the Son could not enter a town openly, or the crowds would become unmanageable. Instead, the Son stayed outside the towns in quiet, hidden places. Yet people still came to him from everywhere.*Mk 1:45* When news about the Son's healing powers spread well north into another region, where the people didn't even know of the Father, people from that region brought the Son all who had diseases. The Son went right ahead and healed even those from well outside the area, and even when they were mentally ill, having seizures, paralyzed, or in severe pain.*Matt 4:24* When the Son approached a town, everyone from that town would gather, bringing their sick along with them so that the Son could heal them no matter what was the illness.*Mk 1:32-34* The Son would sometimes try to withdraw, like when his students returned from sharing the good news and healing the sick, and he wanted to spend some quiet time with them. But the crowds would learn that the Son was nearby and would find him. Rather than chase them away, the Son would welcome them, teach them, and heal those who needed it.*Lk 9:10-11* Large crowds just kept following and gathering, the Son always healing all the ill.*Matt 12:15*

Things got crazy at times. Once, a crowd of many thousands gathered, so that people were trampling one another.*Lk 12:1* When the Son arrived at a place, word would just spread. People would bring all their sick, begging the Son to let the sick touch the edge of his cloak. He healed every one who did so.*Matt 14:34-36, Mk 6:53-56* Even when he crossed the river into the wilderness, large crowds followed for his healing.*Matt 19:1-2* Even when he went up on a mountainside, great crowds brought the lame, blind, mute, and many others to him, laying them at his feet. He would go ahead and heal them, amazing the crowds.*Matt 15:29-31* The Son sometimes entered a house not wanting anyone to know he was in town, but he could not keep his presence secret.*Mk 7:24* The more that the Son told people not to spread news of his healing, the more people kept talking about it, overwhelmed with amazement at how quickly and thoroughly he healed everyone.*Mk 7:36-37* He always taught the crowds that came to him.*Mk 10:1* His teaching delighted the crowds.*Mk 12:37* The Son's wondrous healing delighted the people while humiliating his opponents.*Lk 13:17* No one could miss his popularity.

> ***Keep order.*** The Father is not disorderly but orderly. Keep order when you meet.*1Co 14:33* Speak intelligibly, or have someone interpret.*1Co 14:27* Otherwise, keep quiet, speaking only to yourself and the Father.*1Co 14:28* A few may predict things while others weigh carefully their words.*1Co 14:29* Speak one at a time.*1Co 14:30* Speak in turn so that everyone receives instruction and encouragement.*1Co 14:31* Control your spirit as to when to speak.*1Co 14:32* Some keep quiet, in submission.*1Co 14:34* Ask questions of one another at home, for speaking too much in meetings disgraces.*1Co 14:35* Do everything in fit and orderly way.*1Co 14:40* Follow good models, keeping your eyes on those who live right.*Php 3:17* Follow sound leaders.*1Th 2:10-11* The Father gives you leaders to follow.*Ro 1:1* Listen to your leaders.*Eph 1:1-2* Follow the life and adopt the confidence of your leaders.*Heb 13:7* Leaders who are away physically remain with you in spirit.*1Co 5:1-4* Help leaders whatever they do.*1Co 16:6* Encourage your leaders.*Eph 6:21-22* Ask the Father to restore your leaders.*Heb 13:19* Support and submit to your leaders. Make their work a joy rather than burden.*Heb 13:17* Greet your leaders.*Heb 13:24* Honor your leaders. They deserve it.*1Ti 5:17-18* Do not entertain accusations against your leaders without reliable witnesses.*1Ti 5:19* Correct corrupt leaders in front of everyone to warn others.*1Ti 5:20*

The Son wasn't looking for crowds, though. He wasn't into popularity. He wasn't trying to win an election. The Son would withdraw frequently. The people would search for him, though, find him, and try to keep him from leaving.*Lk 4:42* The Son saw how large the crowds were growing and so hid himself from them, even though he had such compassion for them that he kept healing all their sick.*Matt 14:13-14* When the people planned to force the Son to lead them in revolt, he hid up an out-of-the-way mountain.*Jn 6:14-15* He would often get up very early in the morning to sneak away. His students would have to go looking for him.*Mk 1:35-37* He preferred out-of-the-way places.*Lk 5:16* So many people would crowd around the Son and his students that they couldn't even eat. The Son would sneak them away to hide for rest.*Mk 6:30-32* When the crowds got so persistent that the Son could no longer move about publicly, he took his students into the wilderness.*Jn 11:54* People kept asking why the Son wasn't going public with it.$_{Jn\ 11:55\text{-}56}$ Instead, the Son would hide himself after speaking.$_{Jn\ 12:36}$

> **Rely on the Son, not something senseless.** When you can rely on the creator of the universe, why look instead to senseless things that you and others create?$_{Ro\ 1:23}$ Don't exchange the creator for the created, sense for senselessness.$_{Ro\ 1:25}$ For instance, don't pursue your stomach or lust. They can't fill you, when the Father can.$_{Php\ 3:19}$ I know: telling the difference is hard for those who don't know the Father. Then get to know him.$_{1Co\ 8:7}$ Fine: eat. But food isn't bringing you closer to the Father.$_{1Co\ 8:8}$ That people misunderstand and hate the Son is just so incredibly sad.$_{Php\ 3:18}$ People chasing after so many senseless things is dizzying, distressing. To regain your senses, find people who don't. Find people who talk about the Son coming back to life.$_{Acts\ 17:16\text{-}20}$ Give up senselessness in exchange for the living Father.$_{1Th\ 1:9}$ The Father is everything. Devoting yourself to anything else is senseless.$_{1Co\ 8:4}$ Oddly, people think that senseless things are alive. Then, they let those things rule them.$_{1Co\ 8:5}$ Hold onto your one Father and his Son who together made everything you need.$_{1Co\ 8:6}$ Run from everything else.$_{1Co\ 10:14}$ Don't devote yourself to senseless things. Keep the Father first.$_{1Jn\ 5:20}$ And don't run around with those who devote themselves to senseless things.$_{Eph\ 5:7}$ Truly, rid yourself of devotion to anything but Father and Son.$_{Col\ 3:5}$ Those senseless things get you nowhere.$_{1Co\ 10:19\text{-}20}$ Mixing devotion to the Father with devotion to senseless things doesn't work.$_{2Co\ 6:16}$ If you're not relying on the Son, then senseless things can easily lead you astray.$_{1Co\ 12:2}$ Be careful not to lead others astray even when you're not straying.$_{1Co\ 8:9}$ Don't even look like you're straying. Others may follow you where you're not even going.$_{1Co\ 8:10}$ Just don't mislead the gullible into pursuing senseless things.$_{1Co\ 8:11}$ The Son wants you pointing others to him, not to some senseless thing.$_{1Co\ 8:12}$ Restrain yourself when around someone who might misunderstand your actions.$_{1Co\ 8:13}$ Rely on the Father. Don't make yourself bigger than he is.$_{1Co\ 10:22}$ Pursue senseless things, and the Father and Son will turn you away.$_{Eph\ 5:5}$ Pursuing senseless things angers the Father.$_{Eph\ 5:6}$

Students

The Son attracted students from the start, beginning right after his immersion when two of John's students decided to follow the Son instead.$_{Jn\ 1:35\text{-}37}$ The Son told them to come with him.$_{Jn\ 1:38\text{-}39}$ One of them recruited his brother, telling him that they had found the rescuer.$_{Jn}$

1:40-42 They were fishermen, but the Son told them to follow him and fish for people instead.*Matt 4:18-19, Mk 1:16-18* When the Son astonished the students with a miraculous catch of two boatloads of fish, the leading student Peter asked the Son to leave him, a sinful man. But the Son told him that he would fish for people.*Lk 5:8-10* They immediately left their nets to follow the Son.*Matt 4:20, Mk 1:16-18* The Son had sent them out again to fish after they hadn't caught anything all night. They caught so many fish that the Son's power scared them.*Lk 5:4-11*

> **Teachers may earn a wage.** Those whom you teach may pay for it.*Matt 10:9-10, Mk 6:8, Lk 9:3, 10:7* Let others help support your teaching.*Matt 10:11* Accept whatever those whom you teach offer.*Lk 10:8* If no one supports you, then still tell them the good news, but move on. They should have supported you.*Matt 10:14-15, Mk 6:10-11, Lk 10:10-12* Leave without regret.*Lk 9:4-5, Lk 10:10-11* Those who teach deserve compensation.*1Ti 5:17-18* Teachers may ask for support, just as others earn a wage.*1Co 9:4-7* Let the teacher earn a wage.*1Co 9:8-9* Those who teach should share in the benefit from teaching.*1Co 9:10* Material rewards are appropriate for spiritual teaching.*1Co 9:11* Teachers of the good news should get compensation just as others do for working. You can always decline the offer.*1Co 9:12-13* Fine that you earn a teacher's wage, but fine, too, if you decline it.*1Co 9:14-15* Teach for free, earn a special reward.*1Co 9:17-18* Some teach the good news for free. Good for them and their students.*2Co 2:17* Appreciate rather than condemn those who teach free of charge.*2Co 11:7* Just know that others pay for it when teachers teach you for free.*2Co 11:8* Teaching for free makes it easier for the student.*2Co 11:9*

Going a little farther, the Son quickly recruited two more students, James and John, who were in a boat with their father and hired men. They also immediately left to follow the Son.*Matt 4:21-22, Mk 1:19-20* The Son also recruited Philip, who brought his brother Nathanael to the Son, whom Nathanael called the Father's Son and king of the people, simply because the Son had said that he saw no deceit in Nathanael.*Jn 1:43-49* The Son also recruited Levi, also known as Matthew, out of a tax collector's booth. The Son had dinner at Matthew's house, which surprised the religious leaders.*Matt 9:9, Mk 2:14-15, Lk 5:27-32* The Son drew these students away up a mountainside. He appointed twelve to be with him.*Mk 3:13-14* He told his students that many people would rely on him if they would only go out and talk about relying on the Son.*Matt 9:37-38, Lk 10:2* The Son gave these twelve special students power to make people better physically and mentally.*Matt 10:1-2, Mk 3:16-19, Mk 6:7, Lk 6:12-16, 9:1*

> **Serve the Father.** The Son served the Father rather than himself.*Jn 6:38* Work for the Father.*Jn 9:4* Walk the walk, don't just talk the talk. Do as the Father says.*Matt 7:21-22* The Son notices those who do as his Father says.*Matt 7:23* You are wise when doing as the Son says.*Matt 7:24-25, Lk 6:46-48* Don't be the fool who doesn't do as the Son says.*Matt 7:26-27, Lk 6:49* What you do proves your wisdom.*Matt 11:19* Don't just listen, while deceiving yourself. Do as the Father says.*Jas 1:22* You won't look all that good if you only listen but don't act.*Jas 1:23-24* The Father favors you when you do what he says.*Jas 1:25* Don't just wish someone well. Help them!*Jas 2:15-16* Not doing what you know to do is just plain wrong.*Jas 4:17* Show love by acting, not talking.*1Jn 3:17-18* Be an example for others in doing.*1Ti 4:11* Good deeds get you noticed. Even hidden good deeds eventually come to light.*1Ti 5:25* Sure, be eager to do good. But the Father especially favors you when you suffer for doing right.*1Pe 3:13-14*

Later, when things got hard and many other students left the Son, the Son asked the twelve students if they wanted to leave, too. But Peter answered that they had no one to whom to go, because only the Son could help them live forever.*Jn 6:67-69* The students were afraid of how negatively some responded to the good news. One said that they should return with the Son to the area where the people had tried to stone the Son, so that the students could die with him.*Jn 11:15-16* Yet the students went out boldly telling people to rely on the Son, while they healed many people physically and mentally.*Mk 6:7-13* The Son told his students to keep healing the sick.*Matt 10:8* He wanted them talking about his Father's place as they healed the sick.*Lk 9:2* So the students kept doing so.*Lk 9:6* The Son sent out more and more students.*Lk 10:1* He even told his students to bring the dead back to life.*Matt 10:8* Late in his mission, when they were at a last supper, the Son took off his outer clothing, wrapped a towel around his waist, and washed his students' feet, to show them that they should serve one another.*Jn 13:2-17*

> **You have the Spirit's power.** The Son sent the Father's Spirit as your power.*Lk 24:49* Use the Spirit's power to tell others the good news. It's the best you can possibly do for them.*Acts 1:8* Your power beats all the enemy's power.*Lk 10:19* Rely on that great power.*Eph 6:10* The Father's power keeps you alive and uncorrupted.*2Co 13:4* Your weakness just perfects the Father's power.*2Co 12:8* Admit your weakness so that you have the Son's power.*2Co 12:9* The Spirit does not leave you timid but gives you power.*2Ti 1:7* Overflow with hope by the Spirit's power.*Ro 15:13* Use the Father's power to act appropriately.*2Co 6:6-7* Credit the Spirit's power when you do good.*Ro 15:18-19* The Son's power works in you to

share the good news.*Col 1:28* Ask the Father for his power so that you endure with great patience.*Col 1:10-11*

Feeding

The Son did one more class of wonders beyond sharing the good news, teaching the people, and healing all the sick who came to him. The Son also *fed* the people. The crowd members who followed and listened to the Son would after a time have been without food, hungry. The Son's students once told the Son that he needed to send the hungry crowds away from the remote place where he had been teaching and healing them, so that they could return to villages to buy food.*Matt 14:15, Mk 6:35-36, Lk 9:12* The Son, though, replied that the crowds didn't need to leave the remote place to eat.*Matt 14:16* He instead told his students to give them something to eat, testing his students about their confidence in the Son.*Mk 6:37, Lk 9:13* Already knowing the wonder that he was to do, the Son turned to one student Philip to ask Philip where the students would buy bread for the people to eat. The Son wanted to see if Philip had yet understood what the Son could do.*Jn 6:5-6*

> ***Prove your confidence.*** Claiming confidence in the Son when you do nothing about it won't rescue you.*Jas 2:14* Your good actions should prove your confidence.*Jas 2:18* Confidence dies without supporting actions.*Jas 2:26* Wishing someone well without helping them shows your confidence lacking.*Jas 2:17* Confidence without action is useless. The Father wants to see you rely on your confidence. Then he'll reward you.*Jas 2:20-22* Good actions prove who really gets it among you.*Jas 3:13* Be fully confident, and act like it.*Ro 12:11* Help the poor.*Gal 2:10* Help orphans and widows. That proves your confidence.*Jas 1:27* Help widows who need it.*1Ti 5:3* Care for your family, especially widows.*1Ti 5:4* You show you have zero confidence in the Son when you don't provide for your own household. Get with it.*1Ti 5:8* Help those in need. Produce!*Tit 3:14* Do something useful so that you can help others.*Eph 4:28* Encourage good deeds.*Heb 10:24* Let your confidence overflow into helping others.*Acts 6:1-6* Don't let others go hungry. Lend a hand.*Acts 11:27-30* Just help where you see need. Don't wiggle out of it.*Lk 10:30-37* Risk your life if necessary.*Php 2:30* Supply what others fail to supply.*1Co 16:17-18* Serve everyone to win as many to the Son as possible.*1Co 9:19-21* Do as your employer says as if for the Father. Maybe your work will impress, pointing to the Father.*Col 3:22* Don't threaten subordinates. The Father governs

> both supervisor and worker, favoring neither over the other.*Eph 6:9* Be fair to your workers. The Father protects them.*Col 4:1*

The students failed the Son's test, as they often did as they were learning about the Son's powers. The students replied that buying bread would take more than a half year's wages. They had overlooked the Son's power.*Mk 6:37, Jn 6:7* They did point out, though, that they had found five loaves of bread and two fish, as if that might feed the crowd of thousands.*Lk 9:13* The student Andrew was the one who brought forward a boy with five small barley loaves and two small fish. As he did so, he wondered aloud how far that little bit of food would go.*Jn 6:8-9* The Son took the five loaves of bread and two fish, thanked his Father for providing them, and then broke the loaves. Out of the Son's power from the Father, the bread and fish kept coming until the students had fed five thousand men plus more women and children. The students picked up twelve basketfuls of bread and fish left over, just to show how bountiful is the Father.*Matt 14:17-21, Mk 6:38-44, Lk 9:16-17, Jn 6:10-13* The broken loaves foreshadowed how the Son would feed in spirit all who came to him, out of his own broken body—his sacrifice. Everything that the Son did, he did with greater meaning.

> **Stop worrying.** Stop worrying. Worries make you forget the good news.*Matt 13:22* Don't worry about your lifestyle, like what you eat, drink, or wear. Life is more than food and clothing.*Matt 6:25, Lk 12:22-23* If the birds eat without worrying over it, then won't you, too? You mean a lot more to the Father than a bird does.*Matt 6:26, Lk 12:24* The Father is going to take a lot better care of you than he does his beautiful flowers.*Matt 6:28-30, Lk 12:27-28* Worrying doesn't add a single hour to your life.*Matt 6:27, Lk 12:25-26* Those who reject the good news run after special food, drink, and clothing. The Father supplies you.*Matt 6:31-32, Lk 12:29-30* Do as the Father wishes, and he'll give you what you need.*Matt 6:33, Lk 12:31* Don't worry. The Father's giving you everything.*Lk 12:32* Don't worry about tomorrow. Tomorrow worries about itself.*Matt 6:34* Take each day, one at a time.*Matt 6:34* Anxiety weighs you down. Forget it. Remember that you're going to live forever.*Lk 21:34*

That first feeding wasn't the only time that the Son did such a wonder. The Son later went up on a mountainside in another region, where great crowds of outsiders nonetheless came to him for healing. The crowds lingered for three days without food, glad to be near the Son but growing weak and hungry.*Matt 15:29-32* The Son didn't want to send them home only to collapse on the way, and so he asked his students for the seven loaves of bread and few small fish that they had.$_{Matt\ 15:33-34,\ Mk\ 7:1-5}$ Once again, the Son thanked his Father, broke the loaves, and gave the food to the students, who fed the people until they were all full. This time, the students picked up seven basketfuls of food left over.$_{Matt\ 15:36-37,\ Mk\ 7:6-8}$ Four thousand men had eaten, not counting the women and children who ate.$_{Matt\ 15:38,\ Mk\ 7:9}$ The lesson of the Son's great power was a hard one for his students to learn. Later, when they were puzzling over something that the Son said, once again thinking small when they should have seen the big picture, the Son reminded his students that he had supplied five thousand men out of five loaves and four thousand men out of seven loaves, with basketfuls left over.$_{Matt\ 16:9-10}$ The Son had a mission to share the good news. He also had the means to back it up with teaching, healing, raising the dead, and feeding crowds, so that everyone had good reason to accept it. You don't see these miracles today, but you know about them. Do you need any more convincing?

Help, don't hinder, others. Don't cause anyone to stumble, whether insiders or outsiders.$_{1Co\ 10:32}$ Put nothing in anyone's way.$_{Ro\ 14:13}$ If someone doesn't want to do something, then don't make them do it, especially if it's just a tradition.$_{Ro\ 14:14}$ Don't distress others over what you feel free to do. It just makes trouble for them. The Son died for them, too.$_{Ro\ 14:15}$ You may eat with those who don't yet follow the Son. Maybe they'll come around.$_{1Co\ 10:27}$ Just don't go in for their voodoo. They'll think you're endorsing it.$_{1Co\ 10:28-30}$ Restrain yourself if doing so will help someone stick with the Son. Don't let your freedom drive anyone away.$_{Ro\ 14:20}$ Just hold off when you see that you might upset someone who relies on the Son.$_{Ro\ 14:21}$ You can do as you wish, but keep it between you and the Father rather than upsetting someone who thinks you shouldn't.$_{Ro\ 14:22}$ In other words, don't divide the Son's followers.$_{Acts\ 21:20-26}$

Prayer

The Son was also constantly communicating with his Father while teaching others how to do so. The Son would get up very early in the morning just to talk with his Father.$_{Mk\ 1:35-37}$ The Son would withdraw from all company to talk with his Father.$_{Lk\ 5:16}$ When his students couldn't get something done, the Son would admonish them that they must ask the Father, speak with the Father.$_{Mk\ 9:28-29}$ The Son did everything through the Father. When he brought his friend Lazarus back from dead to alive, the Son first thanked the Father for always hearing him. The Son did so that those present would know that he was doing the Father's work.*Jn 11:41-42* The Son told his students that he had spoken with the Father to save them from the enemy.*Lk 22:31-32* The Son drove dishonest merchants out of the area surrounding the capitol holy city's religious center, saying not to turn his Father's house into a market, when it should be a place to meet the Father.*Jn 2:13-17* A second time, the Son drove out all who bought and sold there. He turned over the money changers' tables, saying that they had turned his Father's house, where one spoke to the Father, into a den of robbers.*Matt 21:12-13, Mk 11:15-17, Lk 19:45-46*

> **Ask confidently.** Ask on all occasions for all kinds of things. Ask especially for those who rely on the Son.*Eph 6:18* Ask thankfully.*Php 4:6* Ask to know what the Father wants you to do.*Col 1:9* Just keep asking.*Col 4:2* Ask for others who rely on the Son and share the good news.*1Th 1:2-3* Ask earnestly night and day that you may supply the confidence others lack.*1Th 3:10* Ask continually.*1Th 5:17* Ask for one another.*1Th 5:25* Constantly ask that the Father enable you to do as he directs.*2Th 1:11* Ask day and night for help.*1Ti 5:5* Night and day, constantly ask for others.*2Ti 1:3* Constantly ask for others and that you rejoin one another.*Ro 1:9-10* Just keep asking.*Ro 12:12* Ask trusting that you will receive.*Matt 21:22* Asking when in right relationship with the Father gets answers.*Jas 5:16-18* Ask anything that the Father wants done.*1Jn 5:14-15* Ask together with others who rely on the Son.*Matt 18:19-20* Don't ask just for others to see you asking.*Matt 6:5* Instead, ask secretly.*Matt 6:6* Keep it brief. More words doesn't help.*Matt 6:7* Your Father knows what you need before you ask him.*Matt 6:8* Ask for all people, including those in authority.*1Ti 2:1-2* Ask for healing.*Jas 5:13-15* Ask for others' healing.*Jas 5:16* Ask for good health for others, especially mental health.*3Jn 2* Ask to gather with others who rely on the Son.*1Th 3:11* Ask to love one another.*1Th 3:12* Wrestle with asking.*Col 4:12* Honor the Father as you ask. Invite his rule. Ask only for today's need.*Lk 11:1-4* Also ask audaciously.*Lk 11:5-8* Ask, and you will receive.*Lk 11:9-10* Ask relentlessly.*Lk 18:1-6* Ask for justice.*Lk 18:7-8* Ask to honor the Son.*2Th 1:12* Ask in reverent submission.*Heb 5:7* Ask to know how great is the Son's love.*Eph 3:17-19* Ask that the good news spread rapidly.*2Th 3:1* Ask that others rely on the Son.*Ro 10:1* Ask the Father to opens doors for the good news.*Col 4:3-4*

The Son also spoke with the Father about himself. He asked the Father that the Son would be able to honor the Father as the Father honored the Son.*Jn 17:1* The Son spoke openly with the Father about how the Father was allowing him to give the Father's chosen ones life forever.*Jn 17:2* The Son told the Father that living forever involves knowing the Father and knowing the Son whom the Father sent.*Jn 17:3* The Son told the Father that his finishing his assigned work had brought the Father honor so that the Father could then honor the Son as the Father had done before they created the world.$_{Jn\ 17:4-5}$ The Son reminded his Father that he had shown the Father to those whom the Father had given him, who obeyed the Father.$_{Jn\ 17:6-8}$

> ***Embrace others who rely on the Son.*** Whoever welcomes a child in the Son's way welcomes the Son.$_{Matt\ 18:5,\ Mk\ 9:36-37,\ Lk\ 9:48}$ Welcome co-workers for the good news.$_{Col\ 4:10-11}$ Welcome one another without complaint.$_{1Pe\ 4:9}$ Speak freely to one another.$_{2Co\ 6:11}$ Don't withhold kindnesses from one another.$_{2Co\ 6:12}$ Open wide your hearts.$_{2Co\ 6:13}$ Make room for one another in your hearts.$_{2Co\ 7:2}$ Be ready to live and die with them.$_{2Co\ 7:3}$ Take great pride in one another.$_{2Co\ 7:4}$ Tell one another about your longing, sorrow, concern, and joy for one another.$_{2Co\ 7:7}$ Show your love for one another. Take pride in one another.$_{2Co\ 8:24}$ When visiting another, be as they wish you to be, and find them as you want them to be.$_{2Co\ 12:20}$ Refresh one another.$_{Phm\ 20}$ Do more than another asks.$_{Phm\ 21}$ Desire their benefit, like a parent saving up for a child.$_{2Co\ 12:14}$ Don't burden one another.$_{2Co\ 12:16}$ Don't exploit one another.$_{2Co\ 12:17-18}$ Act only with consent. Ensure that every favor is voluntary.$_{Phm\ 14}$ Don't grieve one another.$_{2Co\ 2:2}$ Share one another's joy.$_{2Co\ 2:3}$ Show deep love and great compassion for one another.$_{2Co\ 2:4-5}$ Punish the one causing grief, but then comfort and reaffirm that one.$_{2Co\ 2:6-8}$ Submit to one another, revering the Son.$_{Eph\ 5:21}$ Remember one another.$_{Php\ 1:3}$ Be glad that the Son loves and rescues others.$_{Php\ 1:7-8}$ When away from others, think well of them at how much they rely on the Son.$_{Col\ 2:5}$ Make these others your joy and crown.$_{1Th\ 2:19-20}$ Walk in their footsteps.$_{2Co\ 12:18}$ Don't defend yourself to them. Strengthen them.$_{2Co\ 12:19}$ Share news of one another.$_{Col\ 4:7-9}$ Let others know that you still rely on the Son.$_{1Th\ 3:5}$ Share good news about others who rely on the Son. Remember good times together.$_{1Th\ 3:6}$ Make every effort to see one another again.$_{1Th\ 2:17}$ Long to see others.$_{2Ti\ 1:4}$ Ask the Father to connect you again.$_{Ro\ 1:9-10}$ Encourage one another daily. Avoid cynicism.$_{Heb\ 3:13}$ Encourage one another with what the Father has in store for you.$_{1Th\ 4:18}$ Encourage those who love one another.$_{Tit\ 3:15}$ Keep building each other up.$_{1Th\ 5:11}$ Encourage the disheartened.$_{1Th\ 5:14}$ Your love for one another gives great encouragement.$_{Phm\ 7}$ Encourage with confidence.$_{Tit\ 2:15}$ Make your goal encouraging others.$_{Col\ 2:2}$ Encourage patiently and carefully.$_{2Ti\ 4:2}$ Make one another strong.$_{Ro\ 1:11-12}$ Take encouragement from others.$_{2Co\ 7:4}$ Encourage one another.$_{2Co\ 13:11}$ You get a reward for every little encouragement.$_{Matt\ 10:42}$

The Son asked his Father to care for his students rather than the world.$_{Jn\ 17:9-10}$ The Son asked his Father that while he was returning to the Father, the Father would protect the Son's students who remained.

The Son wanted his students to be on the same page as the Father and Son are together.*Jn 17:11* The Son reminded the Father that while he was with his students, he had protected the students, relying on the Father's authority.*Jn 17:12* The Son spoke to his Father not only for the students but for you who rely on the Son. The Son asked his Father that you would all be together, on the same page, just as the Father and Son are in complete unity with one another.*Jn 17:20-23* The Son asked his Father that those whom the Father had given him remain with him to see the honor that the Father gave the Son because the Father loved the Son before creating the world.*Jn 17:24* The Son asked the Father that all would know that the Father had sent the Son. The Son also asked the Father to make the Father apparent to all, so that all would love as Father loves Son.*Jn 17:25-26* The Son spoke continually with his Father.

Give yourself to the Father. The Father wants you. That means you've got to act the part. Restrain yourself, will you, please? Treat others right.*1Th 4:3-6* The Father wants you to be good, not corrupt.*1Th 4:7* Stop lying to each other. That was the old you. You're new.*Col 3:9* Don't lay around doing nothing. Don't over-indulge like those who care nothing for the Father. Wake up, and stay sober, will you?*1Th 5:6-7* Keep the good, get rid of the bad. It's that simple.*1Th 3:19-22* Ask the Father to keep others off your back.*2Th 3:2* Stop the rumors. Stop talking. Clean it up.*1Ti 5:13* Don't mimic fools and the corrupt.*1Ti 5:22* Behave, like someone's watching. The Father is. Be satisfied with what you have, and leave others alone.*Ro 13:13* Partying is alright for the right reasons—for the Son, not for over-indulgence.*1Co 5:8* The Son can clean you up. He's more than up to it.*Php 3:20-21*

6 Character

Sacred

In coming to carry out his mission, the Son revealed his character. Knowing what the Son did in his carrying out his mission, as the prior part describes, is great. You *should* know, for all that you can draw from knowing. Yet knowing not just what the Son *did* but also who the Son *is* can make much more of a difference. And the first thing to know, the overriding thing to keep in mind about the Son's character is that the Son is *sacred*. He is hallowed, different, set apart. He is numinous, supernatural, outside of and above all things. He alone inspires awe, wonder, amazement, astonishment, and reverence. The Son was with the Father before time and place even began. The Son was *with* the Father and *was* the Father in a way that should make you shudder for his otherworldliness._{Jn 1:1-2} The Son himself said that even before the earthly patriarch Abraham was born, the Son already existed. The Son was already the *I am* of individual incorporeal existence without whom none would ever be._{Jn 8:58} The Son who came as the Rescuer is over everything. Indeed, make no secret of it: all will forever honor the Son for being over everything._{Ro 9:5} The Son has every power and every authority. What the Son says, *goes*._{Col 2:10}

Keep it clean. Keep it clean, although you don't have to parade it around. Only the Father needs to see it._{Matt 6:1} Stay pure and patient. Be kind. Love sincerely. Speak truly. Fight with goodness._{2Co 6:6-7} Do the right thing whether people believe you are doing so or not. Don't care what others think. Just keep doing the right thing. Fine to be poor yet make many rich. Fine to have nothing yet possess everything._{2Co 6:8-10} Don't contaminate body or spirit. Practice purity._{2Co 7:1} The Father's word helps you do right._{2Ti 3:16-17} The Spirit helps you clean it up._{Ro 15:16} Ask the Father to help you avoid wrongs. Do right

> even when people think you're doing wrong.₂Co 13:7 Make every effort to do right. You won't see the Father unless you try.Heb 12:14

In coming to carry out his mission, the Son also revealed more of the character of his Father. Whatever you see in the Son, you see *of* the Father. The Son said simply that he and his Father are one. They are the same, one substance, one power, one nature.Jn 10:30 The Son added that whoever looks at him looks at the Father who sent him.Jn 12:45 The Son told his students that if they know him, then they know the Father, and that they did know and see the Father because anyone who has seen the Son has seen the Father.Jn 14:7-9 The Son also said that he is in the Father, and the Father is in him, again, one substance, one nature, one essence.Jn 14:10 Everything belonging to the Father also belongs to the Son.Jn 16:15 While you cannot see the Father, who is invisible, you can see the Son as the invisible Father's perfect image. The Father put the Son over everything just as the Father is over everything.Col 1:15 The Son simply radiates the Father's honor because the Son exactly represents who the Father is. The Son also sustains everything. The whole world was falling apart, meaningless and bound for destruction, until the Son intervened, rescuing everything for the Father.Heb 1:3 The Son is his sacred Father's fullness, everything that the Father is except that the Son lives in bodily form.Col 2:9 The Father loves having all his fullness dwell in the Son.Col 1:19

> **Be like the Son.** The Father invites you to belong to the Son.Ro 1:6 The Father made your destiny to be like the Son. He wanted his Son to have many brothers and sisters.Ro 8:29 When the Father made the Son your destiny, he also invited you, accepted you, and honored you.Ro 8:30 The Father chose you in the Son and then made everything go according to plan.Eph 1:11-12 The Father had this plan for you from the moment your parents conceived you. He wanted others to see his Son in you so that you would share him with those who don't know him.Gal 1:15-16 The Father chose you to listen to the Son with the Spirit's help.1Pe 1:2 Do your best to follow the Father's plan for you. Don't stumble. Earn your rich welcome into the Son's place where you'll live forever.2Pe 1:10-11 Because you belong to the Son, act like it.Eph 4:1 The Father doesn't have anger for you. He has his Son's *rescue* for you.1Th 3:9

Nothing is changing about the Son, either. The Son was the same in the past as he is today. And he will be the same on into the future, indeed forever.Heb 13:8 The Father made it this way from the start, giving the Son every honor, status, power, position, and authority. The Son didn't slowly earn these qualities but had them all from day one.*Jude 24-25* The source wasn't always clear, but those who came before you ate the same spiritual food and drank the same spiritual drink as you do. They drew from the spiritual rock, the Son who was right there with them even if they didn't fully recognize him.*1Co 10:3-4* See, you know about your Rescuer's coming not as a cleverly devised story but from people who saw, heard, and touched him in all his astonishing power.*2Pe 1:16* The Father once spoke to those who came before you, only through seers and sages. But today, the Father speaks to you through his Son, who is his Father's heir through whom the Father made everything.*Heb 1:2* And everything is garbage next to the unsurpassable value of knowing the Son. You should be ready to give up everything for him because he gives you everything.*Php 3:8* The Son came as the true One. The Son came that you might live forever by knowing him and being in him. He is everything that anyone or anything could ever be.*1Jn 5:20* Know the Son's sacred character. He does not disappoint.

> **Don't live for rules.** Rules don't make you the Father's friend.*Ro 2:20* The Father offered you marriage and good food, and yet you make rules not to marry or eat. Shame on you.*1Ti 4:3* The Father picked you before you kept or broke any rules. He did so to show you that your rescue was up to him, not you.*Ro 9:10-12* Your rescue depends on the Father's looking the other way from what you do, not on what you do.*Ro 9:16* Rule-keeping just doesn't explain it. Your relying on the Son explains it.*Gal 2:16* Yet the Son doesn't say to you to throw out the rules. He doesn't want you corrupted.*Gal 2:17* Rule-keeping isn't coming back. It didn't work the first time. The Son's rescue put that to rest.*Gal 2:18* You welcomed the Father's Spirit when you relied on the good news. You didn't earn the Spirit with rule-keeping. Stick with the good news, and the Spirit will stick with you. Don't go back to the old rules.*Gal 3:2-4* To join the Father by rule-keeping, you'd have to be a world-class rule-keeper, and you're just *not*.*Matt 5:20* People thought that the Son broke the letter of some rules, but he never broke the rules' spirit.*Jn 5:9-15*

Human

While the Son is sacred, otherworldly, supernatural, and over everything, the Son is also human, tangible, corporeal. The best way you could know the Father would be to see, hear, touch, and live with his Son. So, the Son, who from the beginning was the Father's Word, took on human flesh—bodily substance and form. The Son did so not to hide from anyone but to live publicly and famously among you *as one of you*, so that you could see how the Father honors the Son. You could see how true, pure, and profound the Son is, even while fully human.*Jn 1:14* You cannot see the Father, but the Son can see the Father, because the Son has the Father's substance and is in closest relationship with the Father. You know the Father through the Son.*Jn 1:18* No one sees the Father except the Son who is from the Father.*Jn 6:46* That's part of why the Son came just as the ancient seer Isaiah predicted, that you would know the Father.*Mk 1:1* That's right: as to his earthly life, the Son officially descended from David, as the seers said that he would.*Ro 1:3* Yet no one knows who the Son truly is—knows all about the Son—other than the Father. And no one knows the Father other than the Son and those to whom the Son reveals the Father, fortunately including you.*Matt 11:27, Lk 10:22* The Father came right out at the Son's immersion to say that the Son is the Father's, the one whom he loves and who pleases him.*2Pe 1:17-18*

> **Meet any place.** The Father's first promise provided for a special meeting place where you could encounter him.*Heb 9:1-2* The special meeting place, curtained off from everything, had symbols representing his first promise.*Heb 9:3-4* The Father designed the special meeting place to show who he was.*Heb 9:5* Many could approach the special meeting place, working outside around it.*Heb 9:6* But only certain persons could enter the special meeting place, and then only once a year, with animal blood.*Heb 9:7* The Father had not yet given his Son as the way to approach him without a special meeting place. He was only foreshadowing what was to come.*Heb 9:8* The gifts and blood that entering the special meeting place took were just temporary rules until the Son's new order.*Heb 9:10* You now need no special meeting place to encounter Father and Son.*Heb 13:10*

The Son shows you how, as the Father's child, you should relate to the Father. The Father plainly loves the Son because he put everything in the Son's hands. Like the Son, be ready to receive the Father's love.*Jn 3:35* The Son gave the reason the Father loves him, which is because the Son gave his life on his own when the Father asked it of him, without the Father having to take the Son's life from him. The Son gave his life only to get it back again.*Jn 10:17-18* The Son himself said that he came from the Father and was going back to the Father.*Jn 16:28* The world doesn't know the Father, who is too good for the world, but the Son knows the Father.*Jn 17:25* The Son gave back to the Father everything that the Father gave to the Son. Everything that each one has is the other's to have, too.*Jn 17:10* Likewise, the Father committed everything to the Son.*Lk 10:22* The Son said that he knows and obeys his Father.*Jn 8:55* The Son repeated to those in the capitol holy city's religious center who tried to stone him that he was the Father's Son, the Father was in him, and he was in the Father.*Jn 10:36-38* So, too, should you share everything that the Father gives you back with the Father, knowing that the Father's Spirit is in you and you in the Spirit. The Father appointed the Son through the same sacred Spirit.*Ro 1:4*

> **You are the Father's child.** All who rely on the Son become the Father's spiritual children.*Jn 1:12-13* Follow the Father's Spirit, and you are the Father's child.*Ro 8:14* The Spirit removes your fear of the Father's anger and brings you close to him.*Ro 8:15* Don't you groan as you wait eagerly for the Father to treat you as his child? So does everything else, everything that he made.*Ro 8:22-23* The Father can't do any better for you than to make you his child.*1Jn 3:1-2* The Father surprises many at whom he chooses as his children.*Ro 9:24-26* Your ancestry doesn't matter. Becoming the Father's child has to do with his promise, not biology.*Ro 9:7-9* You receive everything that a child inherits—everything.*Gal 4:30-31* That's because you are the Father's child.*Gal 4:7* As the Father's child, you receive the Father's Spirit. What better gift could he give you?*Gal 4:6* Trust that you are the Father's child.*1Jn 5:19* Recognize the Father's other children. Help one another.*Phm 9-11* The Father gives everything to his children.*Rev 21:6-7*

The Father chose the Son, just as the Father chose you. The Father named the Son and said he was his Father.*Heb 1:5* The Father gave a pledge, assured you, that he had appointed the Son, whom the Father had made perfect forever.*Heb 7:28* Remember, the Son was the Father's *first born* in the world. When the Father brought his first born into the world, the Father announced that even celestial beings would worship the Son— that's how special the Son is.*Heb 1:6* As the Father's own Son, the Son is way above those beings.*Heb 1:4-5* The Father told the Son, not those beings, to sit beside the Father until the Father put everyone, especially the Son's enemies, under the Son's feet.*Heb 1:13* The Father says that the Son's rule will go on forever. The Son will always be in charge, and not arbitrarily but justly. You'll like the Son's fair-and-equitable rule.*Heb 1:8* The Father made the Son human to begin something new, to start over without death. The Son is above everything including death.*Col 1:18* And yet although the Son has a Father, the Son is without earthly genealogy. The Son has no such beginning or end.*Heb 7:1-17* You must know that the

Son is his Father's human image. Even demons speaking through two violent men called him the Father's Son.*Matt 8:28-29*

> **The Father gives you extraordinary gifts.** The Father loves you. He keeps you for his Son, looking away from your faults while showering you with peace and love.*Jude 1-2* The Father hides treasures in the Son for you, of how to do things right.*Col 2:3* Keep your head on, and make the Son your head, because the head directs the body.*Col 2:19* Your life is in the Son.*2Ti 1:1* Remember the Son, come back to life.*2Ti 2:8* Make the Son your focus.*2Ti 4:1* When you do, everything old and worn out will disappear, so that everything is new.*2Co 5:17* The Father brought you back to him through the Son whom you can now share with others.*2Co 5:18* The Father brought everything back to him in the Son. The Father looked the other way from your faults, having given you good news of new beginnings.*2Co 5:19* The Son protects you from evil when you decide to turn from it.*1Jn 5:18* The Father and Son give you the clearest, truest, and best without finding fault.*2Jn 3* The Son lets you join the Father freely and confidently.*Eph 3:12* Speak the Son's message of getting right again with the Father.*2Co 5:20* The Father made the perfect Son as if the Son was to blame for your faults, so that in the Son you would show the Father's perfection.*2Co 5:21* Let the Son be your credit with the Father, always talking up the Son.*Heb 13:15*

Liberator

Yet the Son didn't come solely to reveal the Father's human image, to show the Father's character. The Son came to rescue you. The Father so loved you that he gave his only Son for you to trust. If you rely on the Son, then you will not die but instead live forever, freed from your greatest enemy *death*.*Jn 3:16* The Son is the way that the Father freed everything and everyone to return to him.*Col 1:20* The Son told the woman at the well in another region that he was the liberator, the one whom the ancient seers had predicted would free everything.*Jn 4:25-26* The Son is the liberator, the emancipator bringing freedom's good news, just as the ancient seer Isaiah predicted.*Mk 1:1* The Son was the liberator whom the Magi from the East followed the star to bow down and honor with treasures.*Matt 2:1-11* Everyone of that day knew that the liberator would first appear in Bethlehem, exactly as the Son did.*Matt 2:4-10* They also knew that the liberator would trace his earthly genealogy through David to Abraham, just as the Son did.*Matt 1:1-17*

Spiritspeak

> **Remain free.** When others see how free the Son has made you, they'll try to enslave you again with the old ways.*Gal 2:4* Don't give in to them for a moment. Just stick with the good news.*Gal 2:5* Their rules not to handle, taste, or touch certain things don't help.*Col 2:21-23* The rules were meant for your good, not to be great burdens imposing constant hardship.*Mk 2:23-28, Lk 6:1-5* So don't let anyone judge you by what you eat or drink, or by special days, which were only shadows of things to come. The Son is the real thing. No more shadows.*Col 2:16* Whether you consider one day special more than another doesn't matter. Just believe what you're going to believe, for the Father.*Ro 14:5-6* Whether you eat meat or abstain doesn't matter if you thank the Father.*Ro 14:6* Eat anything without raising questions of conscience because the earth and everything in it belong to the Father.*1Co 10:25-26* The Father's place is not about eating and drinking.*Ro 14:17*

The ancient seers had long looked for the one who would save the people from their death and bring them back to the Father. Through the Father's Spirit, they had predicted when and how their liberator Son would come and suffer, and then receive the Father's honor.*1Pe 1:10-11* When the Son did come, some people thought the Son was John who had immersed so many, while others thought that the Son might have been the return of one of the ancient seers like Elijah. But the Son's leading student Peter knew exactly who the Son was: their liberator, the one come to rescue them.*Mk 7:27-30, Lk 9:18-20* The religious leaders claimed that the liberator would be King David's son, but the Son pointed out to them that David himself had called the liberator Master.*Matt 22:41-46, Mk 12:35-37, Lk 20:41-44* Even the highest religious official of the day knew of the Son's claim to be the rescuer. When they put the Son on trial, the official charged the Son to say whether he was the liberator, the Father's own Son. The Son replied that the official had rightly said so. The Son added that they would indeed see the Son sitting beside the Father and coming back from above.*Matt 26:63-64* After they killed the Son and the Son rose and returned to the Father, the Son's leading student Peter confirmed that the Son was the only one who would be able to save anyone from death.*Acts 4:12* The Son came to free you. The Son has the character of a liberator, and that character should mean everything to you.

> **It's not about the rules.** Your rescue started with the rules, but rules weren't enough.*1Co 10:1-2* Things were going badly, and so the Father laid down the law. The law, though, only made clear your law-breaking.*Ro 5:13-14* The Father gave the law to show the law-breaking so that you'd know that you

needed him even more.*Ro 5:20* The law defines law-breaking, like when the law says not to covet and yet you covet.*Ro 7:7* The law makes you conscious of your wrong.*Ro 2:20* Rules make you want to break them.*Ro 7:8* Before the rules, no one was a rule-breaker. The rules showed you your wrongs, but you kept on doing them.*Ro 7:8-9* The rules should have helped, but they didn't. They made you worse, convicting you as the rule-breaker you are.*Ro 7:10-11* The rules weren't bad. Your corruption just made the rules look bad. Corruption is the problem, not rules.*Ro 7:13* Things are only getting worse. Didn't you notice? People are far worse today than they once were. They hate the Son more than ever. They don't want *any* rules. They want to make their *own* rules.*2Th 2:3-4* Everyone wants to be their own little god today, making their own rules. That's not going to work. The Son won't let it.*2Th 2:7-8*

Master

The Son didn't come as a sentimental advisor, someone whom you could just as easily ignore. No, the Son came as your boss, your ruler, as the Master. The Son said that his students rightly called him Master because that is who he is. He wasn't faking it, and you can't ignore it.*Jn 13:13* The Son came from ruling, and not mean-spirited ruling but an authority of peace and doing things the right way.*Heb 7:1-17* The Father put the Son as high up as one could. The Father gave the Son a title higher than any other title so that absolutely everyone, no matter who or where, must honor and treat him as their ruler, their Master.*Php 2:9-11* To signify his rule, the Son made a triumphal entry into the capitol holy city, to the shouts of a very large crowd that he was the predicted ruler, the absolute Master. His entry stirred the whole city, although he entered exactly the way that the ancient writings had predicted.*Matt 21:1-11, Mk 11:1-11, Lk 19:28-38, Jn 12:12-16* The religious officials wanted the Son to make everyone quiet down rather than celebrate the Master's coming. But the Son replied that if the crowd kept quiet, then the stones of the streets would cry out in their place. His coming was that assured.*Lk 19:39-40* You are to revere the Son as your Master.*1Pe 3:15*

> **Recognize the Father's children.** The difference between the Father's children and the enemy's children is obvious: the Father's children love one another and stop wrongdoing, while the enemy's children do not.*1Jn 3:9* Just because you have special ancestors doesn't make you the Father's child.*Ro 9:6* Do nothing wrong. Act like the Father's child who you are. Let others do all the

wrong.*Php 2:15* Follow the Father's example as dearly loved children. Love one another. Act like the Son who gave himself up for you.*Eph 5:1* Act like daytime children, doing right, not nighttime children, doing wrong.*1Th 5:5* As obedient children of God, reject the evil desires you had when you didn't know the Father. Instead, be good in all you do, like God is good.*1Pe 1:14-16* Do as the Spirit guides you rather than as the world urges you.*1Co 3:1* You will be like the Son when he returns, even though you can't imagine it.*1Jn 3:2*

The governor at the time called the Son a *king*. In reply, the Son just confirmed that the governor had said so.*Jn 18:37* The Son said that he is greater than the old religious center, Master also over the day that his Father declared for rest.*Matt 12:1-8, Lk 6:1-5* The Son is such a well-known Master that you make no point in teaching one another to treat him as Master because you all, from least to greatest, know that you should do so.*Heb 8:11* The Son trips up those who still try to make rule-keeping and good works your masters. The Son is your only way to get out of this thing alive. Rule-keeping and good works alone won't do it.*Ro 9:32-33* The Son has the say over each one of you, and so you'd better be doing things the Son's way, not your own way.*2Co 5:10* The Father didn't put celestial beings in charge. He put the Son in charge of everything, including you. The Son rules, even though you do not yet see all that he will rule.*Heb 2:5-8* The Son is being patient with you already because he doesn't want any of you to die. Don't make him wait too long for you.*2Pe 3:9* The Son is coming back to decide soon.*Php 4:5* But the good news is that the Son's greatest enemy, the last one whom he will defeat, is death.*1Co 15:26* Yes, the Father puts everything but the Father under the Son, including death.*1Co 15:27* When the Son is done, the Son will put himself under the Father who put everything under him. That way, the Father will be everything in all.*1Co 15:28* Everything will come together under the Son in the end.*Eph 1:8-10* Make the Son your Master because he is.

Trust the Son. You don't get anywhere on your own, even if you do everything that you should. Rely on the Son.*Php 3:9* Don't brag about doing good, following the rules. Brag that you rely on the Son.*Ro 2:27* Relying on the Son is all you need.*Ro 2:28* Relying on the Son takes care of all the rules.*Ro 2:31* Yes, you work for wages. But no one keeps all the rules. Yet the Father still gives you wages—those that the Son earned for you.*Ro 4:4-5* The Father looks the other way from everything you've done wrong and instead gives you credit for everything his Son did right.*Ro 4:6-7* The rules and seers point you the Father's perfect way.*Ro 2:21* Follow the Spirit, and you won't have to worry

> about the rules.*Gal 5:18* Those who have no sense beyond what they see here have no future, having rejected the Son.*Jn 8:21-24*

Celebrant

The Son has another character, role, or attribute, as a celebrant, or if you prefer a *minister*, of what his Father does. The Son is the great celebrant over his Father's house.*Heb 10:21* Your great celebrant the Son empathizes with your weaknesses. Because he is fully human, he too faced every temptation that you face, except that he never succumbed like you did.*Heb 4:15* Yet the Son did not name himself the great celebrant but instead let the Father give him that role. The Father wanted the Son pointing you to him forever.*Heb 5:5-6* The Father designated the Son to be his first and greatest celebrant, over many others who had gone before the Son.*Heb 5:10* The Father made the Son his indestructible celebrant forever, ahead of that long line that had gone before the Son, saying that celebration was all about keeping the law.*Heb 7:1-17* The Son, the one whom you should emulate, got closer to the Father than anyone else so that the Son could be your leading celebrant forever.*Heb 6:19-20*

> **Strive to do right.** Watch carefully that you keep your full reward and do not lose that for which you worked.*2Jn 8* Compete by the rules so that you win.*2Ti 2:5* Fight the good fight to the end. Finish the race.*2Ti 4:6-7* Let everyone who hears about your obedience be happy because of you.*Ro 16:19* All racers run the race, but only one gets the prize. Be the one.*1Co 9:24* But train for a crown that lasts forever, not a temporary crown.*1Co 9:25* Don't run around aimlessly like others or fight like a boxer beating the air.*1Co 9:26* Instead, focus. Win the authentic prize.*1Co 9:27* Stand the test, obedient in everything.*2Co 2:9* Do right in everything and everywhere.*Col 1:10-11* Strive to do what is good for everyone.*1Th 5:15* Follow a good example, working hard not to burden anyone, so that you, too, are a model for others to imitate.*2Th 3:7-10* Be busy rather than idle. Settle down and earn the food you eat.*2Th 3:11* Never tire of doing good.*2Th 3:13* Show the same diligence to the very end.*Heb 6:11* Don't be lazy.*Heb 6:12* Those who do not work won't eat.*2Th 3:10* When done with one job, do the next job. Admit you're not worth much, and then go do your duty.*Lk 17:7-10*

Just as with the Son's other characteristics, the Son's celebration isn't going to change. The Father promised not to change his mind that the Son is the Father's number one fan, his first admirer, his chief celebrant forever.*Heb 7:20-21* Your other celebrants come and go, ending their role in leading you, but the Son lives forever in permanent celebration.*Heb 7:23-24* The Son's celebration is so effective because while he is your participant leader, your one to emulate, he simultaneously intervenes with the Father for you. The Son is always cheering you on while also telling the Father that you're doing the best you can.*Heb 7:25* The chief celebrant Son thus does it all for you. He is as good as anything gets, indeed far better than anything you have around you.*Heb 7:26* The Son doesn't need to keep apologizing to his Father. The Son did nothing wrong. And the Son paid everything, his own life, for your wrong, and so he settled all accounts already. The payments are over, so that all that is left is the celebration.*Heb 7:27* Your chief celebrant Son is already sitting right beside the Father, both as your human representative and also far beyond so.*Heb 8:2* The Son gave his celebration every last thing that he had, right down to his own life. That's why he leads all celebrants. None did as he did.*Heb 8:3-4* Follow the Son in giving the Father all that you have in celebration.

Enjoy your freedom. Thank the Father that you're now free of your old, corrupting desires. Now, you *like* to do good.*Ro 6:17* The Father freed you.*Ro 6:18* Your wrongdoing once consigned you to die. Now, your relying on the Son lets you live forever.*Ro 5:21* Many others have shown you how it's done. Now, do it. Turn from your old ways.*Heb 12:1* Don't give in to wrongdoing. Fight until it hurts, if necessary.*Heb 12:4* Good can beat bad. Trust it, and act on it.*Ro 12:21* You once indulged, more and more. Now, go the other way, more and more.*Ro 6:19* Those who do much wrong have no idea how to do right.*Ro 6:20* Don't get hooked up with wrongdoers. It's like oil and water. No good can come from that.*2Co 6:14* Stand off in the corner, if you must. Don't just go along with the crowd.*2Co 6:17* Breaking man-made traditions won't kill you. Encouraging others to do bad things? Now, that's *wrong*.*Matt 15:10-11*

Guide

Much as the Son leads you in celebrating the good news, the Father's great plan, the Son is also your guide. He doesn't just announce the good news. He also encourages you in how to accept and embrace it. The Son said that he is your good guide. He is so good that he lays down his life for those who follow him—gives himself up entirely to you. The Son says that he came so that his followers would have life to the full, every bit of it.*Jn 10:10-11* You recognize when the Son is the one doing the talking, and you listen. You are on a first-name basis with the Son. He calls you over to him, and you join him right away. You and he are no strangers to one another. From a stranger, you would run away, but to him, you run.*Jn 10:3-5* The Son is the trusted advisor who knows who listens to him. He knows who knows him. The Son and the Father have the same relationship. The Son gives *everything* for those who listen to him. He's not like some hired gun who runs when the real trouble comes. A hired gun does not care what happens to you.*Jn 10:12-15* The Son told you that he is the door, he is the way in to the safe place, the place safe even from death. The Son rescues whoever enters through his door. His door is open. Walk, no *run* through it.*Jn 10:7-9*

> **Accept discipline.** The Father disciplines those whom he loves as his child. Accept it.*Heb 12:6* Endure hardship as discipline. The Father is treating you as his child, as any good father disciplines a child.*Heb 12:7* If the Father did not discipline you, as he does every child, then you would be illegitimate.*Heb 12:8* Don't just accept your human father's discipline. Submit all the more to your spiritual Father's discipline, to truly live.*Heb 12:9* Your human father disciplined you under his own rules, but the Father disciplines you for good.*Heb 12:10* Discipline isn't pleasant but produces great good—if you accept it.*Heb 12:11* So strengthen your weak character.*Heb 12:12* Don't make trouble for yourself. Doing right makes it better for you.*Heb 12:13* The Father's Spirit gives you self-discipline.*2Ti 1:7* Avoid arrogance, or the teacher will discipline you.*1Co 4:21* Delight at how disciplined others are who rely on the Son.*Col 2:5* To lead others, you must be self-disciplined.*Tit 1:8* If you lack discernment, then the Father will discipline you. He'll set you straight.*1Co 11:32* Listen to the Father's words. Don't make light of discipline, and don't lose heart.*Heb 12:5* Those whom the Son loves, he disciplines.*Rev 3:19*

If I were you, then I wouldn't listen to the swindlers and robbers who came before or after the Son and have their own agenda. Their purpose is to steal, kill, and destroy. Oh, sure, they try to befriend you and join you, but they don't walk through the Son's door. They try climbing in through a window! That will never work.*Jn 10:1, 8-10* And don't worry if the Son has opened the door to others who aren't like you. If they're listening to *him,* then they *are* like you.*Jn 10:16* The Son said that some of you will know when he's the one speaking, those of you who wish to know him. If that's you, then you're going to live *forever.* And you know what? No one can can stop the Son and his Father from giving you *paradise* with them forever. That's what they want, and you're going to get it, too—if you want it.*Jn 10:27-29* The Son is the guide. He's the one to whom you must listen.*Heb 13:20* The Son took one look at all of you stumbling around as if you were blind, falling into pits, and he knew that he had to do something, exactly what his Father wanted.*Matt 9:36, Mk 6:33-34*

> **Temptation? Avoid it.** Don't even look. Looking gets you in trouble.*Matt 5:27-28* Don't tease yourself with it. Just turn away. Otherwise, you'll be in over your head before you know it.*Matt 5:29-30* Hands off. Don't touch, and don't walk down that road. Otherwise, you won't be able to resist. You're already caught.*Matt 18:8-9* You think you can dabble with wrongdoing? Better not to dabble than to find yourself enslaved.*Mk 9:43-44* Better to go without the indulgence now than to lose *paradise* later and suffer perpetual torment.*Mk 9:47-48* Leave your wrongdoing now while you can. The Son will forgive it.*Jn 8:11* Don't be overly hard on regretful wrongdoers. Just watch yourself.*Gal 6:1* The enemy tempts. The Father doesn't tempt. Admit it: you like courting your own death.*Jas 1:13-15* You're not so strong, you know? Better watch out.*1Co 10:12* Don't feel sorry for yourself. Everyone faces similar temptations. You can bear it. The Father always gives you a way out. Just take it.*1Co 10:13* Those who rely on the Son shouldn't mess around.*1Ti 6:11* Sexual immorality connects you with someone you shouldn't connect.*1Co 6:15-16* Sexual immorality is deeper than other wrongs. It's on the inside, not just the outside.*1Co 6:18* Don't do the wrongs that others do.*2Co 12:21* Especially avoid sexual immorality.*Heb 12:17* Your body is for the Father, not sexual immorality. He can't reach you when you are sexually immoral.*1Co 6:13* Chasing after riches will lead you to ruin.*1Ti 6:9* Having money is one thing, but loving it is another. Don't love money. It will draw you away from the Father and Son, making trouble for you.*1Ti 6:10*

The Son doesn't do it, doesn't lead and guide you, just for the big crowds. No, if ninety nine of you are right beside him but one of you wanders off, then he'll leave the ninety nine to rescue the one.*Matt 18:12, Lk 15:3-4* And when he finds you, the wandering one, he's happier for finding you than for the ninety nine who never left his side.*Matt 18:13, Lk 15:5-6* The Son said that his Father treats you the same way that the Son treats you. The Father doesn't want to lose one of you, either. He wants you *all* to live with him forever.*Matt 18:14* Everyone under his rule, every celestial being, celebrates more when one of you turns around to follow the Son than over ninety nine who've been following the Son as long as they can remember.*Lk 15:7* Sure, everyone ran off when the religious officials had the Son killed, just as the ancient writings had said that they would. But that was only for the moment. Oh, you didn't notice? The Son is *back*, and like no one had ever come back before him.*Matt 26:31, Mk 14:27* So you, too, be an eager guide like the Son is your guide. The Father will notice and reward you in a way that you can hardly imagine.*1Pe 5:4* Look, everything will come down to the Son deciding whether you were one of those who listened and followed him or instead went off on your own. That's just the way it is.*Matt 25:32* He's got the door open for you. You just need to open *your* door for him. And he's knock-knock-knocking.*Rev 3:20*

> **Father and Son speak through Spirit.** Your soul, meaning your mind, will, and emotions, need not rule you. You will die if they do. Let your spirit, informed by the Father's Spirit, guide you. The Father pours his love into your heart through his Spirit, whom he gave you.*Ro 5:5* If the Father's Spirit lives in you, then you pursue the Spirit rather corrupting desires. If the Spirit who brought the Son right back from dead to alive guides you, then the Father will bring you back to life, too.*Ro 8:11* If the Father's Spirit leads you, then you are the Father's own child.*Ro 8:14* The Spirit gives you courage to speak with the Father, to ask him things.*Ro 8:15* The Spirit began speaking to you as soon as you began relying on the Son. The Spirit makes sure the Father brings you back from death to life.*Eph 1:13-14* The Father gives you his Spirit to teach you.*1Th 4:8* The Father's Spirit shows you what the Father prepares for those who love him, things that no one else has heard, seen, or imagined.*1Co 2:9-10* The Spirit knows the Father's secrets.*1Co 2:10* No one knows the Father's thoughts except his Spirit, just like your spirit knows your thoughts.*1Co 2:11* You listen to the Father's Spirit, not the world's spirit. That's how you know what the Father gives you.*1Co 2:12* Do not offend the Father's Spirit.*Eph 4:30* The Father chose you to share the Spirit's new promise that you receive life.*2Co 3:6* The Spirit is only the beginning. You'll get full life later.*2Co 5:5* The Spirit gives life, next to that which your body wants is nothing.*Jn 6:63* The Spirit is limitless.*Jn 3:34*

Transfigured

The Son has many other profound attributes, more than anyone can count, more than anyone can know. One attribute, though, captures the rest. The Son showed you that he lights the world. He lights every life in and out of the world that wishes to know and follow him.*Jn 8:12* The Son displayed his light-giving, life-giving attribute to his closest students Peter, James, and John, whom he took high up a mountain. There, the Father revealed the Son for who he is. The Father altered the Son's appearance so that his face shone like the sun. The Son's clothes gleamed as brilliant as his face's sunlight.*Matt 17:1-2, Mk 9:2-3, Lk 9:28-29* At the same time, the Father revealed the ancient deliverer Moses and exalted seer Elijah speaking with the Son, right there for the three students to see.*Matt 17:3, Mk 9:4, Lk 9:30* The ancient deliverer and exalted seer spoke about the Son dying soon in the capitol holy city, that horrible but magnificent sacrifice that was about to free everyone.*Lk 9:31*

> **Keep your confidence in the Son.** Stay on the straight and narrow. The enemy successfully offers many broad roads and open ways to destruction. Few stay on the straight and narrow to life.*Matt 7:13-14* The Father wants to rescue many, but few choose rescue. They want their own way to paradise when they must instead accept the Father's way.*Lk 13:22-27* You can't work your way in. You must rely on the Son's rescue.*Ro 9:30-32* The only way that the Father can accept you is for you to have confidence in the Son. Forget working your way in. You're not good enough. No one but the Son is.*Gal 3:11* Your only hope is the Son, not your own rule-keeping.*Php 3:9* If you keep going your own way, then even your zeal for the Father isn't enough. You need him, not you.*Ro 10:2-3*

The extraordinary event frightened the three students, dumbfounding them. They were so shocked that they didn't know what to say.*Mk 9:5-6, Lk 9:33* The event had a dream's quality, but they were fully awake. What they saw was real, genuine, not a vision.*Lk 9:32* The event ended when a bright cloud covered the Son and his ancient visitors, and the Father's voice from the cloud reminded the three students that the Son was who the Father loved and who pleased the Father.*Matt 17:5, Mk 9:7, Lk 9:34-35* When the three students heard the Father's voice, they fell face down in terror. They cowered until the Son touched them and told them to get up rather than be afraid.*Matt 17:6-7* The Son was suddenly alone again, looking normal, no longer brilliant.*Mk 9:8, Lk 9:36* The Son told the three students not to tell anyone what they had seen until the Father had raised the Son from the dead—another revelation.*Matt 17:9, Mk 9:9* The three students had to talk about what the Son meant by rising from the dead. No one had seen it before, so they couldn't even conceive it.*Mk 9:10* They did just as the Son had told them, keeping the Son's transfiguration to themselves.*Lk 9:36* Don't ever think the Son merely human. He is fully human, but he is also his Father's sacred Son, fully of his Father's domain. Know who the Son is. Your rescue depends on it.

> **You can't pay it back.** As much as you might try, you can't pay back to the Father for all the wrong you've done.*Heb 10:1* People have been trying forever,

and it just doesn't work. You can't clean yourself up.*Heb 10:2* The more you try to pay what you owe, the more you discover you still owe.*Heb 10:3* Paying with anything other than the Son just doesn't work. You owe too much.*Heb 10:4* Try and try again, but you'll still not measure up. You are too far behind in payment to ever catch up.*Heb 10:11* The Son made one payment, though, and it was more than enough.*Heb 9:25* The Son doesn't need to do it again. Giving himself once was more than enough.*Heb 9:26* Because the Son is perfect, he made the perfect payment with his own life. You couldn't pay any more.*Heb 10:12-14* You have nothing to pay or fear, when the Father already paid all.*Heb 10:18*

7 Rejection

Opposed

To complete the Father's rescue plan, the Son had to submit to his own sacrifice at human hands, as incredible and unlikely as that plan seemed. Yet sure enough, opposition to the Son quickly built, despite all the Son's powerful teaching and extraordinary healing. Severe opposition even built in his own hometown. After the Son had told his rescue message throughout the countryside, with everyone at first praising him, the Son went to his hometown to tell the same good news in the local religious center.*Lk 4:16* The Son got everyone's attention to read the ancient seer Isaiah's prediction. This prediction was that the Father's Spirit would be on the Son to proclaim the good news, just as the Son was right then doing in his hometown, the good news that would make everyone free and rich.*Lk 4:16-18* When the Son finished reading and sat down, everyone was staring at him, waiting for him to say it. And say it he did, that he had fulfilled the ancient writing that very day, right in front of their eyes.*Lk 4:21*

> **Pursue the good news.** Ask the Son to increase your confidence in the good news.*Lk 17:5* Look for a better place, the Father's place, instead of thinking of what you are leaving.*Heb 11:14-16* Confidence can give back your dead, living again.*Heb 11:35* Trust enabled others to endure torture, face jeers and lashing, and suffer imprisonment.*Heb 11:35-36* Pursuit of the good news enabled others to face death in the worst manner and others to go about dressed in tatters, destitute and mistreated.*Heb 11:37* Look to the Son, your pioneer.*Heb 12:2* Live by right relationship with the Father.*Heb 10:38* Live by relationship, not what you see and desire.*2Co 5:7* Pursue the good news with confidence.*Heb 4:2* Your confidence comes from hearing the good news.*Ro 10:17* Just hold on. The Father is holding on to you.*Heb 10:23* Yes, the Son rescues you and others. But you each still must

Spiritspeak

pursue his rescue.*Jude 3* Continue in your strong pursuit. It's attractive, rescue is, isn't it?*Col 1:23* Show that you rely on your rescue.*1Th 3:8* Have confidence through trials.*2Th 1:4* Rely on the Father's power, not speculation.*1Co 2:5* The Father is trusting you. Prove him right.*1Co 4:2* Talk about it, now that you have confidence.*2Co 4:13*

At first, all spoke well of the Son. His gracious words had amazed them. But immediately, some were reminding others that he was merely their neighbor Joseph's son.*Lk 4:22* The Son knew they were up to no good. He told them that they wouldn't believe his words unless he did the wonders there that he had done everywhere else. He said that they weren't about to give him his due honor.*Lk 4:23-24* The Son added that the Father had sent the ancient seer Elijah to help others, just as now the Son would leave them to help others. They rejected whomever the Father sent.*Lk 4:25-27* Of course, his words made everyone furious.*Lk 4:28* After all, they knew his mother, brothers, and sisters, who were nothing special. Sure, the Son's words had amazed them, but he didn't have any special training to say such things. So they instead took offense at him.*Matt 13:54-57, Mk 6:1-3* The Son could see right through them. Amazed at their lack of faith in him, in what they saw with their own eyes and heard with their own ears, he told them that no one gets honor in their hometown. He had nothing for them—no wonders, no healing, no feeding, nothing but helping a few sick people.*Mk 6:4-6* Well, that was enough. They were going to have no more of him. The people drove the Son out to a hill at the edge of town, ready to throw him off its cliff. Somehow, though, he walked right through the crowd and on his way.*Lk 4:29-30* The Son told everyone that they had seen him and yet still not accepted what they saw.*Jn 6:36*

Check your ambition. Don't presume that you're the Father's darling, his number one. Just serve others humbly like the Son did.*Matt 20:20-28, Mk 10:41-45* Your ambition should be a quiet life. Mind your own business! Just work with your hands. Do as told. Don't become dependent.*1Th 4:11* Take pride that your humiliation calls attention to your diligence. The hard part passes quickly. Just go about your business.*Jas 1:9-11* Others get the credit when you may be just as deserving. Don't worry about it.*2Co 12:11* Just look for the Father's approval. Don't do a lot of patting yourself on the back.*2Co 10:18* No selfish putting yourself above others. Value others more than yourself.*Php 2:3-4* Dress modestly, without a lot of adornment. Let good deeds show who you are.*1Ti 2:9-10* Learn quietly, without assuming authority over those who teach and without giving in to deception.*1Ti 2:11-13* Do not puff yourself up as a follower of one teacher over another.*1Co 4:6* You are no different from anyone else in accomplishments.*1Co 4:7* Submit to the Son, learning from his gentle and humble manner.*Matt 11:29*

For their part, the Son's students grumbled over his hard teaching. They especially didn't like that the Son said he was the *bread of life* whose *flesh they must eat* and whose *blood they must drink*. The thought, the way they took it literally as they took everything too literally, disgusted them.*Jn 6:60-61* Many students just up and left him.*Jn 6:66* His half brothers, sons of Joseph and Mary, told him to stop doing things in secret. They wanted him to be a show off. And when he wouldn't, they rejected him, too.*Jn 7:2-5* The Son told them it wasn't quite the right time yet. Anytime was good for them, but the Son was waiting for the Father to say the time was right. The world hated only him, not them, because the Son was showing that the world filled itself with evil.*Jn 7:6* When the religious officials challenged him, too, saying he couldn't speak for himself, the Son pointed them to his Father's words. He told the officials that they did not know him *or* his Father.*Jn 8:13-19* That's when the officials decided they'd had enough. They threw out of their religious centers anyone who thought much of the Son.*Jn 9:22* The ones in the temple courts asked him to tell them plainly if he was the Rescuer. The Son replied that he *had* told them but that they had refused to listen.*Jn 10:22-26* Opposition built, just as the Father knew it would. The extraordinary plan was working.

Rules reveal your heart. Rules are for rule-breakers, those who flaunt their corruption, kill their parents and others, have sex with whomever they wish, enslave others, and lie for any advantage.*1Ti 1:8-10* Rules show you how corrupt you are.*Ro 2:20* Rules define what's out of bounds, showing how often you go for it.*Ro 7:7* Rules invite the corrupt to break them.*Ro 7:5* Every *do not* becomes a *do*.*Ro 7:8* Rules make you guilty because they reveal your rule-breaking. *Ro 4:14-15* Rules are good even though they reveal rule-breakers.*Ro 7:12* Rules are spiritual in that sense. The problem is that you're *not* spiritual.*Ro 7:14* Sure, you love the rules, but your body urges you to break them.*Ro 7:23* The Son wasn't a rule-breaker. He fulfilled the rules.*Matt 5:17* The Son said that the rules are here to stay until everything else disappears first and his Father accomplishes everything.*Matt 5:18, Lk 16:17* Don't ignore the rules. And don't teach others to do so. Follow the rules, and help others do so. Then the Father will appreciate you.*Matt 5:19*

Divided

Because some opposed the Son, while others saw the Son as he was, the Father's own, the Son divided the people wherever he went. Some in the crowds said the Son was a good man, while others said he deceived the people. All, though, kept quiet for fear of the religious officials, who they knew hated and feared the Son.*Jn 7:12-13* Many in the crowds believed the Son came from the Father because no one else could do the miracles that the Son did. That's why the religious leaders and officials sent guards to arrest the Son—they didn't want the crowds to follow the Son. But the officials weren't going to catch the Son so quickly.*Jn 7:31-44* The crowds remained divided. Some said that the Son was their Rescuer, the one who was going to set everything right. Others disputed that the Rescuer could come from around there rather than that city Bethlehem, as the ancient writings said. They didn't realize that the Son *did* come from Bethlehem.*Jn 7:40-43*

> ***Rules foreshadow the Son.*** The old rules, those that you kept breaking, let you know that the Son was coming to set things straight.*Heb 10:1* You think rules are enough? Forget it. You'll never keep all of them.*Gal 4:21* Rules tell you that you live by doing certain things, when instead you live by relying on the Son.*Gal 3:12* The old rules didn't help. They didn't make you perfect. They just showed you that you needed the Father's help to get there.*Heb 7:18-19* The rule keepers are just doing their jobs, getting you ready to rely on the Son's rescue.*Heb 8:5* The Father didn't want your sacrifices, those that the rules said to pay for breaking the rules. He wanted *you*.*Heb 10:8* You got the rules but didn't keep the rules. What good did *that* do you?*Jn 7:19* You can open yourself up to the Father on his rest day, so why not fix everything else on the Father's rest day?*Jn 7:22-23* The Son didn't get there by keeping rules.*Jn 9:16*

The division worsened. When the guards whom the religious leaders and officials had sent to arrest the Son came back without him, the leaders and officials asked why they hadn't arrested him. The guards answered that no one spoke like the Son!*Jn 7:45-46* The officials retorted that the Son had deceived the guards. The officials and rulers had all rejected the Son, leaving only the accursed mob, the ones who knew nothing of the officials' rituals, accepting the Son. Things were working out exactly as the Son had said that they would.*Jn 7:45-49* One ruling council member Nicodemus, the one who had secretly visited the Son, said to give the Son a chance before condemning him. But the officials replied that no one important could come from the region where the Son lived._{Jn 7:50-52} Yet many others who were not among the ruling class did follow the Son. After all, when they asked the Son who he was, he replied that he was the One, telling it just like his Father told him because the Father was with him. He also hinted about his gruesome death._{Jn 8:25-30}

> **Stop disputing.** Can't you just celebrate the Father without disputing, please?_{1Ti 2:8} Don't quarrel about words. Doing so ruins those who listen._{2Ti 2:14} No useless controversies and arguments about the rules, either._{Tit 3:9} You know what causes disputes? Your desires battling within you for things that you want._{Jas 4:1-2} Just ask the Father for what you want. But don't ask just to spend what you get on your pleasures._{Jas 4:2-3} Just don't grumble or argue._{Php 2:14} Let others do the arguing._{2Ti 2:23} Only the worldly argue._{1Co 3:3} Don't let teachers divide you—from whom you learned or who you follow._{1Co 3:4-5} No resentment, either._{2Ti 2:24} If you must settle a dispute, then get the help of someone who, like you, relies on the Son._{1Co 6:1-2} Those who rely on the Son know how to make sound judgments._{1Co 6:2} Don't let the worldly settle your disputes. They'll do so unjustly._{1Co 6:4} Someone among you is wise enough to judge a dispute._{1Co 6:5} Don't take someone, like you, who relies on the Son, before a judge who does not._{1Co 6:6} You'd be better off letting the other cheat you than to sue in a dishonest judge's court._{1Co 6:7} The worldly judge by appearances. Don't. One who relies on the Son is as good as another._{2Co 10:7} Don't provoke another. Doing so involves conceit._{Gal 5:26} Don't grumble against another, or the Father will grumble against you._{Jas 5:9} Especially don't argue about the good news. You'll put someone off._{Ro 14:1} Disputes destroy one another._{Gal 5:15} Warn a divisive person no more than twice. After that, have nothing to do with them._{Tit 3:10-11} Keep your issues between you and the Father, who knows the truth._{Php 3:15} Warn the disruptive._{1Th 5:14} Keep away from those who disrupt._{Th 3:6} Watch out for those who divide._{Ro 16:17}

The healing that the Son did just worsened the divide. When the Son gave sight to a man born blind, the officials said the Son was not from the Father because he had healed the man on the rest day. But others disagreed because no ordinary person could give sight to a blind man._{Jn 9:16} When the healed man told the officials that the Father doesn't listen to just anyone, the officials shot back that the man was worthless, and they threw him out._{Jn 9:28-34} The man, though, told the Son that he was the One. And the Son said the man was right. The Son was going to help everyone who knew that they needed help but reject those who didn't think they needed it._{Jn 9:35-39} But no matter what the Son said, it always divided the people. When he said he would give his life for the people, some just said he was crazy, while others disagreed because a crazy man cannot open blind eyes.*Jn 10:19-21* Some accepted the Son but others rejected him, even among the leaders, although the leaders who accepted the Son kept it to themselves for fear of losing their positions. They cared more for the here and now than the hereafter.*Jn 12:39-43*

> **Nothing wrong with rules.** While the rules can't rescue you, they are still good rules. Keep them as far as you can. The Father appreciates it.*Ro 2:13* Having the Father's desires makes you naturally follow the rules, even when you don't know all the rules. It's called a *conscience*, and it's good to have one.*Ro 2:14-15* When you follow the rules, you know what the Father approves. You do better. But be careful telling everyone that you know the rules. Truth is, you probably don't. You break the rules all the time and so need the Son.*Ro 2:17-24* Still, nothing wrong with knowing the rules. The Father gave them to you.*Ro 2:2*

Derided

People not only opposed the Son, whose words and healing actions divided the people. People also derided, chided, and mocked the Son—calling him every name in the book. Imagine: they called this traveling, healing, teaching, and preaching itinerant miracle worker a *drunkard* and *glutton*. Sure, he ate and drank what others ate and drank. He was no prude or ascetic. But a drunk?! They didn't like that he ate with government workers, with tax agents and ordinary people.*Matt 11:19, Lk 7:34* When the Son criticized how people loved money more than doing the right thing, the religious leaders who were among the worst offenders sneered at the Son.*Lk 16:14* The teachers of the day called the Son a *blasphemer* because he forgave a paralyzed man whom he had healed.*Matt 9:3, Lk 5:21* They grumbled against the Son for saying that he could feed them—when he did! To them, he was just Joseph's son, another small-town, uneducated rube.*Jn 6:41-43* Even his own family members said that he was completely out of his mind. They even came to take charge of him, to have him committed.*Mk 3:21*

> **Recognize deception.** Watch out that no one deceives you, especially those who claim to be the Son.*Matt 24:4-5, Mk 13:5-6* Don't deceive children against the Son. Better to drown than to do so.*Matt 18:6, Mk 9:42, Lk 17:1-2* Shame on those

who deceive others into wrongs.*Matt 18:7, Lk 17:1* Better not to get it wrong.*Lk 7:23* Watch out for those who make a show of their relationship with the Father. They devour the weak. The Father will punish them severely.*Mk 12:38-40, Lk 20:38-40* Shame on those who mislead seekers.*Lk 11:52* Avoid deceptive influences. Don't listen to the enemy.*1Ti 4:1* Some people pervert the good news.*Gal 1:7* Some introduce lies that deny the good news of the Son's rescue.*1Pe 2:1* Some use the good news for their own gain, exploiting others with fantasies. The Father will punish them.*1Pe 2: 3* Others just like to argue. They make people think that relying on the Son makes you rich.*1Ti 6:4-5* Don't let a wrongdoer worm into your home to control you.*2Ti 3:6* Wrongdoers just get more and more deceptive.*2Ti 3:13* Those who reject the Father speak lies. Everything they touch comes to ruins.*Ro 2:13-16* Speak the good news rather than lies. Enjoy life. The Father watches and responds.*1Pe 3:10-11*

No matter what the Son did, some people mocked him. When a religious center's leader lost his daughter to sickness, a bunch of loudmouths standing around laughed scornfully when the leader asked the Son to bring her back to life—but he did!*Matt 9:23-24, Mk 5:39-40, Lk 8:53* Other religious leaders said that the Son had demons in him and that he worked for the chief demon. Here was the perfect Man, and yet they talking about him as if he were a perfect devil.*Matt 9:34, Mk 3:22* The Son just said he was honoring his Father.*Jn 8:48-49* Teachers of the day said the Son had a dirty spirit—the same Son who was so pure that he gleamed in transfiguration.*Mk 3:29* The Son was right when he told his students that they had better watch out for others who would try to devour them. Just keep to yourself on the road, and be sure not to carry any valuables, the Son told them.*Matt 10:16-17, Lk 10:3* Even when the Son went through the poor districts, the bad parts of town, people refused to welcome him, telling him to get lost.*Lk 9:51-53* Two of the Son's leading students James and John asked if they should rain holy fire on them, but the Son told them to forget it and just walked on.*Lk 9:54-56* The Son and his students faced such constant derision that they found hard, finding places to rest. When a man said that he would follow the Son wherever the Son went, the Son replied to forget it because he'd get no rest, when even animals have places to rest.*Lk 9:57-58*

Ignore the opposition. Some show extreme zeal for traditions. Ignore them.*Gal 1:14* Some will stop at nothing to oppose the Son. Ignore them.*Mk 3:1-6* Some get furious over talk of the Son. Ignore them.*Lk 6:11* They can't make sense of their own traditions, which ultimately have nothing to do with right or

> wrong._{Mk 3:4} Some will oppose fiercely those who follow the Son. Ignore them._{Lk 11:53-54} Correct those who worry about falling out of favor with those who follow religious traditions. Bring them back to the Son._{Gal 2:11-12} Abandoning the Son for tradition is senseless. Don't let it lead others astray._{Gal 2:13} Silence those who make meaningless and deceptive talk, especially those who would have you return to the old traditions. They make a mess of things and are in it just for themselves._{Tit 1:10-11} Shut down the meaningless talkers until they pick up the right talk, giving up their old myths and useless traditions._{Tit 1:12-14}

The Son found right times to give back some of what he got. After all that the Son did, religious officials nonetheless prodded and poked the Son. They demanded that he show them yet another wonder. The Son refused because miracles weren't going to convince them._{Mk 7:12} The Son called them *wicked* and *adulterous* because they were. He was telling the truth, but he sure wasn't going to do miracles to entertain them._{Matt 16:1-2, Lk 11:16, 11:29-32} The leading officials and teachers also tried to keep others, even children, from praising the Son, when the ancient writings had even predicted that children would love him._{Matt 21:15-16} The officials, though, just kept trying to turn the tables on the Son, nitpicking every little word._{Mk 12:13} And this scrutiny wasn't cordial but *fierce*. They *besieged* the Son with questions, and not out of curiosity but to catch him at his word._{Lk 11:53-54} They also told the Son that the governor wanted to kill him, but the Son replied to get out of his way so that he could finish his work and die in the capitol holy city the way that all the great ones did._{Lk 13:31} The Son was right when saying that others would judge him among the worst, just as the ancient writings had predicted._{Lk 22:37}

> **Customs don't help.** Your rescue doesn't depend on following religious customs, although some teach that it does._{Acts 15:1} Listen to those who talk up the Son, not religious customs._{Acts 15:2} Some will still hold onto customs._{Acts 15:5} But the Father's Spirit doesn't see customs. He sees you relying on the Son. Don't burden one another with customs._{Acts 15:7-11} Make it easy on yourself, not hard. Relying on the Son should not bring burdens with it._{Acts 15:12-21} Watch out for wrongdoers who bind you to the hardest customs._{Php 3:2} Keeping customs gains you nothing. Relying on the Son gains you everything._{Php 3:4-7} Custom-keepers will criticize you without reason._{Eph 2:11} Now listen, if you start following religious customs for your rescue, you lose the Son. Then, you're back to rule-keeping._{Gal 5:2-5} Custom-keeping? Have at it. It just doesn't work._{Gal 5:11-12} Don't let customs impress you. They just draw you away from

the Son.*Gal 6:12* Custom-keepers don't really follow the rules. They just want to brag about making you do so.*Gal 6:13* Customs work only if you keep them all, which no one can do.*Ro 2:25* Forget customs. Wait with the Father's Spirit for the Son's rescue.*Gal 5:2-5* The only genuine custom is to serve the Father while relying on the Son.*Php 3:3* The Father is over everyone, custom-keepers or not. And he gives you only one way to rescue: his Son.*Ro 2:29-30* The Son took the spiritual way rather than following an old material custom.*Col 2:11-12* At least customs slowed your corruption—or tried to do so.*Col 2:13* Customs or not means nothing to the Son. Only relying on the Son while showing his love counts.*Gal 5:6* Customs or not means nothing. New life in the Son means everything.*Gal 6:15* Don't even count who's keeping customs and who's not. The only thing that counts is who's relying on the Son.*Col 3:11* When those who don't follow customs do follow the rules, they show that customs means nothing.*Ro 2:26* Those who don't keep customs but do follow the rules shame those who keep customs but break the rules.*Ro 2:27* The custom that counts is inward, spiritual, from the Father's Spirit.*Ro 2:28-29* The Father favors those who rely on the Son, whether custom-keepers or not.*Ro 4:9-10* You can rely on the Son without following the old customs. You can always keep customs later, if you wish.*Ro 4:11-12* Don't worry over customs. Just do as the Father wants.*1Co 7:18-19*

Suffering

The opposition and derision took its toll, but the Son expected it, even if his students didn't. The Son explained to his students that he would take a lot from the religious officials and teachers, who would eventually have him killed. He also said not to worry because he would come right back to life.*Matt 16:21, Mk 8:31-32, Lk 9:21-22* The leading student Peter insisted the Son was wrong, but the Son was having none of it. He said that his students needed to think of the Father's grand plan for rescuing humankind, not their own plans for some kind of cheap worldly honor.*Matt 16:22-23, Mk 8:32-33* The Son kept repeating to his astounded students that an insider would turn him over for execution but not to worry because he would come right back to life.*Matt 17:22-23, Mk 9:30-32* The students just couldn't get it but were afraid to ask what the Son meant. He meant exactly what he said, but they just couldn't believe it.*Lk 9:43-45*

Listen carefully. Listen to the Son to know truth.*Jn 18:37* Be sure that you're hearing correctly.*Mk 4:9, Mk 4:23, Lk 8:8* Consider carefully what you hear.*Mk 4:24-25* Listen to the teacher whom the Son approves, and you hear the Son.*Lk 10:16* You

> belong to the Father if you hear the Father.*Jn 8:47* Listening to teaching is better than serving.*Lk 10:38-42* The Father favors those who hear.*Lk 11:28* Attend carefully to what you hear so as not to drift away.*Heb 2:1* Listen before speaking.*Jas 1:19* Hold your tongue, or your confidence is worthless.*Jas 1:26* Open your heart when you hear.*Eph 4:20-21* Listen to what benefits you and builds you up.*Eph 4:29*

The Son predicted his death another time on the way to the capitol holy city. This time, he was more specific. He told his students that someone would hand him over to the religious leaders, first for condemnation and then for mocking, flogging, and crucifixion. Yet once again, he told them not to worry because he would come right back to life.*Matt 20:17-19, Mk 10:32-34, Lk 18:31-33* The Son's predictions so astonished and scared his students that they almost didn't follow him to the capitol holy city.*Mk 10:32* Things got so bad that the Son did not want to go about the region publicly because he knew the religious leaders wanted to kill him.*Jn 7:1* When the Son did speak publicly, people wondered why the authorities would let him do so when the authorities were trying to kill him. Some even wondered whether the authorities believed that the Son was indeed the great Rescuer.*Jn 7:25-27* The Son played right along, saying that yes, the religious leaders knew that the Father had sent him. Those comments really stirred up the leaders who tried seizing the Son. But once again, the Son slipped away because he had more to do first.*Jn 7:28-30*

> **You don't need religious officials.** The Father once communicated with religious officials.*Heb 5:4* The people would select a religious official to represent them before the Father.*Heb 5:1* But religious officials are just as weak and corrupt as you are.*Heb 5:2-3* They die just as easily as you do.*Heb 7:23* The Son isn't weak or corrupt, though. He's your one and only true religious official. Why not just rely on him?*Heb 7:28* The Son offered himself for you rather than offering something else, as religious officials would do.*Heb 8:3-4* The Son doesn't have to go through motions like religious officials do. The Son rescued you once for all.*Heb 7:27* Your religious official, the Son, is as good as it gets. He's with the Father, both human *and* supernatural.*Heb 8:2* The Son is your permanent official, not a rotating, mortal one.*Heb 7:1-17* The Son lives forever in permanent leadership.*Heb 7:24* The Son also meets your needs as an official, like no other can.*Heb 7:26* The Son came as the number-one, authentic religious official, truly supernatural.*Heb 9:11*

The Son kept right on, despite their efforts to catch and kill him. He even said publicly that they were trying to kill him because of what he was saying.*Jn 8:37* When the Son said that he and the Father are one together, the religious officials in the center's courtyards picked up stones with which to kill him.*Jn 10:30-33* Religious officials in other places also tried to stone the Son.*Jn 11:7-8* The threats had their effect. The Son said that the nearer he got to his death, the more troubled he was. Yet he also said that he wasn't going to ask his Father to save him. No, he'd come for exactly what he was going through.*Jn 12:27-28* He was ready to suffer but just wanted to finish a few other things first, including having one last celebratory supper with his students.*Lk 22:15* Later, the Son's leading student Peter would tell everyone that although the religious officials had stupidly disowned and killed the great Rescuer, the Father had planned the Son's suffering and death just that way, as the ancient writings predicted.*Acts 3:12-18*

> **Be humble.** Don't argue over who is the greatest.*Mk 9:34, Lk 9:46, Lk 22:24* If you want to be first, then be last. Serve everyone.*Mk 9:34-35* The greatest is the one who is least.*Lk 9:48* Don't lord it over others. To the Son, the greatest is like the youngest and the one who rules like the one who serves.*Lk 22:25-26* You must serve others to be great. The Father humbles those who brag but honors those who humble themselves.*Matt 23:11-12* Stop your arrogance—now, quickly. The Son is on his way to correct you.*1Co 4:18-19* Your arrogance will bring your discipline, when you'd much rather have gentle love.*1Co 4:21* If you're rich, then don't be arrogant about it.*1Ti 6:17* Don't toot your own horn. Let others tout you.*2Co 5:12* Be humble when around others.*2Co 10:1* Don't compare yourself with others.*2Co 10:12* The greatest suffer the most to keep them humble.*2Co 12:7* The Father favors the humble.*Matt 5:3,5* Take a child's position.*Matt 18:1-4* First here, last with the Father. Last here, first with the Father.*Matt 19:30* Take the lowest place so that your host doesn't humiliate you by moving you to a lower place but instead calls you to an honored place.*Lk 14:7-10* Braggarts get humbling, while the humble get praise.*Lk 14:11*

See, even though he was the Father's Son, the Son learned obedience from suffering.*Heb 5:8* The Son's suffering simply perfected him. His suffering also perfected you, becoming your source for living forever, when you follow the Son.*Heb 5:9* The Son took care of things for you, paying your full debt.*1Co 5:6-7* The Son had nothing to pay. He'd done nothing wrong and never even lied. He just stood there and took it when accusers hurled insults at him. He knew the Father would take care of him.*1Pe 2:22-23* The Son went through all this suffering to be the go-between for you and the Father, to be your payment in full.*1Ti 2:5* Followers didn't kill the Son. Accusers killed him, just as they killed the ancient seers. Expect them to drive you away, too, even though *they* are the ones who anger the Father and stir everyone up so that you cannot get the good news out. You'd be saving lives, but they'll have none of it.₁ₜₕ ₂:₁₅-₁₆ Just expect to suffer, like the Son suffered. But don't worry. You'll have your huge reward, and they'll get what they deserve from the Father.

> **Don't be a hypocrite.** Some people advocate traditions over rules. Imagine: break the rules, just keep the traditions! Matt 15:1-2, Mk 7:1-5 Know the difference between a tradition and rule. Mk 7:4 Then, keep the rule while not worrying about the tradition. Matt 15:3-4, Mk 7:9-13 Otherwise, you'll be a hypocrite for following traditions that point to rules that you go ahead and break. Follow the Father's rules, not your own traditions. Matt 15:6-9, Mk 7:6-8 Don't worry about eating just the right thing. Worry about *saying* right things and *doing* right things. Matt 15:17-20, Mk 7:20-23 What comes out of you shows you corrupt, not what goes into you. Mk 7:14-15 Food just feeds the heart, but out of the heart comes wrongdoing. Food doesn't count. Wrongdoing counts. Mk 7:17-23 Do what hypocrites say, not what they do. And don't weigh your hearers down with things that neither you nor they can do. Matt 23:1-4, Lk 11:46 Don't do things just for others to see and honor. Matt 23:5-7 You may go ahead and do a good deed on the Father's rest day. Just honor the Father. Lk 13:10-16 Doing something good on the Father's rest day can be both necessary and beneficial, so why stop if the Father favors it? Follow the spirit of the rules, not just their letter. Lk 14:1-6 Some judge others for what they themselves do. Yikes! Acts 23:1-3

Plotting

Plots were certainly afoot to take the Son's life, although those who plotted should have realized that they were only advancing the Father's own plans. No one opposes the Father successfully. The religious leaders wanted to kill the Son to preserve their own monopoly on power and privilege. They used the Son's healing an invalid on the rest day as an excuse to persecute him and plot his death. The Son replied that his Father was always at work, even on the rest day, which just caused the leaders to try all the more to kill the Son for saying that he was from the Father. Jn 5:1-18 What the Son did or said hardly mattered, though, because they just wanted any reason to charge him. They peppered the Son with questions, looking for an excuse. Matt 12:10 Their real purpose was to advance their plot to destroy him, to rid the earth of him. Matt 12:14 When on the rest day the Son healed a man with a shriveled hand, the religious leaders involved government officials in plotting to kill the Son.*Mk 3:1-6* The Son's successes enraged the leaders, who hurried their plotting.*Lk 6:11*

> **Resist deception.** Don't let others deceive you, friends.*Jas 1:16* Don't let another speak evil about what you know is good.*Ro 14:16* Don't let others fool you into abandoning the good news.*Gal 3:1* Others seem zealous to convince you, but for no good, to steal the good news from you so that your zeal is for them.*Gal 4:17* Don't let schemers' cunning and craftiness toss you around.*Eph 4:14* Don't let empty words deceive you. Disobedience angers the Father.*Eph 5:6* Don't let fine-sounding arguments trick you.*Col 2:4* Don't let hollow and deceptive philosophy trap you. Focus on the Son's good news.*Col 2:8* Don't listen to the unspiritual whom idle notions and fantasies puff up.*Col 2:18* Don't use impure motives or tricks to appeal to others.*1Th 2:3* Never use flattery. Don't hide greed.*1Th 2:5* Ignore myths and tales.*1Ti 4:7* Don't listen to idle chatter.*1Ti 6:20* Don't let others deceive or hang out with deceivers. Bad company corrupts good character.*1Co 15:33*

When the religious leaders and teachers saw how the Son amazed whole crowds with his teaching, their fear of the Son's sway grew, and they looked for a new way to kill him.*Mk 11:18* The religious leaders and teachers figured that they would arrest the Son before he said anything more against them to the crowds, but the crowds made them afraid.*Mk 12:12, Lk 20:19* The religious leaders and government officials wanted the Son dead because everyone hung on his words.*Lk 19:47-48* When the Son asked the leaders why they were trying to kill him, they called him deranged and denied that they were up to any such thing, even though they were.*Jn 7:19-20* Finally, when the Son brought his dead friend Lazarus back to life, causing many more people to follow the Son, the religious leaders called a big meeting to approve the plot to kill him so that people would stop going over to him. They didn't want to lose to the occupying Romans their money-making religious center and their power over the people.*Jn 11:46-53*

> **Things go poorly for hypocrites.** Those who turn off people to the Son while pretending to be spiritual teachers—they'll suffer for it.*Matt 23:13* Shame on those who convert others not to relying on the Son but to doing the enemy's work.*Matt 23:15* Shame on those who think religious artifacts mean more than what or whom they represent.*Matt 23:16-21* Shame on those who do just what the rules say about the little things while ignoring the big rules, where the Father focuses.*Matt 23:23, Lk 11:42* Some make a show of working hard to do a little

good while coming naturally to indulgence.*Matt 23:24* Shame on those who gussy themselves up to look good outwardly while being ugly within. Better to be right on the inside than the outside.*Matt 23:25-26, Lk 11:39-40* Shame on those who work hard to make themselves look good while doing little actual good.*Lk 11:43* Shame on those who pretend to honor the Father's workers while instead undermining, opposing, and even killing them.*Matt 23:29-32, Lk 11:47-48* Those who oppose the Father's workers won't escape. They'll get their due.*Matt 23:33* The Son sent teachers whom opponents destroyed, to their never-ending peril.*Matt 23:34-36, Lk 11:49-51* The Son wanted to help, but many rejected him and his workers. They now have nothing.*Matt 23:37-38, Lk 13:34-35*

After the meeting, the religious leaders gave orders that anyone who saw the Son, who by then was keeping a low profile, should report the sighting so that they could arrest him.*Jn 11:57* When a large crowd went to Lazarus's home where the Son had returned for a celebratory dinner, the leaders made plans to kill Lazarus, too, so that more people wouldn't go over to the Son because of him.*Jn 12:9-11* But the crowds just kept talking about the wonders going on through the Son, especially bringing his dead friend back to life. As a result, huge crowds greeted the Son as he entered the capitol holy city for the big annual celebration. The leaders realized that they were getting nowhere with their plotting. They had failed to intimidate the Son or his followers. The whole world was going over to the Son.*Jn 12:17-19* For his part, the Son told everyone who would listen that the religious leaders and government officials would crucify and kill him. He also told everyone, though, that he would then rise back to life.*Matt 16:21, Matt 17:22-23, Matt 20:17-19, Matt 26:1-2, Lk 18:31-33* Plotting against the Father's will is useless, but that doesn't stop people from trying. You are not plotting, are you?

The enemy watches. Sharing the good news exposes some to death repeatedly.*2Co 11:24-26* Some face death every day over the Son's good news.*1Co 15:31* Others receive a death sentence, *knowing* they must rely on the Father who changes the sentence to life. But don't we all face a death sentence?*2Co 1:9* When you think about it the Son's way, death works against you so that life works in you. *2Co 4:12* Until you rely on the Son, all this stuff stinks like death. But when you rely, it smells heavenly because you know it's life.*2Co 2:16* Those who face death for telling the good news, and many do, remind you of the Son's death and his coming right back to life.*2Co 4:10* Those who face death for telling the good news do it for the Son, their dying bodies showing the Son's life._{2Co 4:11} The enemy wants to kill those who share the Son's good news. The enemy wants death, not life._{Rev 2:13}

Anointing

Because the Son saw his death coming, preparing him for his death and burial made sense, as awful as it seemed. But that's exactly what happened. A prostitute came to the Son in utter contrition. On her knees, she cried over the Son's feet, washing his feet with her hair and tears. Then she poured expensive perfume over the Son, which was the custom to prepare a body for burial. The Son told the woman that her confidence had made her good as new, like she'd never done anything wrong in her life._{Lk 7:36-50} The Son said that she was straight with him because she had known what to do, which was to love him. He sent her on her way completely free. The Son pointed out that his religious-leader host hadn't loved him nearly so much._{Lk 7:36-50} This burial preparation happened shortly before the Son's arrest and killing. The students, though, didn't get it, didn't understand the significance of what the woman had done. They said that they should have sold the perfume to give the money to the poor, if you can believe it. The Son, though, said she'd done a beautiful thing preparing him for his burial, something that others would long remember._{Matt 26:6-13, Mk 14:3-9}

Another record gives a similar but subtly different account of the Son's anointing for burial. In this related account, the Son's friend Mary, the sister of Lazarus and Martha whom the Son also loved, anointed the Son's feet with perfume and wiped his feet with her hair. Here, the event took place when the Son attended a dinner at their home given in his honor shortly before the last supper._{Jn 12:1-3} In this account, the student Judas who betrayed the Son was the one who asked why they hadn't instead sold the perfume to give to the poor. Judas asked this question not because he cared for the poor but because he was a thief who helped himself to the money that he carried for the Son and his students._{Jn 12:4-6} The Son said to leave Mary alone because the perfume was for his burial. The Son added that they would always have the poor among them but not always have him. Care for the Son when you have him, while caring for the poor when you don't._{Jn 12:7-8} The Son added that when people spread his good news throughout the world, they would also tell about the woman who anointed him with an expensive perfume to prepare him for burial._{Matt 26:12-13, Mk 14:3-9} The end of the Son's earthly mission was coming. He had prepared for it.

> **Watch out for greed.** Shame on the rich who lived for their comfort._{Lk 6:24-26} Wealth deceives you, choking out the good news, so much better than wealth._{Matt 13:22} Guard against greed. Life isn't about abundant possessions._{Lk 12:13-15} You may think that you'll get richer and richer, but the Father may demand your life tonight. Be rich instead toward the Father._{Lk 12:16-21} Pursuing riches just tempts and traps people to their ruin._{1Ti 6:9} Don't love money. What you have is enough. The Father provides._{Heb 13:5} Loving money tempts you to forget the good news._{1Ti 6:10} Have nothing to do with people who love money._{2Ti 3:2-5} Those who hoard wealth should cry because of their coming misery. Wealth corrodes and corrupts them._{Jas 5:5} Pay workers fair wages, or their complaints will reach the Father._{Jas 5:4} Hoarding wealth and cheating workers to live luxuriously just fattens one for due slaughter._{Jas 5:5-6} Greed is everywhere._{1Co 5:10} The worldly are greedy swindlers._{1Co 5:10} Greed leads to continual wrongs._{1Pe 2:14-16} Don't hoard material riches here. Instead, do things that earn you future rewards from the Father._{Matt 6:19-20} Everyone thinks about riches. You should think of the Father's riches._{Matt 6:21} Those who love money sneer at those who love the Son._{Lk 16:14} Don't covet another's riches._{Acts 20:33} The good news can turn greedy swindlers around._{1Co 6:9-11} Who needs greed when everything is already yours when you rely on the Son?._{1Co 3:21-23} If you are rich, then don't be arrogant. Rely on the Father, not your riches._{1Ti 6:17} Be rich in good deeds. Be generous._{1Ti 6:18-19} You'll lose your mind if you reject the Father. Then you'll fill with greed._{Ro 1:28-29} The Father has no place for the greedy._{1Co 6:9-10} Don't show even a hint of greed._{Eph 5:3} You can't serve both money and the Son._{Matt 6:24, Lk 16:13} Trust with little, trust with much. Dishonest with little, dishonest with much._{Lk 16:10} Don't steal, or the Father won't trust you with his riches, either._{Lk 16:11-12} Some people value highly what the Father detests._{Lk 16:15} Some rich live in luxury with beggars by their gates._{Lk 16:19-21} But the beggars may join the Father while the rich end in hell._{Lk 16:22-23} The rich in hell will get no relief. It's too late, then._{Lk 16:24-31}

Betrayal

The Son predicted that his death would come by betrayal, which is sad but instructive. The Son had also predicted that some of his students would not believe what he said. He knew from the start which ones would reject him and who would be the one to finally betray him. The

Son knows your heart and thus knows your actions even before you do.*Jn 6:64* The Son added that one of his twelve closest students, one of his inner circle, was a mischievous fiend, a devil. Although his other students didn't know it yet, he was referring to Judas Iscariot who would betray the Son.*Jn 6:70* The religious leaders needed a quiet way to arrest the Son, something that a betrayer could supply.*Matt 21:45-46* Just before his arrest, the Son told his students again that someone would hand him over for killing.*Matt 26:1-2* The religious leaders in the high priest's palace were just looking for a way to arrest him secretly for execution, so that people attending the festival wouldn't riot.*Matt 26:3-4, Mk 14:1-2* Even though they knew that they had to get rid of the Son, the religious leaders and teachers still feared the people.*Lk 22:1-2* The religious leaders were glad to have the Son's errant student Judas meet with them secretly to discuss how he might betray the Son. The enemy worked through Judas.*Lk 22:3-4* Remember how Judas loved money? When the religious leaders offered Judas thirty pieces of silver to betray the Son, Judas took the offer, fulfilling yet another ancient prediction.*Matt 26:14-16* That Judas offered to betray the Son, and to watch for an opportunity to hand the Son over to the leaders in secret, delighted the leaders. They were only too glad to pay for the betrayal.*Mk 14:11, Lk 22:5-6*

Resist indulgence. Be careful or drunkenness and carousing will weigh you down.*Lk 21:34* Everyone pursues corrupt indulgences until they learn better.*Eph 2:3* Indulging desires was once natural for you until you realized what you were losing.*Ro 7:5* The desire to indulge in corruption will always be there. Don't pursue those desires while losing life forever.*Gal 5:19-21* Those who indulge entice others to do so with them.*1Pe 2:18* They promise freedom while making themselves slaves.*1Pe 2:19* Desiring to indulge leads one away from the Father.*Ro 8:7* If you make no effort to control desire, then you're a goner.*Col 2:13* Indulgence can't please the Father.*Ro 8:8* The Father says *have at it* to those who reject him, as they degrade their bodies with one another.*Ro 1:24* Shameful lusts flourish among those who reject the Father. It all leads to death.*Ro 1:26-27* Living for pleasure is death, not living.*1Ti 5:6* Rules don't stop those who indulge. Only the Spirit stops indulgence.*Col 2:23*

When the Son gathered with his students for his last meal with them, the Son told them again that one of them would betray him.*Matt 26:17-21, Mk 14:16-17, Lk 22:21, Jn 13:21* When they asked who, the Son told them the one who dipped his hand in the common bowl with him.*Matt 26:22-23, Mk 14:19-20, Lk 22:21* The Son said that the betrayer would be the one to whom he gave a piece of bread after dipping the bread in the dish.*Jn 13:25-26* The Son explained that the moment fulfilled the ancient prediction that the one who shared his bread would turn against him.*Jn 13:18* Judas asked if the Son was referring to him, and the Son said that Judas had said so.*Matt 26:24-25* And that's just the way that the betrayal happened. The moment that the Son gave the dipped bread to Judas, the enemy seized Judas.*Jn 13:26-27* The Son told Judas to do quickly what Judas was going to do.*Jn 13:26* Judas left promptly, in the dark.*Jn 13:30* The Son reassured the other students that they were alright with him, just not Judas who was right then betraying him.*Jn 13:10-11* To the students consternation, the Son told them that in just a little while they would see him no more. He was going to the Father. But then after a little while, they would see him again. The Son was referring to his death and coming back to life, although the students didn't get it then.*Jn 16:16-19* The Son told his students that they would be very glad when he returned again, so glad that no one could take away their joy.*Jn 16:21-22*

> **Corruption counts against you. Avoid it.** Relying on the Son makes everything pure. Rejecting the Son makes everything corruption. You lose your mind and conscience.*Tit 1:15* Some claim to know the Father, but their actions prove that they don't. They are fit for nothing.*Tit 1:16* Don't live in futility like others do. Get with the Son.*Eph 4:17* Rejecting the Son hardens you and darkens your life with ignorance.*Eph 4:18* Those who reject the Son lose sensitivity, instead pursuing sensuality, indulging in every impurity, full of greed.*Eph 4:19* Those who reject sound doctrine do so to suit their own desires. They'll find someone, *anyone*, to tell them what they want to hear.*2Ti 4:3* They turn away from the truth to myths.*2Ti 4:4* Drink up the truth, letting the Father favor you. Reject corruption, and avoid the Father's curse.*Heb 6:8* Those who love the world desert their teachers.*2Ti 4:10* But don't worry. Justice will come in the end. The corrupt won't find any relief.*Rev 21:8*

The Son told his students about the betrayal before it happened as yet another indication that the Son was who he and the ancient writings said he was.*Jn 13:19* The Son knew that everything was going according to the Father's plan, just as the ancient writings had predicted. That didn't mean, though, that Judas was doing the right thing. No, better for Judas that he have never been born.*Matt 26:24, Mk 14:21, Lk 22:22* Remorse seized Judas after the betrayal. He even tried to return the silver to the religious leaders. But they didn't care about him. They even said so. Typical of their hypocrisy, they blamed Judas for their own plot.*Matt 27:3-4* So Judas threw the silver into the religious center and hanged himself.*Matt 27:5* The religious leaders used the blood money to buy the potter's field in which to bury dead foreigners, fulfilling yet another ancient prediction.*Matt 27:6-10* After the Son died and came back to life, the Son's leading student Peter reminded everyone that Judas had fulfilled the ancient predictions.*Acts 1:16*

> **New is better than old.** The old way of doing wrong and then paying for it wasn't pleasing the Father.*Heb 10:8* So, the Son set aside the old way for the new way. No more payback. He was paying it all.*Heb 10:9* The Son's new way is far better than the old way because you get more. You get to live forever.*Heb 8:6* If the old way had nothing wrong with it, then the Father would not have made the new way.*Heb 8:7* The problem wasn't with the old way but with the people who were following it. So, the Father made the new way, the Son's way.*Heb 8:8* The old way rescued people out of material slavery but left them in spiritual slavery. The people were still messing things up, offending the Father. The new way leaves no offense with the Father. You're in with him.*Heb 8:9* The Father calls it the new way because the old way is obsolete. The old, outdated way is disappearing.*Heb 8:13* The Father's new way gives you a heart and mind to do as he wishes, so that you are no longer breaking every rule.*Heb 8:10* The Father has forgotten everything wrong you did.*Heb 8:12* The Son makes sure that's so.*Heb 12:24* In fact, the Son *guarantees* it.*Heb 7:22* The Father made you *want* to do as he wishes so that he could forget about your past.*Heb 10:16* The Son then makes sure that you get the great things the Father promises, living forever in perfect peace. No more payback.*Heb 9:15* The Son wants you even when others don't.*2Co 1:19* The Son does it *all* for you, not just a little bit.*2Co 1:20* Because the Father now *owns* you, you get all he has for you.*2Co 1:22* No one can change it, not even the old rules.*Gal 3:15-17*

At this last meal, on the night of his betrayal, the Son took bread, thanked the Father, broke the bread, and gave the bread to his students, telling them to eat the bread as his body.*Matt 26:26, Mk 14:22, Lk 22:19* He then took a cup of wine, thanked the Father, passed the cup to them, and told them to drink from it as his blood poured to excuse corruption.*Matt 26:27-28, Mk 14:23-24, Lk 22:17-20* The Son called it the new promise of his blood, his death for you.*Lk 22:20* The Son said that he would not drink again with them until they were together in his Father's place.*Matt 26:29, Mk 14:25, Lk 22:18* The Son had thus said that the bread is his body broken for you. The Son added that you should do as he just did to remember him.*1Co 11:23-24* The Son confirmed that the cup of wine represents the new promise in his blood, his death, which you are to drink to remember him.*1Co 11:25*

> ***Remember the Son.*** Breaking bread shares the Son's broken body, his death.*1Co 10:16* Sharing a cup of wine shares the Son's blood, his death.*1Co 10:16,18* Whenever you eat the broken bread and drink the shared cup, you remember the Son's death.*1Co 11:26* Eat the Son's spiritual food and drink his spiritual drink as others have before you.*1Co 10:3-4* When you do so, you live forever. The Son's food and drink are real, authentic.*Jn 6:52-55* Eating and drinking this way keeps you alive in the Son.*Jn 6:56-57* Eat and drink this way together, respectfully.*1Co 11:20-21* When you gather, eat together.*1Co 11:33* Don't eat before others eat, just because you're hungry.*1Co 11:34* Examine yourself before eating and drinking this way. Have a conscience.*1Co 11:28* The enemy has his own cup. Don't drink from it.*1Co 10:21* Rely on the Son when eating and drinking this way. Be honest and genuine, or things will not go well for you.*1Co 11:27-30*

Garden

The Son's final betrayal happened in a garden, a favorite place to which the Son would go for prayer and rest. On the night of his betrayal, the Son took his students from the last meal to the garden, the place of his betrayal, asking them to sit while he talked with the Father nearby.*Matt 26:36, Mk 14:32, Lk 22:39, Jn 18:1* The Son also told his students to speak with the Father that they, too, not fall into temptation, like Judas had fallen.*Lk 22:40* He then took his leading disciples Peter, James, and John aside with him. The Son told them that sorrow overwhelmed him right up to the point of death. He asked that they watch with him.*Matt 26:37-38, Mk 14:33-34* The Son then went about a stone's throw away to kneel and talk with the Father.*Lk 22:41* He fell facedown to ask that his Father relieve him of his awful duty but then asked that his Father do as his Father willed, not as he wished.*Matt 26:39, Mk 14:35-36, Lk 22:42* Right then, the Father sent a celestial messenger to strengthen the Son.*Lk 22:43* The Son continued to talk to his Father in anguish, even more earnestly, his sweat like falling drops of blood.*Lk 22:44*

The Son returned to his students but found them sleeping.*Matt 26:40, Mk 14:37* Sorrow had exhausted them.*Lk 22:45* The Son asked Peter whether Peter couldn't keep watch for just one hour to help the Son in his horrible anguish.*Matt 26:40, Mk 14:37* The Son also asked them to get up, watch, and speak with the Father so as not to fall into temptation.*Matt 26:41, Mk 14:38, Lk 22:46* The Son added that the spirit is willing but the flesh weak.*Matt 26:41, Mk 14:38* The Son then went aside again, asked the same again from the

Father, and came back to find his students sleeping again.*Matt 26:42-43, Mk 14:39-40* The Son went aside a third time, asked the same again, and came back to find his students sleeping once again. This time, though, he told them to rise because the hour had come for the betrayer to deliver the Son into the enemy's hands.*Matt 26:44-46, Mk 14:41-42* The Son's rejection was now complete. All that remained for his enemies to accomplish was his execution.

> ***You have the strength to continue.*** Don't worry what to say in trials. The Spirit will give you what to say and will speak for you.*Mk 13:11* The Spirit will give you words and wisdom that your adversaries cannot contradict.*Lk 21:14-15* Consider the martyer Stephen who spoke with the Spirit's wisdom.*Acts 6:8-10* Be strong, but don't fight as others fight.*Lk 22:35-38* Be strong in the Father's power.*Eph 6:10* Truth helps you stand firm. Right relationship with the Father also helps. And the good news always serves you well.*Eph 6:14-15* Ask for the Father's strength. Then you'll endure.*Col 1:10-11* Don't let trials unsettle you. Expect them.*1Th 3:3-4* Remember the confidence others have in you. That'll help.*1Ti 1:18* Even the best teachers face trials. The Father rescues all.*2Ti 3:10-11* The Father strengthens you. That's how the good news spreads.*2Ti 4:17* Be strong. Have courage.*1Co 16:13* The Father rescues from every attack.*2Ti 4:18*

8 Execution

Arrest

The Son's execution was swift. From arrest to death took less than a day, hardly due process. Evil doesn't wait. Here's how it happened. The betrayer Judas knew the garden where the Son spoke with his Father because the Son had often met there with his students.*Jn 18:2* The Son was still speaking to the students in the garden after speaking with the Father in such anguish, when Judas arrived with a large, armed crowd that the religious leaders had sent.*Matt 26:47, Mk 14:43, Lk 22:47* Soldiers and officials accompanied the crowd, carrying torches and lanterns along with their weapons.*Jn 18:3* The Son knew all that would happen. He remained in complete control and so went out to ask them whom they wanted.*Jn 18:4* When they said that they wanted the Son, and he told them that he was the Son, they fell back to the ground. They couldn't stand up to his presence.*Jn 18:5-6* So the Son asked again whom they wanted, and when they again answered the Son, he again said that he was the Son. But he added to let the others go. The Son gave that command so that he would lose none of his students, as he had predicted.*Jn 18:7-8*

> **Comfort is coming.** Don't worry. The Son's coming back for you. He's prepared a special place for you where he is.*Jn 14:1-3* You know the way to that place: it's *him*, the Son.*Jn 14:4-6* The Son gives you peace—*his* peace, not a worldly peace that isn't really peace. So just hang on.*Jn 14:27* You may find it hard now, but if so, then the Father will especially favor you later.*Lk 6:21* The Father comforts you in trouble. Then, you can comfort others in trouble, using his comfort.*2Co 1:4* Yes, you'll share some of the Son's suffering. But then you'll enjoy all of the Son's comfort.*2Co 1:5* Better to suffer for the comfort and rescue of others. Comfort in distress promotes endurance.*2Co 1:6* Hope for one

another. Share in one another's suffering. Then, you'll also share in comfort.*2Co 1:7* The Father comforts those who mourn.*Matt 5:4*

The betrayer Judas had arranged a signal with the crowd to be sure that they arrested the right one. They were to arrest the one whom Judas kissed, of all things. So, Judas went straight up to the Son, greeting him with a kiss. The Son highlighted the ugly irony, asking Judas if Judas intended to betray the Son with a kiss.*Lk 22:47-48* Yet the Son wasn't resisting. Instead, he also said for Judas to do that for which Judas came.*Matt 26:48-50, Mk 14:44-45* Then, other men from the crowd stepped forward to make the arrest.*Matt 26:50* At that point, one of the Son's students drew a sword with which he cut off the ear of a religious official's servant.*Matt 26:51, Lk 22:49-50* The leading student Peter was the one who drew the sword.*Jn 18:10* Peter apparently had big plans for a fight and rescue. But the Son told Peter to put away the sword. The Son said that he must do that which the Father had given him. The plan was his arrest and death, and the Son was going through with it.*Jn 18:11* The Son also warned Peter to put away the sword because those who live by the sword die by it. You stick a sword in someone, then someone will stick a sword in you. The Son also said that he could have called on his Father to send legions of powerful celestial beings but that instead the Son was going to do as the ancient writings predicted.*Matt 26:52-54*

> **The enemy holds no greater power.** All power comes from the Father. The enemy has no power.*Jn 19:10-11* The Son overthrows and destroys the enemy's supposed power.*2Th 2:7-8* The enemy's power is temptation.*Ro 2:8-11* The Son broke the enemy's power.*Heb 2:14* The enemy's power is in deception.*2Th 2:9* The Father permits those who reject the Son to suffer powerful delusion. They believe lies.*2Th 2:11-12* Your struggle isn't with your health. Your struggle is against the enemy's power of deception.*Eph 6:12* You've beaten death's power with the Son's freedom from condemning rules.*1Co 15:55-56* Rules have no power to free you from guilt. The Son gave you that power. Rely on it.*Ro 8:3-4* No power can separate you from the Father's love shown in his Son.*Ro 8:38-39* The Son disarmed and triumphed over enemy powers, making a spectacle of them.*Col 2:15* The deadliest attacks hold no power next to the Father's power.*Acts 28:1-6*

The Son remained in complete control, true to his mission. After the Son ended any thoughts of fighting, he touched the servant's ear, instantly healing the servant. Whom do you think that servant was now going to follow?*Lk 22:51* The Son then told the crowd that he was not leading a rebellion. They didn't need swords and clubs. The Son had just taught openly in the capitol holy city's religious center. No one had bothered to arrest him then. So why did anyone think that he would lead a secret rebellion now?*Matt 26:55, Mk 14:48, Lk 22:52-53* The Son added that darkness was their time and their way of doing things—secret and furtive because shameful.*Lk 22:53* But the Son repeated that his arrest must happen to follow the ancient writings' predictions.*Matt 26:56, Mk 14:49* And that was the end of it. At the religious officials' behest, the soldiers with their commander arrested and bound the Son like some common criminal.*Jn 18:12* The students all then ran for their lives.*Matt 26:56, Mk 14:50* Indeed, a young man who had followed the Son fled naked when they tried to seize him. He left his only garment behind.*Mk 14:51-52* All on both sides were acting like the cowards who they were, except the Son, who though submitting to arrest had complete control of the awful situation.

> **You have an enemy.** The enemy killed the Son, but it backfired on him when the Son came right back to life. The killing just proved that the Son would give everything for his Father—and you!*Jn 14:30-31* Make no mistake, though: the enemy is a murderer. He's a liar, too.*Jn 8:44* The enemy lies naturally, all the time. He wants you lying, too.*Jn 8:44* Don't let the enemy cause you to lie to one another. But especially don't lie to the Father. That'll cost you—maybe everything.*Acts 5:1-6* The enemy lies in wait to destroy you. Watch for him.*1Pe 5:8* The enemy knows the Father but just doesn't respect him. Don't let that be you.*Jas 2:19* The Son's words stop the enemy in his tracks. Know those words. You'll need them.*2Ti 2:25-26* Grasp the Son's words, really grasp them, or the enemy will get you.*Matt 13:19* The enemy loves to tempt you. That's how he works.*1Th 3:5* The enemy also tries to keep you apart from others who know the Son's words.*1Th 2:17* Don't underestimate the enemy. His tricks are subtle and powerful.*2Th 2:9* Those who follow the enemy hate and indulge, while those who follow the Son love and resist.*1Jn 3:9* The enemy pretends to be good just to fool you.*2Co 11:14* Those who follow the enemy pretend to do good but do not.*2Co 11:15* The enemy promotes envy and selfishness.*Jas 3:14-16* The enemy can also torment your body, though not your spirit.*2Co 12:7* Listen to the Father's Spirit who shows you the enemy's tricks.*1Ti 4:1* The enemy uses lust to draw you away.*1Ti 5:14-15* Sometimes, you've got to let someone pursue the enemy when they just won't listen. That'll teach them.*1Ti 1:20* The enemy is conceited. Don't be that way, or you'll catch it.*1Ti 3:6* A good reputation can keep you from the enemy, like an inoculation.*1Ti 3:7* Don't work for the enemy. Do the Father's work.*1Co 10:20* The enemy has his troops.*Matt 9:34* The enemy most wants to stop the good news.*Matt 16:22-23* The student who betrayed the Son followed the

> enemy.*Jn 6:70* The enemy prompted him to do so.*Jn 13:2* The enemy got him. That's how he works.*Jn 13:26-27* The enemy wants to get you, too. The Son won't let him. He's asked the Father to protect you.*Lk 22:31-32* It's over for the enemy. The Son's condemned him.*Jn 16:8-11*

Trial

A nighttime trial followed, although the trial was a charade, not a real trial. Everyone knew the outcome even before it started. Those who arrested the Son first took him to a relative of the highest religious leader. This relative, who had been the highest religious official earlier, had recommended that the Son die for the people. He didn't mean it in the sacrificial way that the Father planned. He was just trying to keep the leaders in power. But he was right nonetheless.*Jn 18:13-14* The relative questioned the Son about his students and teaching, as if anyone had any need to ask, when the Son had spoken openly to everyone, everywhere, with nothing in secret. The Son told the relative so and said to ask those who heard him.*Jn 18:19-21* An official slapped the Son for speaking impertinently, but the Son replied that the official should testify to what the Son had said that was wrong and, because he spoke truth, should explain why the official struck him. The official had no good answer, showing once again that the Son was in complete control.*Jn 18:22-23*

The mob then took the Son to the highest religious official, where the teachers and other leaders had assembled.*Matt 26:57, Mk 14:53, Lk 22:54* The student John knew the highest official and so went along with the Son.*Jn 18:15* The other leading student Peter followed at a distance. He sat outside until John came back, talked with the servant girl there, and brought Peter into the courtyard.*Jn 18:16* Peter then sat with the guards in the courtyard to see what would happen.*Matt 26:58, Mk 14:54, Lk 22:54, Jn 18:16* The religious leaders looked for false evidence with which to convict the Son to put him to death.*Matt 26:59, Mk 14:55* One after another, many false witnesses testified, but none brought forward any convicting evidence.*Matt 26:60, Mk 14:56* Two witnesses testified that the Son had said he could destroy the temple to rebuild in three days, which of course was preposterous, except that they didn't know that the Son was referring to his death and coming back to life again. *Matt 26:60, Mk 14:57* Yet even their testimony did not agree.*Mk 14:58*

> ***Don't desert the Son even if it gets hard.*** Many leave the Son over his hard teaching.*Jn 6:60-66* Truly, though, you have no other place to go. Only the Son helps you live forever. No one or nothing else can.*Jn 6:67-69* Everyone lapses when things get hard. Just don't make your lapse permanent.*Matt 26:31, Mk 14:27* None are better than another. All abandon the Son at some point—except the Father.*Jn 16:31-32* The Son prayed to keep and restore you so that you can encourage others.*Lk 22:31-32* You may think that you are especially brave, but you're not.*Matt 26:33, Mk 14:29, Lk 22:33* You may even think that you'd give your life for the Son like he gave his life for you.*Jn 13:37* You're probably not that brave, though.*Matt 26:34, Mk 14:30, Lk 22:34, Jn 13:38* You may brag about your commitment, but be careful. The Son's the committed one. You're relying on his commitment, not yours.*Matt 26:35, Mk 14:31* All run away at some point.*Matt 26:56* When pressed, you may even deny that you know the Son.*Matt 26:69-74, Mk 14:66-71, Lk 22:56-60, Jn 18:17, 25-27* And the Son already knows it.*Matt 26:74-75, Mk 14:72, Lk 22:60, Jn 18:27* He's watching you.*Lk 22:61* But you'll be getting back on track already if you promptly regret it.*Matt 26:74-75, Mk 14:72, Lk 22:62*

The highest religious official then demanded that the Son answer for himself—no right to remain silent, apparently. But that's just what the Son did, saying nothing.*Matt 26:61-63, Mk 14:60-61* The highest official then charged the Son to say whether the Son was the great Rescuer whom the ancient writings predicted.*Matt 26:63, Mk 14:61* The rest of the religious leaders joined in, demanding that the Son tell them. See, they knew exactly who the Son was but just were refusing to admit it.*Lk 22:66-67* The Son replied that they would not believe him if he told them.*Lk 22:67* The Son also replied that he was indeed the great Rescuer. They were right.*Mk 14:62* The Son also replied that the highest official had himself said as much.*Matt 26:64* The Son added that they would indeed see the Son sitting at his Father's side and also coming down from above as utter ruler.*Matt 26:64, Mk 14:62, Lk 22:69* They all asked him together whether he was then the Father's Son, to which the Son said that they had just said that he was. They knew full well who he was.*Lk 22:70*

The highest official then tore his clothes to express angry judgment over the Son. The highest official said that they needed no evidence. They could convict the Son from his own words because he had said what they refused to accept, claiming an authority that he had but to which they refused to submit.*Matt 26:65, Mk 14:63-64, Lk 22:71* The rest agreed that they should have the Son killed. That's when they really began to treat him most badly. They spit in his face, struck him with fists, and slapped his face, while mocking him to say again that he was the great Rescuer. Of course, the Son said nothing more because everyone knew who he was. He had repeatedly said it *and* proven it with wonder after wonder, which was the reason why they were killing him.*Matt 26:66-68, Mk 14:64-65* They blindfolded the Son so that guards could take him, mock him, and beat him. Many others heaped insults on him, which is what people do, joining any angry mob, even the worst one.*Mk 14:65, Lk 22:63-65* As the beating went on, the religious leaders planned the Son's execution. The guards finally led the Son away bound, to the governor.*Matt 27:1-2, Mk 15:1*

> **Resist the enemy.** The Son asked the Father to protect you against the enemy.*Jn 17:15* Your struggle isn't truly against your hunger and lust. It's against the enemy who tries to influence you.*Eph 6:12* Don't look left or right. Keep your focus where it should be. The enemy's trying to distract you.*Matt 6:22-23* Good thing: the enemy runs when you resist him.*Jas 4:7-8* The Father beats back your enemy.*Col 1:13* Leave the fight to your Father. He's stronger than you.*Jude 8:10* Let the Father protect you. You'll need him because the enemy's powerful.*Eph 6:11* Resist the enemy. Rely on the Son. You're no different. Everyone's in the same battle.*1Pe 5:9* When the enemy shows up, you'll manage if you're relying on Father and Son.*Eph 6:13* Anger gives the enemy a chance to beat you. Rid yourself of anger.*Eph 4:27* Careful! Your enemy is right there, daily. Take all the help you can get.*Eph 5:15-16* Relying on the Son turns away the enemy's thrusts.*Eph 6:16* The Father pulls you back from the cliff.*2Ti 4:17* The Father is crushing your enemy, *crushing* him.*Ro 16:20* The enemy finds plenty of foolish people to do his ugly work.*Matt 13:36-38* In the end, though, the enemy gets left with nothing but destruction. You'll still be standing.*Matt 13:40-43* The Father is ready to blister the enemy, just *destroy* him.*Matt 25:41* You know, even if the enemy captures and kills you, you'll be fine. Paradise is waiting for you for relying on the Son. The enemy's got nothing on you.*Rev 2:9-10* The enemy may be all around you, but you'll be alright with the Son.*Rev 2:13-16* Don't let the enemy impress you. The end's coming for anyone who does.*Rev 2:19-24*

Sentence

With the Son's trial over, sentencing was the next brief step on the way to sure execution. The religious leaders needed government help to execute the Son. So, the religious leaders marched the Son before the governor in the early morning. They made the governor come outside his palace so that the leaders could pretend to be pure of the governor's corruption. Can you believe their hypocrisy?$_{Jn\ 18:28}$ When the governor came out to ask the charges, the leaders said that they wouldn't have handed over the Son unless he were a criminal. They weren't even going to tell the governor the reason to execute the Son. Not one for their games, the governor replied to judge the Son on their own then.$_{Jn\ 18:29-31}$ The leaders replied that they could not execute anyone, which just confirmed their corrupt intentions to kill the Son as predicted.$_{Jn\ 18:31-32}$ The governor then brought the Son into the palace, where the officials had refused to go.$_{Jn\ 18:33}$

The governor asked the Son privately if he was the religious ruler, to which the Son replied that the governor had said so. The Son would turn the table on the governor, just as the Son had done in the officials' mock trial.$_{Matt\ 27:11,\ Mk\ 15:2,\ Lk\ 23:3}$ The Son asked the governor if the Son's being the religious ruler was his own idea or others had told him so.$_{Jn\ 18:33}$ The governor asked why the Son's own people had handed him over. The Son replied that he, the Son, had otherworldly authority. The Son was, in other words, over everything, not just the earth or the governor's puny kingdom.$_{Jn\ 18:35-36}$ The governor replied that the Son was indeed a ruler then, to which the Son replied that the governor had said so. But the Son added that he came to talk truth, not just to rule. The Son was sharing the good news.$_{Jn\ 18:37}$ The governor retorted asking what truth is. Yet the governor then went out to tell the religious leaders that the Son had done nothing wrong, which was true.$_{Jn\ 18:38}$

> **Find truth in the Son.** The Son said to leave those who guide you into the old traditions. You'll end up in a pit.$_{Matt\ 15:14}$ The blind cannot lead the blind without them both falling into a pit.$_{Lk\ 6:39}$ The Son said that deceivers will abound just before the end.$_{Matt\ 24:11}$ Deceivers deny that the Father sent the Son. Watch out for them.$_{2Jn\ 7}$ Deceivers who reject the Son will try to slip in among you, spreading their immorality.$_{Jude\ 4}$ Some will say that the Son has already returned.$_{2Th\ 2:2-3}$ Those who say that whomever is coming back to life already has, are making up things.$_{2Ti\ 2:18}$ Rely on it if the Son said it. Don't rely on things that contradict the Son. They're lies.$_{1Ti\ 6:3-4}$ The harder someone argues against the Son, the harder you should oppose them.$_{2Ti\ 4:15}$ The enemy tries to lead you away from the Son. That's his gambit.$_{2Co\ 11:3}$ Reject those who teach about a good news or Son other than the one you know. They're just making things up.$_{2Co\ 11:4}$

The religious leaders finally made some serious accusations, starting with that the Son claimed to be ruler. They also said that the Son opposed paying taxes, which wasn't true.*Matt 27:12, Mk 15:1-2, Lk 23:1-2* Yet the Son did not respond, even when the amazed governor asked if he didn't hear the serious charges.*Matt 27:13-14, Mk 15:5* The governor still told the religious leaders that he found no evidence supporting the charges. But the religious leaders insisted that the Son stirs everyone up with his teaching.*Lk 23:4-5* When the governor heard that the Son was a Galilean, he decided to send the Son to the corrupt ruler of that region. The governor's referral greatly pleased the corrupt ruler who expected to see signs or magic of some sort from the Son.*Lk 23:6-8* But the Son said nothing to the corrupt ruler's many questions, even with the religious leaders and teachers vehemently accusing the Son.*Lk 23:9-10* So the corrupt ruler and his soldiers ridiculed and mocked the Son before sending him back to the governor in an elegant robe.*Lk 23:11-12*

The governor repeated to the religious leaders that neither he nor the corrupt ruler to which the governor had referred the Son had found any basis for a charge. The governor told the religious leaders that he would punish and release the Son. But the crowd kept shouting to crucify the Son, until the governor relented.*Lk 23:13-23* The governor typically released a prisoner to honor the crowd at the festival, so he asked the crowd whether he should release a notorious prisoner who had taken part in an uprising, or release the Son whom the governor knew the religious leaders had handed over for their own interests.*Matt 27:15-18, Mk 15:6-10, Jn 18:39* The governor's wife sent the governor a message saying not to mistreat the innocent Son because she had suffered a great deal over a dream for him.*Matt 27:19-20* Yet the religious leaders had convinced the crowd to demand the notorious prisoner's release instead and the Son's execution.*Matt 27:22-23, Mk 15:11-14, Jn 18:40* And so, the governor washed his hands of the Son's innocent blood, leaving the crowd responsible.*Matt 27:23-24* In an irony that the people surely did not appreciate, the people agreed that the Son's blood was on them and their children. Indeed, the Father had planned his Son's sacrifice for that very reason, although the people didn't intend that meaning when accepting the Son's blood.*Matt 27:25* The governor thus had the Son flogged and sent for crucifixion.*Matt 27:26, Mk 15:15, Jn 19:1*

Don't misunderstand the enemy. He understands you. The enemy does the enemy's work. You can't use the enemy's ways to do the Son's good works. Haters destroy. Lovers repair.*Matt 12:25-26, Mk 3:22-26, Lk 11:17-18* Don't attribute good works to the enemy.*Matt 12:27-28, Lk 11:19-20* Don't fight the enemy. Banish him.*Matt*

Spiritspeak

> *12:29, Mk 3:27, Lk 11:21-22* Getting rid of the enemy isn't enough, though. You must replace the enemy with a friend—the Father's Spirit.*Matt 12:43-44, Lk 11:24-26* You don't have to be an insider to do an insider's good works. Outsiders do the Son's work, too. Leave them to their good works. They're not your enemies.*Mk 9:38-40, Lk 9:49-50* Unknowing people may accuse you of following the enemy.*Matt 11:18* They'll especially accuse you of following the enemy when your good work threatens their bad work.*Jn 7:19-20* Reject the Son, and you do follow the enemy. It's inevitable. If you're not on the Son's side, then you're on the other side, following the enemy as your leader.*Jn 8:39-44* The enemy submits to the Son and those who rely on the Son, not to others. Be sure you rely on the Son when taking on the enemy.*Acts 19:13-16*

The soldiers first led the Son into the palace before the whole company of soldiers.*Mk 15:16* There the soldiers stripped and robed the Son, jammed a crown of thorns on his head, put a staff in his hand, and knelt before him to mock him cruelly as the people's supposed king. They also spit on him and struck him with the staff. Then they led him away for crucifixion.*Matt 27:27-31, Mk 15:17-20, Jn 19:2-3* When the Son came out wearing the crown of thorns and purple robe, the governor repeated to the people that he found no basis for a charge. But the religious leaders shouted again to crucify him because he claimed to be the Father's Son. Their law said he must die. The shouting that the Son was from the Father made the governor even more afraid.*Jn 19:4-8*

The governor questioned the Son yet again, but the Son gave no answer.*Jn 19:9-10* When the governor told the Son that he had the power to crucify him, the Son finally said that the governor's only power was what came from above. The Son also said that the betrayer who had handed him over to the governor was guilty of greater wrong.*Jn 19:10-11* The governor kept trying to set the Son free, but the religious leaders said that if the governor did so, then he would not be Caesar's friend because the Son had claimed to be a ruler opposed to Caesar.*Jn 19:12-13* The governor replied that the Son was their ruler, but the religious leaders said they have no ruler other than Caesar and to crucify the Son. Can you believe it—a religious people rejecting their own Father in favor of an earthly tyrant as their only ruler? That's how desperate were the religious leaders to see the Son killed. The governor finally handed the Son over for execution.*Jn 19:14-16* All that remained was the awful act.

> **The Son beat the enemy. So can you.** The Son used the word to beat the enemy. Know the word so you can, too.*Matt 4:3-11, Lk 4:3-12* The enemy knows the

Son's premier status. So shouldn't you?*Mk 3:11-12, Lk 4:41* The Son saw his Father throw the enemy out of the Father's place.*Lk 10:18* The Son beat the enemy back so that you could step forward.*Jn 12:30-32* The Son made a public spectacle of the enemy. Can't you see it?*Col 2:15* The Son and your enemy have nothing in common.*2Co 6:15* You must choose one side or the other. No playing both sides.*1Co 10:21* And don't let the enemy fool you into turning from the Son.*2Co 11:3* The Son made himself like you so that he could come right back to life after the enemy killed him, to give *you* new life after death.*Heb 2:14* The Father protects you from the enemy.*2Th 3:3* Just let anyone corrupt among you be fully corrupt. That'll teach them to give it up for better things.*1Co 5:4-5* Don't hold things over others. You aid the enemy when you do.*2Co 2:10-11* Do what you see the Son doing. Don't do what the enemy does.*1Jn 3:7-8* The Son's got you. The enemy doesn't.*Ro 8:38-39*

Crucifixion

The religious leaders, government officials, and soldiers killed the Son by the most hideous of means, carrying out a prediction the ancient writings had made hundred of years before humans invented crucifixion. The Son carried his own cross toward the crucifixion place known as the Skull, a stony outcrop looking that way from a distance.*Jn 19:16-17* As the guards led the Son to the crucifixion place, they forced a man from the crowd to carry the Son's cross.*Matt 27:32-33, Mk 15:21, Lk 23:26* The man was Simon from Cyrene, whose sons were Alexander and Rufus.*Mk 15:21* A large number of people followed the sordid procession, including women who mourned and wailed for the Son. The Son finally turned to them, saying to weep for themselves and their children. The Son had prepared himself. The women could not.*Lk 23:27-31* At the crucifixion place, they first offered the Son a sedative drink and then, after he refused, they stripped him and nailed his hands and feet to the cross. The soldiers then cast lots for his clothes as they watched the Son die, fulfilling another of the ancient writings' predictions.

Ask the Father to excuse wrongs. Ask that the Father excuse your wrongs. But you be ready to excuse others.*Matt 6:12* Ask that nothing tempt you.*Matt 6:13* Admit to the Father that you need his excuse, that you've done wrong.*Lk 18:9-13* Humble yourself as you ask. Don't ask based on pride.*Lk 18:14* Ask that the Father excuse others, too.*Jas 5:13-15* Ask that the Father excuse others who rely on the Son.*1Jn 5:16-17* Ask that the Father make others strong enough to avoid

> temptation.*1Th 3:13* Ask that others keep a clean conscience.*Heb 13:18* Ask for protection from wrongdoers.*2Th 3:2* Ask that the Father protect teachers.*Ro 15:31-32* Ask that the Father overcome your challenges.*2Co 1:11* Ask that the Father restore you.*2Co 13:9* Ask that the Father restore your leaders.*Heb 13:19*

A sign on the cross said that the Son was the people's ruler.*Matt 27:34-37, Mk 15:23-26, Jn 19:19-24* The religious leaders protested to the governor not to write that the Son was their ruler but only that he *claimed* to be ruler. But the governor said that he had written what he had written.*Jn 19:21-22* The sign was in three languages so that many people could read it as they passed by.*Jn 19:19-20* The guards also crucified two rebels, one on either side of the Son.*Matt 27:38, Mk 15:27, Lk 23:32-33, Jn 19:18* As the soldiers were doing their awful work, the Son prayed to his Father to forgive them for not knowing what they were doing.*Lk 23:34* The rebels, passersby, and the religious leaders and teachers, though, mocked and insulted the Son for saying he was going to destroy and rebuild the temple when he apparently couldn't even save himself.*Matt 27:39-40, Mk 15:29-32* The people watched the leaders sneer, saying that if the Son was the Father's great Rescuer, then he should go ahead and rescue himself.*Lk 23:35* The soldiers also mocked the Son, saying that if he was the people's ruler, as the sign above him said, then he should save himself.*Lk 23:36-38*

> **Avoid anger.** Your anger with a friend judges you, not your friend. Better stop it, or the Father will judge you, too.*Matt 5:21-22* Control your anger. Anger doesn't make you any better.*Jas 1:20* Hating follows wrongdoing, not doing right.*1Jn 3:12* You either love or hate. Those who hate die, while those who love live forever with the Son.*1Jn 3:14-15* Just get rid of your wanting to harm others. Stop it. Now.*1Pe 2:1* Be especially careful when you're angry. Anger leads to wrongs. Cool off before you go to sleep at night, or you'll be even hotter in the morning.*Eph 4:26* Don't be bitter. Don't rage. Just don't have it in for others.*Eph 4:31* You used to get away with it—all the anger and foul language. You can't now. And that's a *good* thing.*Col 3:7-8* Isn't talking with the Father and honoring him better than anger?*1Ti 2:8* If you love, then it's hard to hate.*1Co 13:5*

When one of the crucified criminals continued to hurl insults at the Son to save himself and them, the other criminal, who had initially also insulted the Son, finally rebuked the first criminal. The second criminal said that they should both fear for their just punishment, but the Son had done nothing wrong.*Lk 23:39-41* That criminal then said to the Son to remember him when returning to his rule. The criminal had a change of heart on the cross, at the last possible moment deciding to join rather than reject the Son. To show you that he forgives everything, right up to your last moment, the Son replied that the criminal would that day be with the Son in his paradise.*Lk 23:42-43* The Son's mother, his mother's sister, and other women who had cared for the Son during his mission work stood near, weeping and mourning as the Son died above them on the cross.*Jn 19:25* When the Son noticed his mother and the student John, he told his mother that John was her son and John that the Son's mother was John's mother. From that moment on, John took the Son's mother under his care.*Jn 19:26-27*

Thus, religious and government rulers killed the glorious Son, the perfect Man who has all the Father's power.*1Co 2:8* To make himself a complete sacrifice, the Son assumed every human characteristic, made himself fully human even to the last human weakness *death,* and not any death but the most-disgraceful possible death. Yet the Son lives by the Father's power.*2Co 13:4* By giving himself to death, even death on a cross, the Son defeated every contrary power and authority. The Son competed on *your* terms, the dirty terms, and still won.*Col 2:15* The Son put up with such pain because he knew he was turning that pain to the greatest joy. He didn't care about the cross's shame because he knew the honor that followed, joining his Father.*Heb 12:2* The Son was putting everything back together, ending every dispute.*Eph 2:15-16* The Father was bringing it all home to him through what his Son did in dying on the cross.*Col 1:20* What earthly rulers did as they always do in their corrupt nature, the Son undid and set right forever, even for those earthly rulers, indeed for all of you.

> **The cross is your victory symbol.** When the liberator Moses lifted a snake on a pole to heal the people from snake bite, he foreshadowed the people nailing the Son to the cross so that the Son would heal everyone to the point of living forever.*Jn 3:14-15* The Son predicted that men would crucify him but that he would then draw everyone to him.*Jn 12:32-33* The Son said that he would spend three days and nights dead, like Jonah spent three days and nights inside a whale.*Matt 12:40* The Father nailed your debt to the cross.*Col 2:14* The cross gave the Son victory over evil, even death.*Col 2:15* Many reject the whole cross thing.*Php 3:18* But for you, the cross crucified everything else but the Son.*Gal 6:14* The Son did it to bring together in him one big peace, ending warring.*Eph 2:15-16* The cross is foolishness to those who will die. That's how the Father does things. He makes worldly wisdom foolish while creating incredible power, even over death, through the cross.*1Co 1:18-19* Don't be foolish, letting others bewitch you into abandoning the cross's message.*Gal 3:1* Those who reject the Father's

gift crucify the Son all over again, disgracing him again.*Heb 6:6* Don't follow those whom no one crucified. Follow the crucified Son.*1Co 1:11-15* When you follow the Son, you crucify the ugly desires that destroy you.*Gal 5:24*

Death

Here's how the Son's earthly life ended, much as it had begun in perfect wonder. While the Son was still alive on the cross, darkness fell for three hours right in mid-day. The sun simply stopped shining, as the Father turned away.*Matt 27:45, Mk 15:33, Lk 23:44-45* The Son cried out in anguish, asking why the Father had turned away, although knowing that the Father must turn from the corruption that the Son had endured for the great rescue plan.*Matt 27:46, Mk 15:34* Bystanders said he was calling an ancient seer, although he was not. The Son was instead talking to his Father.*Matt 27:47, Mk 15:35* Then, knowing that he had finished everything, the Son said that he was thirsty.*Jn 19:28* One nearby put vinegar in a sponge on a staff to offer to the Son as drink.*Matt 27:48, Mk 15:36, Jn 19:29* That one said to leave the Son alone to see if the ancient seer would come take him down from the cross.*Mk 15:36* Others joined in saying to leave the Son alone for the ancient seer to come.*Matt 27:49* After the Son received the drink, he said that he had finished his work. He bowed his head and died.*Jn 19:30* The Son cried out, took his last breath, and was done.*Matt 27:50, Mk 15:37* The Son called out that he had given himself back to his Father.*Lk 23:46*

Fittingly, the moment of the Son's death was cataclysmic. The great curtain that had separated the people from the inner area of the capitol holy city's religious center tore in two. The people suddenly had access to the Father through the Son. The rescue was complete.*Matt 27:51, Mk 15:38, Lk 23:45* The earth shook, rocks split, and tombs broke open. Many saints and seers would walk out of those tombs after the Son came back to life, where the people could see them.*Matt 27:51-53* When the centurion and other guards saw everything happen at the moment of the Son's death, they exclaimed that surely the Son was the great Rescuer, the Father's own Son.*Matt 27:54, Mk 15:39* The centurion added that surely the Son was a perfectly good man.*Lk 23:47* When all the gathered people saw what happened, they cried out in anguish before slinking away.*Lk 23:48* The women who had cared for the Son watched everything from a distance.*Matt 27:55, Mk 15:40-41* The students and others who had followed the Son also watched from a distance.*Lk 23:49*

The religious leaders, though, were still thinking of their ritual duties. They didn't want any bodies on crosses during the next day, their rest day. So the religious leaders asked the governor to order the legs broken and bodies taken down. Breaking the legs ensured that the dying prisoners suffocated to death if they were somehow still alive.*Jn 19:31* Soldiers broke the legs of the two criminals but not the Son, who was plainly already dead.*Jn 19:32-33* Instead, to be sure that the Son was dead, a soldier pierced the Son's side with a spear. Blood and bodily fluids poured out of the Son's side. These things happened to meet the ancient writings' predictions that no one would break the Son's bones and that they would look on the Son whom they pierced.*Jn 19:34, 36-37* The leading student Peter, who had fled at the first sign of trouble, would later courageously proclaim in front of crowds that the religious leaders killed the Son by hanging him on a cross.*Acts 10:39* The Son was dead. He had accomplished his great rescue work.

The Son died to make you faultless. The Father gave his Son's life to pay for everything that you owed the Father.*Ro 2:25-26* The Father had the Son die in your place as you should have died.*Ro 4:25* The Son's love dying for you should convince you to give up your old broken life for him.*2Co 5:14* The Son is your payment and protection.*1Co 5:6-7* You should give up your old mess in the way that the Son gave up everything for you, so that you can live with the Son's life.*Gal 2:20* Don't let anyone make fancy theories out of the simple power of the Son's willing death.*1Co 1:17* Share a cup with others who rely on the Son, to remember his blood, and break bread, too, to remember his broken body.*1Co 10:16,18* The Father uses his Son's death to restore you to him as faultless like the Son.*Col 1:22* The Son's death is your life made spotless, the Father's way of giving you riches you didn't deserve.*Eph 1:7-8* You couldn't afford all that you owe, so the Son used his life to pay, lifting you out of that generational debt.*1Pe 1:18-19* The Son made himself human because you are human, so that by dying as a human dies, he would defeat death.*Heb 2:14* The Son fixed your every violation with his horrible death.*Gal 3:13* So tell this good news not with fancy words but just as simple as it is, showing your awe for it.*1Co 2:1-3* Some want wonders, others philosophy, but you just tell the good news over which the wonder-seekers and philosophers stumble but from which you draw the Father's power.*1Co 1:22-24*

Burial

The Son's body had a proper burial. The Son had a rich follower Joseph of Arimathea who was a prominent member of the ruling religious council. Joseph had objected to the council's trial of the Son. He instead saw the Son for who he was—the great Rescuer and ultimate ruler. That evening, after the Son had died on the cross, Joseph went boldly to the governor asking for the Son's body.*Matt 27:57, Mk 15:42-43, Lk 23:50-52, Jn 19:38* Joseph had kept secret his conviction that the Son was the one. He, too, feared the Jewish leaders. But now that the Son had died, Joseph was ready for bold action.*Jn 19:38* The governor was surprised to hear that the Son had already died. Some prisoners survive longer before suffocating on the cross. So the governor first confirmed with the centurion that the Son was indeed dead. The governor then granted Joseph's request for the Son's body.*Mk 15:44-45*

> **The Son had to die.** The Son had to bleed and die to pay for your blood. How generous the Father was to you!*Eph 1:7-8* The Son's blood was worth more than anything. The Son's death rescued you from the empty life your family handed down to you.*1Pe 1:18-19* The Son returned to the Father once for all and forever by his own blood.*Heb 9:12* The old traditions used animal blood as a sacrifice, burning the animal bodies outside the area.*Heb 13:11* And so the Son died outside the city gate to rescue everyone through his own blood.*Heb 13:12* Go to the Son outside your comfort zone, outside your natural area, bearing the disgrace he bore. You have no enduring city here. Look instead for what's to come.*Heb 13:14* The Son's one sacrifice made perfect forever those whom the Father chooses.*Heb 10:14* Be confident approaching the Father, while relying on the Son. His body, his death, opened for you a new and living way.*Heb 10:19-20* The Son is your way.*1Co 1:30*

Another ruling-council member Nicodemus, who had visited the Son secretly at night, accompanied Joseph to help retrieve, prepare, and entomb the Son's body. They following the religious burial customs, bringing seventy-five pounds of myrhh and aloes with which to do so.*Jn 19:39-40* Joseph took the body, wrapped it in linen strips, and placed it in Joseph's new tomb cut out of the rock in a garden, rolling a huge stone across the tomb's tiny entrance.*Matt 27:58-60, Mk 15:45-46, Lk 23:53, Jn 19:41-42* Two of the women who had cared for the Son sat opposite the tomb, seeing where they laid the body.*Matt 27:61, Mk 15:47, Lk 23:55* Those women went home to prepare spices and perfumes but rested the next day, as religious law and custom required.*Lk 23:56* The next day, the religious leaders went to the governor saying that the Son had predicted that he would come back to life in three days. They asked the governor to secure the tomb against the students stealing the body to perpetrate a resurrection hoax.*Matt 27:62-64* The governor ordered the tomb secured with a seal and guard.*Matt 27:65-66* Everything was in place for the Son's extraordinary victory.

> **The Son paid all that you owe.** The Son dying for you when you were doing nothing for him showed how much he loves you.*Ro 5:6-8* The Son made sure that the Father wouldn't hold anything against you.*Ro 5:9* The Son's dying for you encourages you to live right for him.*1Pe 2:24-25* The Son's dying for you opened your way again to the Father. The Son gave you new life, forever life.*Ro 5:10* You should be glad for what the Son did getting you back on the Father's good side—*very* glad.*Ro 5:11* The Son makes you innocent when you are guilty.*Ro 10:4* The Son is your go-between with the Father. The Father lets the Son do that because the Son earned it with his own death.*1Ti 2:5* Put up with any trouble you face if that trouble is over the good news. It's worth it.*2Ti 1:8* The Son ended the whole death thing. The Son did the impossible, making you immortal.*2Ti 1:10*

9 Restoration

Resurrection

He came right back. The Son lived again right after his death. He had predicted it. The Son said repeatedly that although others would kill him, would cruelly *crucify* him, he would then come right back to life._{Matt 16:21, Matt 17:22-23, Matt 20:17-19} Here's how it happened, this glorious *resurrection*. Two of the women went to the tomb after the rest day. The earth shook, the sky opened, and a celestial being in brilliant white clothing appeared like lightning. He shoved the great stone aside from the tomb's mouth and then sat on the stone, satisfied._{Matt 28:1-3} The stunned guards shook with such fear that they looked as if they had died or turned to stone._{Matt 28:4} The celestial being, though, told the women not to fear. The women thought of looking for the crucified body inside the now-opened tomb. The being said to go ahead and look but that they'd find nothing because the Son had come back to life just as he predicted. They should instead go meet the Son in his old home region. The amazed women ran to tell the students._{Matt 28:5-8} As the women hurried away, excited but still frightened, the Son himself stopped and greeted them. The women didn't know what to do but to fall down to clasp his feet in elated honor._{Matt 28:9} The Son repeated the being's instruction to tell his students to meet him in his old home region by the lake._{Matt 28:10}

The women ran off to tell the Son's students. The stunned guards, though, reported to the religious leaders the extraordinary opening of the tomb. The religious leaders didn't know what to do. So they paid the guards a lot of money to say instead that the students had come and stolen the body while the guards slept. The religious leaders promised to keep the guards out of trouble with the governor._{Matt 28:11-15} The women told the eleven students who had been the Son's closest followers. The students did not believe the women.*Lk 24:9-10* The leading student Peter, though, ran to the tomb. There, he saw the cast-off linen strips that had wrapped the missing body. He couldn't, though, believe what had happened.*Lk 24:12*

> **You can live forever.** Accept that the Father brought the Son right back to life, rather than say he never did.*1Co 15:12* Only those who are dying do not accept the good news.*2Co 4:3* Culture blinds those who reject the Son. They don't see the incredibly good news.*2Co 4:4* Reject the worldly perspective.*2Co 5:16* Accept the good news, confirmed by so many eyewitnesses.*Heb 2:3* The Father told it in advance and then showed so many wonders around it.*Heb 2:4* The ancient writings show not only how the first natural human lived and died but also how the first *supernatural* human *died and lived*.*1Co 15:45* The spiritual supersedes the natural.*1Co 15:46* The Father made the first natural human out of dust but made the first supernatural human out of spirit.*1Co 15:47* You can remain earthly and die if you wish, but why not live forever?*1Co 15:48* Everyone begins earthly, but everyone can take on spiritual form.*1Co 15:49* The mystery is that you will not all die, but the Father will change all of you.*1Co 15:51* Your change will come instantly when the Father decides that time is right to make the dead permanently alive.*1Co 15:52* Your old dead body must take on spiritual form to live forever.*1Co 15:53* When your old dead body takes spiritual form, to live forever, then you, too, like the Son, will have defeated death.*1Co 15:54* Death only hurts when you have no way on your own around it, with your only way to receive the Son's perfect form.*1Co 15:55-56* Thank the Father that he's given you permanent life through his Son.*1Co 15:57*

Another account reports that three of the women who had cared for the Son bought spices and went to the tomb to anoint the body, wondering who would roll the stone away.*Mk 16:1-3, Lk 24:1* But when they got to the tomb, they saw the stone already rolled back.*Mk 16:4, Lk 24:2* When they entered the tomb, the Son's body was not there.*Lk 24:3* Instead, inside the tomb, the fear-stricken women saw a young white-robed man. The man told them not to be afraid because the Son had risen.*Mk 16:5-6* He also told the stunned women to go tell the students and their leader Peter that the Son was going ahead of them into his home region. They all would see the Son there. The women, of course, were shocked senseless, but the man assured them that they must believe his word, just as he had told them.*Mk 16:7* Another account reports that the women saw two men in clothes gleaming like lightning.*Lk 24:4* The women bowed reverently. But the two men asked why they looked for the living among the dead. They told the women that the Son had risen just as he said that he would, on the third day after his death.*Lk 24:5-7* The trembling and bewildered women fled. They didn't even reply to the two gleaming men because they were so afraid.*Mk 16:8*

Another account reports that one of the women who had cared for the Son, Mary from the village of Magdala, went to the tomb early while still dark. There, she saw that the stone no longer covered the entrance.*Jn 20:1* So she ran to tell the leading student Peter and the student John whom Jesus especially loved. Mary told them both that someone had removed the Son's body from the tomb. The body was gone, who knows where, she said.*Jn 20:2* Peter and John ran to the tomb. There, they saw the linen strips and cloth that had wound around the Son's head.*Jn 20:3-8* They grasped only part of what they saw. As they walked away, they still did not see that the Son had just fulfilled the ancient writings predicting that he would come back to life.*Jn 20:8-9*

Mary of Magdala wept outside the tomb. But then she saw two celestial beings in bright white, seated inside the tomb. They asked her why she cried.*Jn 20:11-13* She told them that someone must have taken the Son's body away. But when she turned around to leave, the Son stood right there, although in her amazement at everything she didn't realize who he was.*Jn 20:13-14* The Son asked her why she cried. Mary, thinking the Son was instead the gardener caring for the tomb, asked where he might have put the Son's body.*Jn 20:15* At that moment, though, the Son called her name *Mary*. She then recognized the Son's familiar voice. In her amazement and joy, she cried out *Teacher!*.*Jn 20:16* The Son had come back to life, just as he predicted. All things were now possible. All things were now new. The Son had eliminated human destiny in death, offering life forever, for anyone who would accept it.

The Son lives forever, so you will, too. Because the Father raised the Son from the dead, the Son cannot die again. Death no longer masters him.*Ro 6:9* The Son defeated death, bringing immortality.*2Ti 1:10* Those who die with the Son will live forever with him.*2Ti 2:11* You who remain earthly will return to earthly dust, but you who are of the Son's rule will live forever as the Son lives.*1Co 15:48* Thank the Father for victory through the Son.*1Co 15:57* The Father won't ever change how he gave life back to the Son.*Heb 13:20* You have the Father's unchangeable promise, now that the Son died to pay your penalty, setting you free from your sodden past.*Heb 9:15* The Son did it to make you perfect forever, good for the Father.*Heb 10:14* Just rely on the Son's will and you, too, will live forever.*Jude 20-21* The Father and Son gave you every reason to hope for the best, which is to live forever.*2Th 2:16-17* You will do so if you rely on the Son.*1Ti 1:16* Rather than pointing out your many faults, the Son will honor you forever.*2Ti 2:10* The Son is that generous to give you life forever.*Ro 5:21* The Father gave you the Son's gift of living forever.*Ro 6:21-22* The Son rules with the Father forever.*Heb 1:8* Everything else wears out, but the Father remains.*Heb 1:11* The Father will end everything but remain the same forever.*Heb 1:12* The Father wants everyone looking to his Son so the Son can give them life forever.*Jn 6:40* You will live forever if you rely on the Son.*Jn 6:47* You can eat all you want, and you'll still die, but if you let the Son sustain you, then you will live forever.*Jn 6:50-51* You will live forever letting the Son sustain you because he is real living.*Jn 6:52-55* Letting the Son sustain you gives you his endless life.*Jn 6:56-57* Draw your sustenance from the Son to live forever.*Jn 6:58*

Appearance

The Son didn't just make a fleeting appearance and then disappear again. He instead showed himself to as many as it took to make a solid historical record of it. The Son especially presented himself to his core group of students, proving to them in many ways over a period of forty days that he was fully alive. As he did so, he kept talking about the place of his Father's unquestioned rule.*Acts 1:3* For example, the same day as the women discovered the empty tomb, two students were walking away disconsolately to a village about seven miles from the capitol holy city. As they walked, they talked about everything that had just happened leading to the Son's death. The Son came up and walked along with them, even though they didn't recognize him.*Lk 24:13-16* The students explained to the Son what had happened including the empty tomb's discovery.*Lk 24:17-24* The Son told them how foolish and slow they were. He explained again everything that the ancient writings had predicted about him, including his death and coming back to life again.*Lk 24:25-27* As they approached the village, the Son planned to continue on, but the two students urged him strongly to stay with them. So the Son joined them for a meal. When the Son broke the bread for the meal, the students suddenly recognized him, and, job finished, he disappeared from their sight.*Lk 24:28-31*

Tell others your good news. The Father promised you life forever when you told others that you rely on the Son.*1Ti 6:12* Just keep saying so without letting others make you feel bad about it.*2Ti 1:8* The good and generous way you act leads others to celebrate that you rely on the Son.*2Co 9:13* Your willingness to accept the Son puts you right with the Father, and then your willingness to say so rescues you.*Ro 10:10-11* Just keep relying on the Son to offer the Father his due.*Heb 13:15* Hold tight to the Son because you can trust the Father.*Heb 10:23* The Father gave you his Spirit who helps you rely on and speak about the Son as rescuer.*1Jn 4:13-14* Celebrate when others speak about relying on the Son.*3Jn 3-4* Keep it simple: know only that the Son died to rescue you. Don't get fancy with the truth.*1Co 2:1-3* Be bold about your rescue.*2Co 3:12* Talk it up.*2Co 4:13* The Father will give you more than you think when you do—not just a bed but a city.*Heb 11:16* Especially talk up relying on the Son when you meet those who don't.*Php 1:20*

The two students hurried back to the capitol holy city to tell the other students that the Son had indeed come back to life.*Lk 24:33-35* While they were still excitedly telling the other students, though, the Son appeared right there, standing among them. His appearance so shocked the frightened students that the Son had to reassure them that peace was with them.*Lk 24:36, Jn 20:19* The students had all been together behind locked doors, hiding from the religious officials, when the Son had just appeared straight through the locked doors.*Jn 20:19* The terrified students couldn't believe that it was him. So the Son told the students to look at his hands and feet, pierced from the crucifixion. When they still thought that he was some apparition, a figment of their overactive imagination, the Son told them to touch him to confirm that he was real.*Lk 24:37-40* When the Son showed them the wounds in his hands and side, the students were ecstatic that he was alive and with them.*Jn 20:20* The students asked the Son if he was going at that moment to put everything under his Father's rule, but the Son said the time was secret and up to his Father.*Acts 1:6-7* The Son had told the religious leaders who said no one could live again that his Father isn't interested in leading a bunch of dead people but instead would indeed make dead persons like celestial beings.*Matt 22:29-32*

Your new body will differ. Don't worry foolishly about how the Father brings you back to life.*1Co 15:35-36* It works for plants, and so why not humans? The Son explained that to produce seeds, a plant must first die.*Jn 12:24* The plant dies, sowing seed that comes to life.*1Co 15:36* To sow is not to plant what will be but instead to plant only the seed of what will be.*1Co 15:37* The Father gives the seed a form as he determines, giving each seed its own form.*1Co 15:38* It's like that, although not exactly like that. Forms differ. People have one kind of

> flesh, animals another, birds another, and fish another.*1Co 15:39* Celestial bodies differ from earthly bodies.*1Co 15:40* The sun has one form, the moon another, and the stars another, while star differs from star in splendor.*1Co 15:41* Coming back to life is the same way. Your body dies but returns unable to die.*1Co 15:42* The Father turns your dead body into special form. It dies powerless but returns powerful.*1Co 15:43* Your body goes from natural to spiritual, just as you sense your spirit now.*1Co 15:44* The Son told the religious leaders that when you're with the Father, you won't worry about earthly things like to whom you were once married. You'll be like a celestial being.*Matt 22:23-30, Lk 20:27-36*

To remove all doubt about what the students were seeing, the Son asked for something to eat and then took and ate the broiled fish that they gave him. As he did so, he reminded them that he had said that he would do everything that the ancient writings had predicted about him.*Lk 24:41-44* The Son taught them again so that they knew what the ancient writings meant. He explained again how he had to die that horrible death, to come back to life after three days. He repeated that the whole point was so that they could tell others the good news that if they turned to the Son, everything was forgiven, everything was new, a clean slate and fresh start for everyone, even the worst among them.*Lk 24:45-47* The Son said that the students had now seen it firsthand, with their own eyes, so that they could trust it.*Lk 24:48* The Son repeated that he wanted them to be confident and assured, not afraid and doubting, when he sent them on their way with this incredibly good news.*Jn 20:21* The Son told them that he was going send them what his Father had promised. They were to stay in the capitol holy city until power came down on them.*Lk 24:49* The Son then did an amazing thing: he breathed on them. As he did so, he told them to receive the Father's Spirit. The Son had given them everything, the power and authority of Father and Son.*Jn 20:22* The Son added that they could now decide whether others should get the fresh start and good news.*Jn 20:23*

> **You can have the Son's immortality.** The Father's power that gave the Son life again is the same power that gives you new life.*Ro 6:3-4* The Father does the same for you that he did for his Son, which was the point, to rescue you from your dead condition.*Col 2:13* The Father gave you new life when he gave his Son new life.*Col 3:1* You need only die relying on the Father like the Son did to certainly come back to life like he did.*Ro 6:5* When you die with the Son, you live with the Son.*Ro 6:8* When you rely on the Son, your old body dies, but the Spirit gives you the Son's new life.*Ro 8:10* You only need the same Spirit of the Father

> who brought the Son back to life. Just let the Father's Spirit live in you, and you'll come right back to life, too.*Ro 8:11* Don't rely on the old rules. Rely instead on the Son's new life. Then you'll please the Father.*Ro 7:4* When the Son brought his dead friend back to life and said to remove the grave clothes to let him go, the Son was talking about you, too. Give up your dead attitude to embrace immortal life.*Jn 11:43-44*

The student Thomas, who was always questioning things, was not with the other students when the Son first appeared. When Thomas joined them, he did not believe the others when they told him that they had seen the Son. Thomas said that he would not believe unless he could put his fingers where the nails were and his hands in the Son's pierced side. Little did Thomas know that he would soon do exactly that.*Jn 20:24-25* A week later, the Son appeared again to the students, again through locked doors, again telling them not to be afraid that he had come back.*Jn 20:26* The Son told Thomas to put his fingers in the wounds in the Son's hands and side. Thomas did so, crying out that the Son was indeed everything. The Son replied that Thomas had believed because he saw but those who believe without seeing would be even better.*Jn 20:27-29* The Son told the students that they would receive the Father's Spirit so that they would have power to tell everyone, everywhere, that they had seen the dead Son back alive.*Acts 1:8*

> **Accept the good news. It's true.** Asking the Father for things doesn't work when you don't even believe him.*Jas 1:6* Those who doubt don't get anything from the Father. *Jas 1:7* Doubters are unstable in everything.*Jas 1:8* The Father has made himself obvious.*Ro 1:19* Everyone can see the Father's qualities from what he made. You have no excuse.*Ro 1:20* Don't be foolish. Use your mind. You know the Father. So give him his due.*Ro 1:21* Those who reject the good news are fools.*Ro 1:22* Don't condemn yourself with doubts.*Ro 14:23* Help those who doubt. Snatch them from the fire.*Jude 22* Don't require the Son to personally appear to you. He already appeared to hundreds of others. You believe many others whom you'll never meet.*Jn 20:24-25* Those who rely on the Son without his personal appearance have special favor.*Jn 20:27-29*

Later, the Son appeared to the students yet again by the lake in his home region, as he had said that he would. The students had fished all night without catching anything, wasting their time plying their old trade.*Jn 21:1-3* They didn't recognize him at first, but the Son stood on the shore watching them come in from their fruitless night. He called to them to throw their net on the boat's right side. Still not recognizing the

Son, the bemused students did as he said. And when they pulled in the net, they had caught so many fish that they couldn't get the net into the boat.*Jn 21:4-6* Only then did the student John realize who had called to them. John turned to the leading student Peter, telling him that the figure on the beach was the Son. Peter was so excited that he jumped in the water fully clad to make for shore.*Jn 21:7* When the other students landed the boat with the net full of fish, the Son already had a fire with fish and bread cooking for them on the beach. The Son invited them to join him to eat.*Jn 21:9-14* The Son came back to life, real, active, and capable, not in imagination. Those who deny it are imagining things as they are not.

> **Death has you unless you rely on the Son.** You'll die if you don't rely on the Son. That's it. Over and done with.*Jn 8:21* You must admit that the Son came from the Father, or you're not going anywhere but back to dust.*Jn 8:24* Your body without the Spirit is no good for anything but desires that lead to death.*Ro 7:5* The rules show that you can't make yourself perfect on your own. No one but the Son keeps all the rules.*Ro 7:8-9* Rules are fine, but they just show that you're a rule-breaker, headed the wrong way.*Ro 7:13* You think you can be good enough to avoid death? No way. You can't even follow the rules.*Ro 7:10-11* Better to let the rules show you that you need the Father's help. Let the rules point you to the Father's solution.*Gal 2:19* Rules can't help you once you're dead.*Ro 7:1* Marry another when your spouse dies. See? Rules don't apply to the dead.*Ro 7:2-3* The Son did the same for you: the rules don't kill you anymore when you rely on the Son's death. He came right back to life and brought you, dead in your rule-breaking, with him.*Ro 7:4* So stop living for your body and the old rules. Start living for the Spirit.*Ro 7:6* Wrongdoers know that they're doomed. They just do wrong anyway.*Ro 1:32* Wrongdoers *earn* their death.*Ro 6:21-22* Live for the body, you die. Live for the Spirit, you live. Pretty simple. Try it.*Ro 8:12-13* Pursue spiritual life. Let those who care nothing for the spirit die and keep burying their dead.*Matt 8:21-22, Lk 9:59-60* You can't cheat death. You can't fool the Spirit. Accept and tell the truth straight up, or you, too, may die.*Acts 5:1-6* Don't oppose those who share the good news. It's over for you if you do.*Acts 12:19* Don't think that you're god. You're not. That thinking gets you nothing but death.*Acts 12:19-23*

When the students had finished eating with the restored Son, the Son asked Peter if he loved the Son more than others, to which Peter replied that the Son knew that he loved him.*Jn 21:15* The Son told Peter to care for his weak little students.*Jn 21:15* The Son then repeated his question to Peter whether Peter loved him, to which Peter again replied that the Son knew that Peter loved him.*Jn 21:16* Again, the Son told Peter to care for his students.*Jn 21:16* The Son then repeated his question to Peter a third time, asking whether Peter loved him, hurting Peter, who answered that the Son knew that he loved him.*Jn 21:17* The Son said again to care for his students. The Son added that when Peter was old, others would stretch out his hands and lead him where he would not want to go, indicating the death on the cross that Peter would suffer for the Son.*Jn 21:17-19* The Son then said to follow him.*Jn 21:19* When Peter asked what about John, who was walking behind, the Son said that if John remained until the Son returned, his doing so made no difference to Peter.*Jn 21:20-22*

> ***The Son's death restores everything.*** When the Son died, the Father received back everything that he made.*Col 1:20* The Son endured his ignominious death knowing that he'd have the reward of rejoining his Father.*Heb 12:2* The Son rejoined his Father permanently, not through something else's sacrifice but his own sacrifice.*Heb 9:12* When the Father gave his own Son for you, he showered you with everything.*Ro 8:32* Your corrupt old self died with the Son's death, freeing you from its slavery.*Ro 6:6-7* You died, and you now live in the Son.*Col 3:3* The Son died for everything, so don't go on living for yourself but for him. After all, he lived again.*2Co 5:15* The Son died as a prisoner to make you free.*Heb 13:12* Don't give a care to the world, but instead live and die free like the Son, for your permanent life to come.*Heb 13:14* By dying, the perfect Son made you perfect, too.*Heb 10:14* Go straight to the Father as the Son did when he died for you.*Heb 10:19-20* You have no reason to fear death.*Heb 2:15* You need only deny yourself and follow him where he went.*Matt 16:24, Mk 8:34, Lk 9:23* It won't work trying to save your own life. Instead, lose your life for the Son, and then you'll find permanent life.*Matt 16:25, Mk 8:35, Lk 9:24* Love your old life, and you'll lose your new life. Hate your old life, and you'll gain permanent new life.*Jn 12:25* The whole world gains you nothing. Only the Son can win you your soul.*Matt 16:26, Mk 8:36-37, Lk 9:25*

Witnesses

After coming back to life, the Son appeared to hundreds of others. The Son first appeared several times to the leading student Peter and the other core group of students, even eating with them. But the Son also appeared to more than five hundred others at the same time. And reliable authors wrote these things down right after they happened. Indeed, most of the hundreds of eyewitnesses were still living and talking about it at the time author witnesses wrote the earliest reliable records.*1Co 15:5-6* The

Son also appeared to his brother James. The last one to whom the Son appeared was the great student Paul.*1Co 15:7-8* Because of the Son's many appearances, the leading student Peter was able to say to a great crowd in the capitol holy city at the next religious festival that they were *all* witnesses to the Father bringing the Son back to life—and the great crowd agreed.*Acts 2:32* Peter proclaimed openly that the Father brought the Son right back to life after three days so that these many special witnesses would see.*Acts 10:40-41* Peter and the core group of students had plenty of candidates among whom to choose, when they decided to replace the dead betrayer Judas, with another witness to the Son coming back to life.*Acts 1:21-22*

The Son indeed rose on the third day after burial, as the ancient writings say.*1Co 15:3* The Father raised the Son from dead.*Heb 13:20* The Father's Spirit has that power to give life back to dead persons.*Ro 8:11* The Father simply did it, bringing the Son back from dead.*Gal 1:1, Ro 4:22-24, Col 2:22* The Father did it to make you right with him.*Ro 4:25* The Father gave the Son life again to lead you.*Ro 1:4* The Father gave the Son life again to give you new life, too.*1Pe 1:3* Your hope in the Father is from his giving the Son life again.*1Pe 1:21* The Son's new life saves you from death because the Son has the Father's approval and power.*1Pe 3:21-22* Better believe it: the Father exerted tremendous strength when giving the dead Son new life.*Eph 1:19-21* You had better rely on the Father's Son because the Father literally brought him back from the dead.*1Th 1:10* The Son died and came back to life so that he would control both the living and dead.*Ro 14:9* When by his power the Father gave new life to the dead Son, the Father showed that he will raise you, too, from dead.*1Co 6:14* The Father only made the Son the first whom he will give new life after death.*1Co 15:20* The Father who gave new life to the dead Son will also give you new life so that he may have you as his gift.*2Co 4:14*

> **The Son beat death, offering immortality.** If he had not come right back to life, then the Son would still be in the grave.*1Co 15:13* And if the Son is still dead, then talking about him and relying on him are useless. You'd also be lying about the Father.*1Co 15:14-15* If no one can come back to life, then the Son hasn't done so, and you may as well forget it. You remain broken, and those already dead are gone forever.*1Co 15:16-18* If thinking about the Son is good to you only for this life, then pity on you—but it's not so.*1Co 15:19* The Father instead promptly gave the Son new life after he died, with many more to follow.*1Co 15:20* Yes, the Father gives life back to the dead.*Ro 4:17* Because the

Father gave the Son life again when the Son was dead, the Son will never die again. Death is over for him._Ro 6:9_ The Son died once, and that was it. Now, he lives for the Father._Ro 6:10_ The Son died and lived again for you so that you can live with him._1Th 3:10_ Those who die with the Son then get to live with him._2Ti 2:11_ The Son died and came right back to life so that he ruled over those dead and those living._Ro 14:9_ The great rescuer Son destroyed death, making immortaility possible._2Ti 1:10_ The Father doesn't want to rule over a bunch of dead people. The Father rules over the living._Mk 12:26-27, Lk 20:37-40_ Both Father and Son now have this power to give life right back to the dead._Jn 5:21_ The Son came not to condemn the world but to rescue it._Jn 12:47_

Ascension

The Son had repeatedly told his students that he was going to ascend again to rejoin his Father._Jn 6:60-62_ The Son told them plainly that he was going to the Father._Jn 14:12_ The Son had repeated that he was going to the Father so that when it happened, his students would believe what they saw rather than treat it as an apparition._Jn 14:28-29_ The Son also explained that he was returning to the Father for their good. Although they wanted him to stay, they were better off with him going._Jn 16:5-7_ And so, after having made many appearances to hundreds of witnesses, the Son indeed returned to his Father. He did so before his core students. Here's how it happened. When Mary from the village of Magdala met the alive-again Son outside the tomb, she had wanted to clasp his feet in reverent honor. Yet the Son told her not to hold onto him. He needed instead to return to his Father and their Father. She must instead go tell the students that the Son was alive again and to meet him in his home region, as she did._Jn 20:17-18_ After the Son made other appearances to the students and others in the capitol holy city, the students went to the mountain in the Son's home region. There, they met and honored the Son again._Matt 28:16-17_

You have the same power now. The Father's power for you now is the same as that which he showed when he brought the Son back to life. The Father and Son rule everything, not only now but in the future._Eph 1:19-21_ The Father has not yet brought back to life everyone who is dying or has died._2Ti 2:18_ You have a way yet to go to get this new life that comes with following the Son. Just keep on pressing toward that incomparable goal that the Son gave you._Php 3:12-13_ Your rescuer the Son is going to use his utter power to turn your dead body into celestial form like his form._Php 3:20-21_ You need only wait expectantly for the Son to do so, just like his Father did for him.*1Th 1:10* The Father used his power to give the Son life again after the Son had died. The Father will do the same for you.*1Co 6:14* The Father who gave new life to the Son will do the same for you so that he can present you to himself.*2Co 4:14* So for you, to live is to follow the Son but to die is to gain everything.*Php 1:20-21* That truth makes hard whether to live or die because living means helping others live while dying means to be with the Son, which everyone knows is far better.*Php 1:22-23*

The Son told them that his Father had given him authority over everything, to make everything new. The students should go teach everyone, everywhere, about the Son's good news. They should also immerse everyone into the way of the Father, Son, and Spirit. They should teach others to do as the Son said. And they should know that the Son would be with them as long as they did so.*Matt 28:18-20* The Son led his core group of students out, lifted his hands, and told them that he would be caring for them. Then he rose upward until they could no longer see him. The students returned to the capitol holy city unable to contain themselves with excitement.*Lk 24:50-53* The Father took up the Son right before their very eyes, hiding him in a cloud as he did so.*Acts 1:9* When the Son rejoined the Father, many people were amazed, so much that they decided to rely on the Son, which was great for them.*Eph 4:8* The Son rejoining the Father was no small thing. It was instead the biggest thing that ever happened, especially in that the Son had been here on earth.*Eph 4:9-10* The Son's rejoining the Father was spectacular.*1Ti 3:16* The students kept looking intently up until two men dressed in white suddenly stood beside them. The men asked why the students looked up when the Son would come back in the same way that they saw him leave.*Acts 1:10-11*

The Son living again makes everything matter. The Son said to be glad that he was going to the Father because the Father is greater than the Son.*Jn 14:28* The Father let men kill the Son to pay your debt and then gave him life again so that you could live, too.*Ro 4:25* Accept the power that brought the Son right back to life. It's yours. Act like the Son as he died so that you can live forever with him.*Php 3:10-11* Thank the Father for being willing to take you back with the Son's coming back to him.*1Pe 1:3* The Son lets you know and rely on the Father for giving the Son life again, honoring him.*1Pe 1:21* The Son coming back to life rescued you because the Son is now in complete charge.*1Pe 3:21-22* So don't live and die for yourself but instead live and die for the Son. You belong to him either way.*Ro 14:7-8* It makes sense that because death was a human condition, a human would have to overcome it.*1Co 15:21* Humans all died until the Son came so all could live.*1Co 15:22* Nothing matters without the Son coming back to life.*1Co 15:29* If the Son hadn't come right back to life, then you might as well just live easy.*1Co 15:30* If the Son hadn't come right back to life, then you might as well quit talking about him and instead just eat and drink until you die.*1Co 15:32* Some believe in nothing, while others believe in these authentic things, these true things.*Acts 23:8*

Alighting

Remember the immersion in both water and spirit? Not just coming clean but also having new life from the Father's own Spirit? After the Son came back to life and returned to the Father, Father and Son sent the Spirit, just as promised. Here's how it happened. The Son's students were all together in one place at the time of a religious festival, waiting for the Spirit, just as the Son had told them to do. From above they heard a great sound like a tornado, filling the whole building where they sat.*Acts 2:1-2* Then, extraordinarily, what looked like tongues of fire descended and separated, alighting right down on each of them. They weren't burned, though. Instead, the Spirit filled each of them so that they began speaking in other languages.*Acts 2:3-4* A bewildered crowd gathered from among the many foreigners from different nations who were then visiting the capitol holy city. They couldn't believe that they each heard the students speaking in their own foreign language.*Acts 2:5-6* That simple local students could tell of the Father's wonders in so many languages utterly amazed them. They wondered what it all meant, although some made fun that the students were just drunk.*Acts 2:7-13*

Indulge and die. Pursue the Spirit and live. You once indulged your appetites, preparing to die. But now you have the Spirit's new way.*Ro 7:6* Those who live to indulge think only of their appetites. Those who live for the Spirit think instead of what the Spirit desires.*Ro 8:5* Flee the corrupting desires of youth.*2Ti 2:22* Do not get drunk. It only makes you stupidly corrupt.*Eph 5:18* Appetites kill the mind, while the Spirit gives the mind life and peace.*Ro 8:6* Do as the Spirit says. Don't do whatever you want to satisfy your appetites.*Gal 5:16-17* Just cut it out, that trying to satisfy every craving. You'll die if you try.*Ro 8:12-13* Natural instincts lead to corrupting appetites.*Jude 17-18* Indulging in secret doesn't help.*Eph 5:11-12* Don't cozy up to indulgence. Stay as far away from it as you can. It'll kill you.*Jude 23*

The leading student Peter stood up with the other students, though, explaining that they were not drunk—at only nine in the morning! Instead, the event was fulfilling a prediction of the ancient writings that the Father would give his Spirit to all people to rescue everyone who relied on the Son.*Acts 2:14-21* Peter explained that the Father had let the Son show them wonders, to get them to accept the Son. But instead, they had killed the Son in gruesome manner. Yet the Father had promptly brought the Son back to life. Death had no control over the Son, just as the ancient writings had predicted.*Acts 2:22-31* Peter added that all those present had seen the Father bring the Son back to life. So they all knew that the Son had the power to send them the Spirit that they had just heard and seen descend.*Acts 2:32-33* Peter's telling them that they had killed the Father's own Son cut them to the quick. Heartbroken, they asked what they could possibly now do. Peter reassured them that they need only turn around now to rely on the Son. They should immerse themselves in the Son so that the Son could rescue them, too. Then, they, too, would have the Spirit's help.*Acts 2:36-38* Peter's warning worked. The students were able to immerse thousands that same day, and many more followed day by day.*Acts 2:39-41, 47*

> **The Spirit cleans you up.** The Spirit cleans up your act, rescuing you.*2Th 2:13* The Spirit cleans up not just anyone but those who listen to the good news.*Ro 15:16* The Spirit scrubbed you clean until you were someone the Father could accept.*1Co 6:11* Treat yourself like the Spirit's special container—because you are.*1Co 6:19* Better that the Spirit rescue you than the law condemn you.*2Co 3:8-9* The Spirit says to listen to his voice rather than go your own dead way.*Heb 3:7-8* The Spirit says that doing the right thing is now on your mind rather than out of the way. The Spirit doesn't even remember how awful you once were.*Heb 10:16* Look, how the Spirit works is mysterious, but the Son showed that it works—spectacularly. Good enough for you?*1Ti 3:16* Get your act together. You've now finally got the Spirit to do it.*2Co 6:6-7* Getting there, truly *arriving*, isn't about where you can eat out whenever you want to. You know you've arrived when you're at peace and happy about doing the good stuff the Spirit shows you.*Ro 14:17* The Spirit, or bust. That's it. You have no other way.*Mk 3:29*

Empowering

The Spirit did not just alight once on the students and then leave them to their challenges. The Spirit instead continued to work through them, giving them confidence that they had never before had. For example, the Spirit filled Peter when the religious leaders seized and jailed him for questioning. Rather than rejecting the Son as he had done before, Peter repeated to their face that they had gruesomely killed the Father's own Son. He also told them that the Father had promptly brought the Son back to life to rescue *everyone*—courageous truths and remarkable affronts spoken straight to the religious leaders.*Acts 4:8-12* For another example, when the religious leaders jailed, threatened, and released both Peter and another leading student John, Peter and John simply rejoined the other students asking that the Father help them speak with *even greater* boldness. And what happened? The Father's power shook the place as the Spirit filled them.*Acts 4:22-31* The students devoted themselves to their common work.*Acts 2:42* They stayed together, sharing everything they had.*Acts 2:44* They continued to meet and ate together happily, honoring the Father while enjoying popularity.*Acts 2:46-47*

> ***Forego food to focus on the Father.*** Forego food not for others' attention but to focus on the Father.*Matt 6:16* Look fresh as if eating, so that only your Father notices you're not eating and he rewards you.*Matt 6:17-18* The Son's students forego eating when the Son is not with them.*Matt 9:14-16, Mk 2:18-19, Lk 5:33-34* Foregoing eating is hard. Don't make it too hard.*Matt 9:16-17, Lk 5:36-39* Don't forego food to justify yourself.*Lk 18:9-14* Teachers and seers forego food to prepare for further work.*Acts 13:1-3* Forego food to commit leaders to the Father's work.*Acts 14:23*

The Spirit kept the students courageous to the end. Peter and the other students marched right up to the ruling religious body to tell its members that the Father gives his Spirit to those who obey him.*Acts 5:32* For yet another example, the Spirit filled another student Stephen, who not only performed great wonders but also spoke with incontrovertible wisdom.*Acts 6:8-10* Another student Philip told everyone in another region about the Son's rescue work, causing many to accept immersion. Peter and John visited the same region, asking the Father to give them the Spirit, too, and the Father promptly did so as soon as Peter and John touched them.*Acts 8:14-17* Peter castigated one, though, who offered to pay money for the Spirit.*Acts 8:18-24* The Spirit continued to descend on people all over the region. When Peter told the good news of the Son's rescue to a Roman military leader and other outsiders with him, the Spirit descended on all of them. Peter's close acquaintances couldn't believe that the Spirit would accept outsiders, but the Spirit clearly did.*Acts 10:36-48*

Spiritspeak

> ***The Spirit makes you wise, not just smart.*** The Spirit shows you what's real, true, full of meaning. He doesn't say whatever he thinks but what the Father says and plans.*Jn 16:13* The Son taught his students to rely on the Spirit.*Acts 1:2* The Spirit helps you help others to do as the Father says.*Ro 15:18-19* Forget your own wisdom. The Spirit is the wise one. Rely on reality, not your made-up stuff.*1Co 2:13* You need the Spirit to accept the Father's way. Otherwise, the Father's way looks foolish. It isn't.*1Co 2:14* The Spirit helps you see as the Son sees. Then, no one can tell you what to do. Only the Father and his Spirit know.*1Co 2:15-16* Ask the Father for the Spirit to make you smart *and* wise.*Col 1:9* The Spirit will tell you: don't stop relying on the Son. He's all you've got.*1Ti 4:1* Do it the Spirit's way. Stop making rules out of it.*Ro 7:6* The Spirit tells you what's going on where it counts, in the Father's place.*1Pe 1:12* The good news? It's more than news. You get the Spirit with it. And the Spirit will change you forever, for the better.*1Th 1:5* People can read you, see you've got something special from the Son, because they pick up the Spirit from you. You're *alive*, not cold, hard stone.*2Co 3:3*

One event, though, was a special turning point. One religious leader Paul had pursued those who rely on the Son, with the high official's letters to the religious centers to help Paul take the Son's followers prisoner. But a light flashed, Paul fell blind, and the Son's voice asked Paul why Paul opposed him.*Acts 9:1-5* The Son sent Paul into a major city, led by the speechless men who had accompanied Paul. For three days, Paul could not see.*Acts 9:6-9* In the city, the Son in a vision called a follower to visit Paul to restore Paul's sight.*Acts 9:10-14* The Son said that he had chosen Paul to share the good news widely.*Acts 9:15-16* The follower went to Paul, placed his hands on him, and told him that the Son had sent him so that Paul could see again and receive the Spirit.*Acts 9:17* Paul could then indeed see again and got up for immersion, to rely on the Son.*Acts 9:18-19* Paul began sharing the good news, astonishing all while growing more and more powerful.*Acts 9:20-22* Paul shared the good news fearlessly.*Acts 9:27-28*

Others whom persecution had scattered began to speak in other regions about the good news. A great number turned to the Son.*Acts 11:19-21* Paul and another, full of the Spirit and relying on the Son taught great numbers of people who then trusted the Son.*Acts 11:22-26* Paul turned farther afield when religious insiders rejected him. Many outsiders relied on the Son because of Paul.*Acts 13:46-48* The Spirit gave Paul and another powers like Peter and John showed, with which to share the good news.*Acts 13:2-4* When Paul found some who relied on the Son in another region, but who hadn't heard of the Spirit's descent, Paul immersed them in the Son. Then, when he touched them, the Spirit descended on them so hard that they started speaking in foreign languages, predicting things.*Acts 19:1-7* The Spirit made Paul go back to the capitol holy city, warning him that he faced prison and hardships, but Paul obeyed.*Acts 20:22* Some urged Paul not to go, one predicting correctly that religious officials there would hand Paul over to the Romans for prosecution.*Acts 21:4* Yet those with the Spirit had such confidence and courage that they were ready to do anything that the Spirit directed.

> **The Spirit brings gifts.** The Spirit gives different persons different gifts.*1Co 12:4* The Spirit's gifts, though, work for the common good.*1Co 12:7* The Spirit gives one wisdom, another knowledge, another faith, another the ability to heal, and to others miracle power, predicting things, distinguishing good from bad, figuring out what others are trying to say, or applying what they're saying—all great gifts!*1Co 12:8-10* The Spirit decides what you each get, and it's all good.*1Co 12:11* The Spirit knows what you need, and he asks the Father to supply it before you even think of it, as slow as you are.*Ro 8:26* Here's who the Spirit is: the Spirit brings you love, joy, peace, patience, kindness, goodness, faithfulness, gentleness, and self-control. These things are all so good that none have any limit.*Gal 5:22-23* The Spirit keeps you alive, truly *alive*.*Gal 5:25* You are weak, quite weak. But the Spirit knows it and fixes it, making you strong, loving, and self-controlled, just what you need to be.*2Ti 1:7* Funny, strange, but the Spirit actually lives in you, showing you what to believe.*2Ti 1:13-14* Your hope should overflow. You have the Spirit's power!*Ro 15:13* Let the Spirit run free, truly free.*1Th 5:19* Let the Spirit fill you up until you sing to one another.*Eph 5:18-19* See, love is from the Spirit.*Col 1:8* The Spirit helps you move freely, here and there, like the wind.*Jn 3:8*

The students did amazing things with the Son's power. When a man lame from birth begged Peter and John for money, Peter instantly healed the man's legs so that he could walk and jump.*Acts 3:1-10* The students did many wonders among the people. More and more believed. They brought their sick into the streets so that Peter's shadow would fall on them and heal them. Crowds brought the sick and mentally ill, and all enjoyed healing.*Acts 5:12-16* Philip taught of the Son in a different region, where many paralyzed and lame enjoyed healing.*Acts 8:5-8* Peter met a paralyzed and bedridden man whom he told to get up and roll up his mat, which the man promptly did. Many accepted the Son's rescue because of the healing.*Acts 9:32-35* Paul looked straight at a man lame from birth and, seeing his confidence in healing, told him to stand on his feet, at which the man jumped up to walk.*Acts 14:8-9* The Father did extraordinary things through Paul, so that handkerchiefs and aprons that touched him cured the sick.*Acts 19:11-12* Paul healed the sick father of a chief official, after speaking to the Father. Paul also cured the rest of the sick on the island when they came to him.*Acts 28:7-9*

Persecution

The Son's student John later had a vision of how the Son's good news would spread through the body of ones whom the Son called out, that body that the Son called his *church*. Yes, the good news would begin with an oppressed chosen people.*Rev 12:1-3* The great oppressor would indeed wait to destroy the Son as soon as he had come, and to destroy everyone who heard the good news and decided to rely on the Son.*Rev 12:4* But just as happened, the Father would protect the Son when he had come, until the Son could complete his earthly mission and return to the Father. The Son's students who remained would remain oppressed but in their flight to safe places spread across the earth.*Rev 12:5-6* The Father would settle the outcome. The great oppressor would fight against the Son's people only for a time on earth.*Rev 12:7-9* The Father's power and rule would ultimately rescue everyone who relied on the Son, defeating permanently the great oppressor, through the Son's great sacrifice.*Rev 12:10-11* The great oppressor knows of his ultimate defeat and so fills the earth with his fury.*Rev 12:12* The oppressor pursues the members of the church who continue to rely on the Son, while all await the Son's return and the Father's final victory.*Rev 12:13-17*

The Son predicted that people would hate and persecute his students, who would flee from town to town.*Matt 10:22-23* Persecutors indeed handed over the Son's students to be killed.*Matt 24:9* But don't worry what to say or how to say it when persecution comes. The Father's Spirit will speak through you. And the Father will rescue you.*Matt 10:19-20, Mk 13:11, Lk 12:11-12* Religious leaders seized, jailed, and questioned the Son's students Peter and John.*Acts 4:1-21* Then, the religious leaders jailed the students again, but the Father's messenger freed them to stand in the religious center's courtyards telling the people the good news.*Acts 5:17-20* Officers brought the students in again for orders not to teach in the Son's name, but the students refused. The religious leaders nearly put them to death but flogged them instead.*Acts 5:25-40* The religious leaders conspired to kill the converted student Paul, too, but he barely escaped.*Acts 9:23-25* When Paul debated with other traditionalists, they tried to kill him.*Acts 9:29* The local governor arrested Peter and put him in prison, but with the church asking the Father to release him, the Father's messenger rescued him.*Acts 12:3-17*

> **Don't lead a cursed life.** Shame on anyone who does not love the Father.*1Co 16:22* The Father curses those who distort the good news.*Gal 1:8* Stick with the good news that you know. Don't suffer the Father's curse for distorting it.*Gal 1:9* Rule-keeping doesn't get you to the Father's place. Rules ultimately only curse because you can't satisfy every rule.*Gal 3:10* The Son lifted the rule's curse. His murder cursed the Son to lift your curse.*Gal 3:13* The Father lets those who reject him go crazy, corrupt and cursed.*Ro 1:28-29* Weep for the cursed who reject the Son, especially those close to you.*Ro 9:2-5* Those who do nothing for others may suffer a curse that they not even live.*Matt 21:18-19*

Wherever the students went, they faced persecution. A crowd in another region stoned Paul, dragging him outside the city thinking he was dead. But Paul got up and returned to the city before leaving the next day.*Acts 14:19-20* When Paul rebuked a future-predicting spirit out of a female slave, her owners, realizing that they had lost their way of making money with the slave, had Paul and Silas severely flogged and thrown into prison.*Acts 16:19-24* Traditionalists in another region opposed Paul, became abusive toward him, and made a united attack on him, bringing him before the proconsul, who drove them off because it had to do with their own law.*Acts 18:12-17* Traditionalists in another region plotted against Paul.*Acts 20:3* Others at the main religious center stirred up the crowd to seize Paul and try to kill him, putting the whole capitol holy city into an uproar. The Roman commander saved Paul by arresting him.*Acts 21:27-36* The commander nearly had Paul flogged until Paul showed himself a Roman citizen, at which the commander arranged for Paul to face a religious trial.*Acts 22:22-30*

The good news nonetheless spread. When Peter healed a paralyzed and bedridden man, all those who saw the healing turned to the Son.*Acts 9:32-35* Many more turned to the Son when Peter raised a dead follower.*Acts 9:42* Peter told all that the Father appointed the Son to decide who lives forever.*Acts 10:42-43* When one region's leader saw Paul blind an opponent for a time, the leader promptly accepted the powerful good news, amazed at its effect.*Acts 13:6-12* Paul and a helper spread the good news across a wide region, making many have confidence in the good news.*Acts 15:3* The Father opened the hearts of whole households to respond to the good news that Paul shared.*Acts 16:13-15* Even a jailer and his household came to rely on the Son after the imprisoned Paul and another helper asked the Father to free them, and he promptly did.*Acts 16:25-34* Some received Paul's good news eagerly, many of them coming to rely on the Son.*Acts 17:10-12* Even in the heart of the distant cosmopolitan city Athens, Paul was able with proof to foster the confidence of many in the Son.*Acts 17:22-31* Opposition just seemed to draw more attention to and greater confidence in the good news.*Acts 18:5-8* Wonders happened in Paul's presence and around the Son's other students that caused many others to trust the Son.*Acts 19:13-18*

Keep a good attitude. Don't fear persecutors.*Matt 10:26* Stand firm. You'll get your rescue when you do.*Matt 24:9-13, Lk 21:12-19* Some, though, won't be up to it. They'll forget that it's worth it.*Matt 13:20-21* Expect hardship before your great rest. That's just the way it is.*Acts 14:22* Don't be afraid but keep on speaking the good news. The Father is with you.*Acts 18:9-11* Serve humbly, even if with tears over hardships.*Acts 20:19* Consider your present life worth nothing. Shoot higher.*Acts 20:23-24* Guard against infiltrators.*Acts 20:29-31* Be ready not only to be bound but to die for the Son.*Acts 21:13* Whatever happens, act worthy of the good news.*Php 1:27* Delight in persecutions for the Son's sake.*2Co 12:10* When others curse you, bless them, while when others persecute you, just endure it.*1Co 4:12* Bless rather than curse those who persecute you.*Ro 12:14* When others slander, answer kindly.*1Co 4:13* When those who oppose you fail to frighten you, show them a sign that the Father will rescue you but destroy them.*Php 1:28* You may at times find no rest, harassed at every turn, conflicts on the outside, fears within.*2Co 7:5* Suffer for the Son, struggling as others struggle.*Php 1:29-30* Rely on your rescue against spiritual attack.*Eph 6:17* Yes, they killed the Son. So they may also drive you out.*1Th 2:15-16* Just keep on through persecutions.*2Th 1:4* Warn one another of persecution.*1Co 4:14* The Father delivers you from deadly peril.*2Co 1:10* Ask the Father to help one another defeat persecution.*2Co 1:11* Stand firm for your rescue.*Mk 13:13*

Martyrs

Some then formed a conspiracy, binding themselves with an oath to kill Paul, and so the Roman commander transferred Paul to the governor in another region, before whom Paul stood trial.*Acts 23:12-31, Acts 24* When

Paul also stood trial before the governor's successor, and the religious leaders made false charges against him, Paul appealed to Caesar.*Acts 25:1-12* The governor brought Paul before the region's king to determine the charges on which to send Paul to Rome.*Acts 25:13-27* Paul said that he stood trial because of his hope in coming back to life as the Father had promised their ancestors.*Acts 26:1-8* After Paul's trial, the Son appeared to Paul to tell him to take courage because Paul would testify about him in Rome.*Acts 23:9-11* Paul told the religious leaders in Rome that chains bound him because of his hope.*Acts 28:17-20* The Son's students become scum, garbage in the world's eyes.*1Co 4:13* The Father puts them on display, like those condemned to die, to call attention to the good news beating back death.*1Co 4:9* The students are a spectacle to everyone, everywhere.*1Co 4:9* They appear fools for the Son, while others appear wise, strong, and honored in the Son.*1Co 4:10* The students went hungry and thirsty, in rags, brutally treated, and homeless, while working hard with their own hands.*1Co 4:11-12* They were imprisoned, flogged severely, and exposed to death repeatedly, while facing many other hardships.*2Co 11:24-26*

> **You'll feel weak.** You carry the good news in a weak body. That's to show the Father's power. It's not you. It's him.*2Co 4:7* Things will look like it's over for you, but it won't be over yet. You'll make it through.*2Co 4:8-9* Death threatens you so that you can show you have the Son's permanent life.*2Co 4:10* Face death for the Son's sake. Then you'll reveal his life.*2Co 4:11* Keep at it. You may look like you're losing, but you're winning. The Father's on your side.*2Co 4:16* This little trouble you face now is nothing compared to what it's earning you.*2Co 4:17* When you make it through the hardest troubles, you show that you work for the Father.*2Co 6:4-5* Don't feel sorry for yourself. Others keep sharing the good news without sleep, while hungry and thirsty, and while cold and naked.*2Co 11:27* Be happy about your weakness. Laugh at insults and hardships. When you look weak, you are actually strong.*2Co 12:10* Just ask the Father to restore you.*2Co 13:9*

The Father's power filled another who relied on the Son, Stephen, who performed great signs and wonders. No one could stand against Stephen as he spoke with the Spirit's wisdom. But some used false witnesses to stir the people up against him.*Acts 6:8-12* False witnesses told the religious leaders, before whom they brought Stephen, that he had spoken against their law. Stephen just kept quiet, looking completely innocent.*Acts 6:12-15* Finally, when asked if the charges were true, Stephen gave the leaders their own history. That history condemned them as stubborn. They resisted the Father's Spirit, betrayed and murdered the wonderful Son, and disobeyed their own law.*Acts 7:1-53* The leaders were furious. But the Spirit filled Stephen, who looked up, saying that he saw the sky open with the Son standing at the Father's side.*Acts 7:54-56* The leaders covered their ears, yelled, rushed at Stephen, and dragged him out and stoned him. Stephen prayed that the Son would receive his spirit and not hold his murder against the leaders.*Acts 7:57-60, Acts 8:1* A great persecution broke out against the church, scattering all except a few leading students.*Acts 8:1-3* The religious leaders had the Son's followers imprisoned.*Acts 9:1-2* Paul, who later followed the Son, was initially among the leading persecutors.*1Co 15:9* The region's king had the student John's brother James put to death.*Acts 12:1-2* Another follower Antipas was killed.*Rev 2:13* Many lost their lives for the Son as his good news spread like wildfire.

> **It's not easy now but will be later.** At some point, everyone will hate you because of the Son.*Mk 13:13* Just remember that worldly people hated the Son first.*Jn 15:18* If you act worldly, then people won't hate you. But because you rely on the Son, the worldly hate you.*Jn 15:19* Because the worldly persecuted the Son, they'll persecute you, too.*Jn 15:20-21* But that persecution just gets you the Father's favor.*Matt 5:10* The Father rewards you when people insult and persecute you because of the Son.*Matt 5:11, Lk 6:22* So be glad for persecution because of the Son. You'll get a great reward.*Matt 5:12, Lk 6:23* Some who rely on the Son face death daily because of it.*1Co 15:31* Your persecution may spread the good news.*Php 1:12* Persecutors, at least, know you rely wholeheartedly on the Son.*Php 1:13* But your persecution makes confident others who also rely on the Son.*Php 1:14* The Spirit will rescue you. Asking the Father for protection helps, too.*Php 1:19* Know how hard it gets for those who rely on the Son.*2Co 1:8* The persecution can feel like a death sentence. But it just throws you back on the Father who gives life right back to the dead.*2Co 1:9* Some will intensely persecute the church, trying to destroy it.*Gal 1:13* Yet those who persecute the church initially, may soon preach the good news that they formerly tried to destroy.*Gal 1:23* Turnabouts of that kind are amazing.*Gal 1:24* The Father forgives even a violent persecutor who acts in ignorance and unbelief.*1Ti 1:13* Remember one another's hardship.*Col 4:18*

Outsiders

The Son's rescue was not just for the insiders but for everyone. A devout centurion had a vision from the Father's messenger who told him to send for the leading student Peter.*Acts 10:1-8* The next day, Peter fell into a trance, during which the Father told him that he could break the old rules about not eating certain meat.*Acts 10:9-16* The centurion's men then arrived, and Peter went with them to the centurion.*Acts 10:19-25* Peter explained to the centurion that the Father had shown Peter that the Father would have no more insiders and outsiders, rule-keepers and rule-breakers, clean and unclean. The Son would make all clean.*Acts 10:26-28* Peter continued that the Father shows no favoritism but accepts the people of every nation when they fear him and do right.*Acts 10:34-35* Peter proclaimed the Son's good news.*Acts 10:36-43*

> **Appoint sound leaders.** Appoint sound leaders for the body, who will rely on the Son.*Acts 14:23* Follow the instructions of those sound leaders.*Acts 16:1-5* Let those sound leaders keep order.*Tit 1:6* Choose humble, patient, temperate, gentle, and honest leaders.*Tit 1:7* Choose hospitable, self-controlled leaders who love good.*Tit 1:8* Leaders, don't order people around. Instead, appeal to them gently.*Phm 8-9* Leaders, stick with the good news.*Tit 1:9* Daily challenges press these leaders. Help them.*2Co 11:28* Leaders feel great compassion.*2Co 11:29* Volunteers should also be sound.*1Ti 3:8* Volunteers should serve only if decent.*1Ti 3:10* Volunteers must also stick with the good news.*1Ti 3:9* Volunteers should lead their own households well, too.*1Ti 3:12* Be confident volunteers.*Col 4:7* Finish what you start.*Col 4:17* Managers should be eager, too.*Eph 3:1-2* Managers, watch over your precious members.*Acts 20:28* Choose managers who are above reproach.*1Ti 3:2-3* Choose managers who lead their own family well.*1Ti 3:4* Don't choose a manager with a mess of a family.*1Ti 3:5* Don't choose as a manager someone who just started relying on the Son. It may go to that person's head.*1Ti 3:6* Choose managers who have good reputations.*1Ti 3:7* Managing the Father's body is noble.*1Ti 3:1* Only those who can manage their own family can manage the Father's body.*1Ti 3:5*

The Spirit came on all who heard Peter's message, including the outsiders, astonishing the insiders. And so they immersed the outsiders in the Son, just as they would have the insiders.*Acts 10:44-48* When other leading insiders throughout the region heard that the outsiders had received the Father, the insiders at first criticized Peter. But after Peter explained what had happened, the insiders relented and instead honored the Father for granting outsiders the same chance for enduring life.*Acts 11:1-18* Some whom persecution had scattered to far regions began to speak in those regions the Son's good news. Because the Father's hand was with them, a great number turned to rely on the Son.*Acts 11:19-21* As students shared the good news, full of the Spirit and confidence, great numbers of people came to rely on the Son.*Acts 11:22-26*

Think clearly about yourself. Don't think too highly of yourself. Use sober judgment with appropriate confidence.*Ro 12:3* Don't fool yourself. You may not be all that much. Test your own actions. Just do the best you can without comparing yourself to someone else.*Gal 6:3-4* Don't stop trying. You have more to accomplish.*1Co 4:8* Truth keeps you humble. Know the truth.*Ro 11:25-26* No pride, and no conceit. Associate easily and frequently with people of low position.*Ro 12:16* Humble yourself. Put the Father above yourself. Then, he'll lift you.*1Pe 5:6* Be completely humble, gentle, and patient with others.*Eph 4:2* Your rescue isn't your doing. The Father did it.*2Ti 1:9* Remember who and what you once were—not much.*1Co 1:26* You're only human.*Acts 14:11-18* Serve the Father with great humility, even tears over your own inadequacy.*Acts 20:19*

10 Return

Recovery

Although the Son left, ascended, he is coming back to recover and restore what is his—everything.*2Pe 3:9* The Son will return in just a little while. He's not taking too long.*Heb 10:37* Here's how it will be. The Son will descend much like he ascended. You'll hear a loud command from the greatest celestial being along with a great siren. You won't miss it. Then, all hell will break loose. Those who died relying on the Son will come up out of their graves.*1Th 4:16* As these dead are coming up, living, those who are living relying on the Son will rise with them to meet and join the Son—forever.*1Th 4:17* You who know the Son have been waiting for it.*1Th 5:4* The Father will open the sky showing the blazing Son surrounded with powerful celestial beings.*2Th 1:7* You've been looking forward to the Son's promise of a new everything, as soon as he returns.*2Pe 3:13* The Son's second appearance, after his mission work on earth and ascension, will not be to give everything up for you. He's already done that. This time, he's coming for your complete rescue.*Heb 9:27-28*

> **You are the Son's sibling.** You are in the Father's family forever.*Jn 8:34-35* Children always see their Father's face.*Matt 18:10* The Father wants none of his children to die.*Matt 18:14* The Son is first among many brothers and sisters.*Ro 8:29* The Son brings you with him to the Father, as another of the Father's children.*Heb 2:13* The Son said that his students who do as he says are his family.*Matt 12:46-50, Mk 3:31-35, Lk 8:19-21* Calling you a brother or sister doesn't embarrass the Son because you are all the same family.*Heb 2:12* The Son tells his other brothers and sisters that you are one of the family. He sings your praises.*Heb 2:12* The Spirit says that you are the Father's child. If you suffer with

> the Son, then you inherit the Son's honor.*Ro 8:16-17* You are the Father's child because you have confidence to rely on the Son.*Gal 3:26* When you rely on the Son, you become the Father's child.*Gal 3:29* Without the Son, you receive only the elemental things that the world offers.*Gal 4:1-3* But with the Son, the Father adopts you as his child.*Gal 4:4-5* The Father calls peacemakers his children.*Matt 5:9* The Son doesn't leave you as an orphan.*Jn 14:18*

By coming, dying, returning to life, ascending, and then returning, the Son opens your way to his Father's paradise. No person had joined the Father's paradise until the Son who came from there did so.*Jn 3:13* The Son told one of his students that he opens the way to his Father's place so that you can see celestial beings coming and going.*Jn 1:50* The Son rejoined the Father in his paradise until the Father restores everything.*Acts 3:21* The Son did not just enter a place that people made. He entered the Father's place from which the Son had come. And he did so to advocate for you, that you join the Father, too.*Heb 9:24* His was a one-time sacrifice of himself, not like people sacrificing animals for their own wrongs. What good does that do?*Heb 9:25*

When the Son returns, spectacularly, with his Father's greatness and many celestial beings, the Son isn't putting up with anyone who doesn't put up with him. He'll find many of those because that's the way it's been lately.*Mk 8:38* When the Son returns, you'll be different, too. You'll be like him, this time seeing him just as he is. Wow. Imagine.*1Jn 3:2* See, you're still a work in progress. The Father hasn't yet stopped molding you for that day that the Son returns.*Php 1:6* When the Son appears, you'll be ready for him, ready to be like he is, spectacular.*Col 3:4* Just keep pursuing him, doing as he says, so that you'll be ready when the Son returns. He'll gather you up with his others.*1Th 3:13* Then, the Son in all his spectacular power will put a stop to all the fooling around, all the evil. That stuff will be over—for good.*2Th 2:7-8* Just remember that the Son comes first, then those like you who belong to him.*1Co 15:23*

> **Work at being ready.** Because the end exposes everything, you better live right now. The Son's coming soon, as you know.*2Pe 3:11-12* Don't let the Son be ashamed of you when he comes back with his great company. Stick up for the Son now, when doing so counts. Not many of you do.*Mk 8:38, Lk 9:26* When the Son returns, things will be tough for those who don't know and rely on him. He'll have no part with them. For them, it'll be over, all over.*2Th 1:8-10* So do everything you can to be good and right now, as you wait for things to end. You've read and heard about the Son's return, so don't let ignorant and

> unstable people distort what you know.*2Pe 3:14-16* You've had this warning. Don't throw it all away for a little bit of short-term fun. Stick with what you know, and learn more about the phenomenal Son.*2Pe 3:17-18* Be smart about things so that you are ready for the Son's return.*Php 1:9-10* Don't give the Father any reason to leave you behind when the Son comes back for his friends.*1Th 3:13* Be on your best behavior for the Son's return.*1Th 5:23*

Fulfillment

Now, you're not there yet. You are in between, waiting for it to happen, like the spiritual nature once waited for the Son. But now he's already come and you're just waiting for his return. The Father gave his word, though, and so did the Son. The Son's coming back. You've heard even more of what's coming from a messenger who told the student John. It's coming—trust it.*Rev 1:1-2* The Father will treat you special if you do rely on what's coming.*Rev 1:3* John, who followed the Son around closely to write it down, heard the messenger say to write down and share widely even more about what's coming, so no one misses the chance to prepare.*Rev 1:9-11, 19* The wise Father wanted it that way. He wasn't keeping secrets, surprising it on you. No, you'll have seen it coming from a long way off. In the coming end, which is close, the Father is putting everything under his beloved Son.*Eph 1:8-10*

You'll love it that way, that is, if you decide to be part of the Son's spectacular return.*2Pe 3:13* Join the party. Those who join with you, especially those who join *because of* you, will make it very good for you when the Son returns.*1Th 2:20* So, tell others how good the Son's return will be for them if they're part of the party, too. The Father will treat them royally, just as he treats you.*1Th 4:18* Oh, yes, the day that the Son comes back, the Father is putting this great, big crown on your head like you're the greatest thing going, if you're one of those who wanted the Son to return. You just have to want it.*2Ti 4:8* The Son said that he's coming to finish everything as soon as everyone hears the good news, so that everyone has a chance to join the party.*Matt 24:14* The Son is coming with a crowd of celestial beings, ready to take over, unchallenged.*Matt 25:31* You have no getting around it. Anyone, anywhere, faces the same thing. That day comes for all.*Lk 21:35*

Let the Father judge, not you. Don't condemn another, or you, too, face judgment._{Matt 7:1} If you do not condemn, then you will not face condemnation._{Lk 6:37} You must meet the same measure by which you measure others._{Matt 7:2} Don't try fixing the little problems others have while the ignoring your own bigger problems._{Matt 7:2-4, Lk 6:41-42} Fix your own big problems first. Then help others._{Matt 7:5} Don't judge from the outside but instead by the inside, correctly._{Jn 7:24} Only the perfect one can condemn others, and no one but Father and Son is perfect._{Jn 8:7} When you condemn another, you lose all excuse and condemn yourself because you do the same things._{Ro 2:1} When you judge others for doing what you do, then the Father judges you._{Ro 2:2-3} Don't judge those who know less than you do about the Father and Son. The Father accepts them._{Ro 14:2-3} Others serve the Father, not you, so you have no business judging them. The Father will take care of that, treating them better than you would._{Ro 14:4} Don't judge or mistreat another because you all face the same Father._{Ro 14:10} Stop judging one another._{Ro 14:13} And no more slander. Talking down about others breaks the rules._{Jas 4:11} Your judging makes no sense because you can't do anything about it, anyway. Only the Father rescues or destroys._{Jas 4:12} The Father pays others back for what they did to you, so let him do it, not you._{2Th 1:6-7} Others who run down your loyalty to the Father will pay for it._{1Th 2:16} But you should not repay. Let the Father do it for you._{Ro 12:17} Do not take revenge. The Father will handle it better than you._{Ro 12:19} Do the opposite. Kill your opponent with kindness._{Ro 12:20} Overcome wrong with right._{Ro 12:21} Two wrongs don't make right._{1Th 5:15} Put up with one another. The Father puts up with you._{Col 3:13} And don't worry about it if no one defends you. The Father does so._{2Ti 4:16}

Succession

These things have an order to them. First, the Son returns. Once he returns, then he gets together those who are his, who rely on him._{1Co 15:23} Then the Son takes over everything, every bit of authority and power so that he has it *all*. Finally, the Son hands everything over to the Father. And that's it, when everything comes together as it always should have been._{1Co 15:24} The Son, though, has to start it. He's got to get everything in order, everything under his control._{1Co 15:25} And that includes death, getting rid of death._{1Co 15:26} The Father made it that way, giving the Son all power and control other than control over the Father._{1Co 15:27} When the Son is done, the Son is getting right back under his Father who put everything under him. See, everything must be under the Father to be as it should.*1Co 15:28* So come on and do it, Son!*1Co 16:22*

Don't be mistaken. The Son has not yet given new life to those who died relying on him.*2Ti 2:18* But know that the Son will do so. You shouldn't grieve like others who reject the Son and thus have no hope.*1Th 4:13* Because you are relying on the Son living again, the Father will give you the Son's new life.*1Th 4:14* The Father has given his word that those who died relying on the Son will live to meet him on his return. Then you who are living will join the Son, too, each in turn.*1Th 4:15* When the Son returns with great fanfare, those who died relying on the Son will come right back to life first.*1Th 4:16* Then, your turn is next. The Father will draw you up with those who have just come back to life. Then, you'll all be together with the Son—forever.*1Th 4:17* The Father rescues your spirit on the Son's return.*1Co 5:4-5*

You can start now. Talk up those around you who want the Son to come back. Then, when he does, you'll have a *lot* about which to boast.*2Co 1:14* Keep encouraging one another, all the more as the Son's return approaches.*Heb 10:25* The Son said that he will come with all his Father's spectacular appearance and with many celestial beings. When he gets here, he's going to reward you just as you deserve, no more, no less.*Matt 16:27* The Son warned you that his Father judges those who reject him, to rely on their own puny powers. They should have listened to the Son. The Father told the Son what to say, and what the Son said will judge them lacking in the end.*Jn 12:48* The Son warns you that his return is soon. He's bringing your reward if reward you deserve. No one else judges you like he judges you. He started it all, and he's going to finish it all.*Rev 22:12-13* Oh, yes, he's said it: the Son is coming back to recover and restore everything soon.*Rev 22:20*

> **You can join the Son.** You can do it. Just talk with the Father about escaping an awful end and instead joining his Son.*Lk 21:36* When the Son returns, you can step right up and join his great parade.*Col 3:4* Anyone who relies on him, trusts and listens to him, will be able to celebrate his return.*2Th 1:10-11* You'll enjoy his return so much that you'll be right alongside him.*1Jn 3:2* Don't look to things you own or that entertain you because whoever looks back to their old life will lose everything, old and new, while those who look to the Son will both preserve and gain everything.*Lk 17:31-33* Expecting his return keeps you sober.*1Jn 3:3* Waiting patiently for his return lets your good work ripen.*Jas 5:7-8,10* The Father will watch out for you while you wait for your great rescue.*1Pe 1:5* Just

stay alert and sober so that you can see what the Son has for you. Then, you won't miss it.*1Pe 1:13* Be ready to show off when he comes so your homework is obvious.*Php 2:16* The Father will continue to help you along the way while you wait. The waiting isn't all up to you.*Php 1:6* The Father will give you the supplies that you need while you wait for the Son to come back.*1Co 1:7* The Father will help you be ready so that you're looking good when the Son returns.*1Co 1:8*

End

When the Son returns, it's all over. Things have an end, and it's the best end. Just don't let anyone fool you. Some will say that they are the Son when they aren't the Son. Others will say that the end is here when it's not yet here.*Matt 24:3-4, Mk 13:3-5, Lk 21:7-8* Don't worry when things go haywire and seem to be coming to an awful end. A huge mess has to happen before things end.*Matt 24:6-8, Mk 13:7-8, Lk 21:9-11* The Son just said to run for the hills when things get bad, even among those who await the Son's return. Don't try to go back patching things up because doing so won't work when things get so bad, worse than they've ever been.*Matt 24:15-21, Mk 13:14-19* Armies will surround the capitol holy city just before its destruction. That's when you should flee to avoid getting caught up in its destruction.*Lk 21:20-22* The Father will keep it livable, survivable, though, just for the sake of those who rely on the Son. Otherwise, everyone would succumb.*Matt 24:22, Mk 13:20*

Don't believe it then, when people point here and there to the supposed Son. You'll see a lot of fakers, some of whom will do fancy things to try to fool those who follow the Son.*Matt 24:23-26, Mk 13:21-23* No, you'll be able to tell the real thing, the authentic Son. He'll light up the whole sky, not just some ordinary pyrotechnics, when he comes.*Matt 24:27, Lk 17:24* You won't even see the moon, sun, or stars anymore.*Matt 24:29, Mk 13:24-25* Not only will the sky be different, but the oceans will roar, too, scaring everyone. People will faint from terror.*Lk 21:25-26* Then you'll know that the Son is about to come.*Matt 24:32-34* Then you'll see the Son. The sky will open up, and you'll see his spectacular power.*Matt 24:30, Mk 13:26* Then the Son will send celestial beings to gather everyone who relied on the Son, no matter where they are. He isn't going to overlook you. He'll find you.*Matt 24:31, Mk 13:27* Just stand up and look up when you see him coming. Enjoy its sight, the sight of his great power. He's about to rescue you.*Lk 21:27* Everyone will look for him, and everyone will see him, even those who rejected him, although they'll be the sorry ones.*Rev 1:7*

The Son chooses whom he rescues. The Son said he would judge those who did not trust him.*Jn 8:26* The Son said that he came to judge so that those who knew that they needed him would survive while those who thought they were fine on their own would not.*Jn 9:35-39* The Son said he divides even family members against one another.*Lk 12:51-53* When the Son returns, he will separate everyone, good to one side, bad to the other.*Matt 25:32* To the good, the Son will say that his Father has nothing but good for them, prepared long ago.*Matt 25:34* The Son approves of those who feed the hungry, give drink to the thirsty, shelter the homeless, clothe the naked, heal the sick, and visit the prisoner.*Matt 25:35-36* The Son says that doing good to one of these is like doing good to him.*Matt 25:37-40* The Son disapproves of wrongdoers, condemning them forever.*Matt 25:41* The Son says that refusing to help those who need it is effectively refusing to help him.*Matt 25:42-43* Every time you fail to help those who need it most, you fail to help the Son.*Matt 25:44-45* The good will have a great time forever, but for the bad, it's over.*Matt 25:46* When wrongdoers see what's in store for the do-gooders, they will weep at their loss.*Lk 13:28-29*

Timing

Only the Father knows the day and hour when the end will come. He hasn't shared it with anyone, so don't go thinking that someone else knows.*Matt 24:36, Mk 13:32* The Son will return when you do not expect him.*Lk 12:40* His return will be like the great flood, no one suspecting it—but it came anyway.*Matt 24:37-39, Lk 17:27* The Son's return will especially catch unawares those who continue just going about their business like nothing is going to happen.*Lk 17:28-30* Two people will be working side by side, and the Father will take one up with the Son, leaving the other just standing there alone. Two people will be in bed side by side, and the Father will take one but not the other.*Matt 24:40-41, Lk 17:34-35* You don't know the Father's time because time differs to him. To him, a day can be like a thousand years or a thousand years like a day. You plod along day by day, but he thinks way forward.*2Pe 3:8* The Son in waiting to come back isn't undecided. He's coming but just being patient because he wants everyone to turn to him rather than get left behind to die.*2Pe 3:9*

Yes, the last days before the Son's return will be awful.₂Ti 3:1 But the Son's return will come sneaking up. Then, his fire will destroy and lay bare everything.₂Pe 3:10 That time is near.Php 4:5 So wait for the Son's rescue from those awful end times. Can't you see them coming?1Th 1:10 Don't look for date and time because you can't predict it, but just know that it's coming.1Th 5:1-2 Don't worry as some do that the Son has already come because he hasn't.₂Th 2:2-3 The Son will return when a great rebellion occurs and people think they can do whatever they want, no matter who gets hurt.₂Th 2:3-6 Don't be one of those lawless evildoers because the Son will surely take care of them when he comes back.1Ti 6:14-15 The Son's return will not surprise you who rely on him and wait for him.1Th 5:4 Don't be your own judge but just wait for him.1Co 4:5 Each will get their own when he comes.1Co 4:5 Some of the Son's students won't have to die to see him return.Matt 16:28, Mk 9:1, Lk 9:27 But most won't see it and so should not go running around when people say that he is here or there.Lk 17:22-23 You will not know in advance when he comes.Rev 3:3

Watch for the Son's return. Because you won't know until the Son comes, you've got to watch for him.Matt 24:42, Mk 13:33, Lk 21:36 Keep on the lookout, stay awake, and be ready. Don't get caught naked and exposed.Rev 16:15 Be like a homeowner guarding the house because you won't know until he comes.Matt 24:43-44, Mk 13:34-35 Watch out!Mk 13:37 Be the security guard who watches everything. Run a tight ship where everything is ready and on time.Matt 24:45, Lk 12:42-43 The Father will put you in charge if you're ready for the Son's return.Matt 24:46-47, Lk 12:44 On the other hand, the Father will punish those who don't care if the Son's coming back and aren't ready when he does return.Matt 24:49-51, Lk 12:45-46 Some will be ready, in the right frame of mind and spirit, but others won't.Matt 25:1-4 Those who have the right frame and spirit will jump to attention when the Son comes.Matt 25:5-7 Those who don't see it coming will ask what's going on but not get a good answer.Matt 25:8-9 Those who see it coming will promptly join the Son, leaving behind those who don't and are all confused at his return.Matt 25:10-12 So just be ready to join the Son and go to work for him, and he'll go to work for you.Lk 12:35-37 Keep watch because you don't know when he's coming.Matt 25:13 Keep doing the Father's work while the Son's away so that you get his big reward when the Son returns.Matt 25:14-23 Don't be lazy and worthless, thinking that the Father doesn't deserve your work. If you are, then when the Son comes, the Father will take away the little that you have.Matt 25:24-30 Be alert and aware. Talk with the Father about it because everything is about to end.1Pe 4:7 Wake up because the good things you expect are getting closer.Ro 13:11

Way

Remember that this whole thing about the Son coming, dying, coming back to life, ascending, and then returning is for you. Oh, yes, it's all for Father and Son, too, but the Father wants you with them in his place, his paradise, which you gain through the Son.*Php 3:13-14* So make your allegiance to the Father's paradise, not this earthly mess. Look forward to your true destination, rescued by the Son, rather than getting stuck here.*Php 3:20-21* The Father made it that way for you, giving you a seat at his great table, where he's ready to show you even more of his incomparable riches.*Eph 2:6-7* The Father keeps those riches there with him so that they don't spoil here.*1Pe 1:4* When the Son returns from the Father's place, he'll take you all back, living and dead, all you who relied on the Son.*1Th 4:17* Just be sure that the Father will do it for you, taking you safely and securely to his paradise.*2Ti 4:18* Don't worry if you're one of those who dies first because the Father is still taking you to his permanent house, his forever dwelling, the one that he built.*2Co 5:1*

> ***Avoid schemes.*** You live only briefly with no real idea of tomorrow. So avoid money-making schemes. Do what the Father wants.*Jas 4:13-16* Don't swear to do this or that. Just go do it.*Jas 5:12* Shame on those who profit by undermining the good news.*Jude 11* Shame on those who feed only themselves without the slightest qualm, producing nothing for others.*Jude 12-13* Watch for those who boast about themselves while flattering you, all for their own advantage.*Jude 14-15* Use worldly wealth to make friends so that when the wealth is gone, you still have the good news of living forever.*Lk 16:1-9*

Here, you groan with burden, facing death every day, when you know you'll face nothing of the sort with the Father.*2Co 5:4* Your reward for relying on the Son is to enter the Father's secure house, so secure that nothing disturbs it.*Heb 12:28-29* You sense how special that permanent security will be, from the peril that you face here, constantly feeling exposed.*2Co 5:2-3* You should look forward to the Father's promised place, his perfect new place, everything united and restored.*2Pe 3:13* That hope of joining him feeds your confidence in the good news that really will happen, no matter what anyone says to the contrary.*Col 1:5* Hold onto that hope of joining the Son beside the Father.*Col 3:1* In fact, do everything now as if you were doing those things in the Father's place so that it goes better for you when you get there.*Matt 18:18* Remember, too, that you've got that chance of joining the Father, right until your end. Never give up hope._{Lk 23:42-43}

> **The Father judges justly.** The Father doesn't shoot from the hip. He judges justly._{Ro 2:5-6} The Father sees everything, laid bare before him. He knows what to do about it._{Heb 4:13} The Father judges your secrets._{Ro 2:16} You can't second-guess the Father._{Ro 11:33} You can see plainly that the Father is always right._{2Th 1:5} The Father repays you for what you do._{Ro 2:6} The Father avenges, too, making up for wrongs._{Heb 10:30} The Father pays back for those who feast, carouse, and revel over wrongs._{1Pe 2:13} So let the Father's Spirit help you do as you should, like the Son did. Don't think that satisfying others is enough. Satisfy the Father._{1Co 2:15-16} Care little if others judge you. And don't condemn yourself._{1Co 4:3} Don't let your conscience be your only guide. Let the Father guide you because he judges._{1Co 4:4} The Father uncovers what people try to hide. He shows your true motives. He'll praise those with right motives._{1Co 4:5} When the Father judges, all account for every word they've spoken. Words either acquit or condemn._{Matt 12:36-37}

Power

Consider the student John's glimpse into the Father's place, an extraordinary revelation. Take it for what you will, but never underestimate the Father. A great voice said to John, from an open door to the Father's place, to see what would happen next._{Rev 4:1} The Father sat regally, royally, looking as if made of the most precious jewels. Brilliant colored light encircled him. Twenty-four prominent others sat in a circle around the Father._{Rev 4:2-4} Lightning flashed and thunder pealed from where the Father sat, while spirit fires danced in front of him on a crystal-clear sea of glass._{Rev 4:5-6} Four extraordinary winged creatures surrounded the Father, chanting endlessly how phenomenal he was, is, and will be._{Rev 4:6-8} With each chant, the twenty-four others fell down to honor and thank the Father for creating everything and giving you your being._{Rev 4:9-11}

And never underestimate the Son. John saw that the Father held a sealed writing. A great celestial being asked loudly who could break the seals to read the writing._{Rev 5:1-2} John wept because no one looked ready, but one of those surrounding the Father said that the Son could handle it._{Rev 5:3-5} The Son, looking dead, sacrificed as you know that he was, approached the Father. Bearing the Father's seven spirits, the Son took the writing from the Father. As soon as the Son had the writing in hand, the extraordinary creatures and others all fell down, honoring the Son._{Rev 5:6-7} They were now singing a new song, saying the Son could open the sealed writing. They sang that the Son had died to bring persons from around the world to honor and serve the Father, taking over the new earth._{Rev 5:8-10} One-hundred-million celestial beings joined the song that the slain Son now had the Father's power and honor._{Rev 5:11-12} Then every living being everywhere sang the Son's praises._{Rev 5:13-14}

> **Don't be a scoffer.** Near the end, scoffers will do the evil that they please. They'll say that the Son isn't coming back. They'll say that the Father doesn't care about you._{2Pe 3:3-4} But they ignore that the Father's word created everything. They ignore that the Father started over after the great flood. And they ignore that the Father is going to wrap it all up, destroying those who have no patience for him._{2Pe 3:5-7} The Father will judge all when the Son returns._{2Th 1:7} When the Son returns, the Father will destroy those who do not know him and accept the good news._{2Th 1:8-10} Father and Son will judge both living and dead._{2Ti 4:1} The Son will rescue the good while destroying the bad._{Matt 3:12} The Father judges rightly, rewarding all who wait for the Son to reappear._{2Ti 4:8} The Father rescues his Son's followers while destroying the wrongdoers. It'll be just like the old days when the Father destroyed the lawless._{1Pe 2:7-9} Don't be stubborn. The Father's anger will get you if you are._{Ro 2:5} No one faces judgment until the Son comes. Then everyone faces judgment._{1Co 4:5} Everyone. The Son rewards good and punishes bad. It's that simple._{2Co 5:10} No one who relies on the Son gets condemned._{Ro 8:1} The Son judges just as the Father wishes._{Jn 5:30}

Rescue

The Father then gave the Son's student John a glimpse of the future, when the Son comes. First, a great call issued for the Son to return, to come. And so the Son opened the writing's first seal, causing the Father's judgment to spread across the earth, a judgment the Father committed to the Son._{Rev 6:1-2} When the Son opened the second seal at another call for him to come, the Father's judgment again spread across the earth so that evildoers killed each other._{Rev 6:3-4} When the Son opened the third seal at a third call for him to come, famine and misery spread across the earth from all the evil that people had done._{Rev 6:5-6} When the Son opened the fourth seal at a fourth call to come, death and its dark region spread across the earth from the people's evil, with a fourth of the earth dying at war or in plague or famine.*Rev 6:7-8* Those who do not rely on the Son will face horrible times.

> **The Son's rescue means freedom.** The Father sent his Son to rescue you, not condemn you.*Jn 3:17* Relying on the Son gets around condemnation. Rejecting the Son leaves you condemned.*Jn 3:18* That's why the Father named him *Jesus*, or Yeshua if you prefer, meaning *he rescues*.*Matt 1:21* Your rescue comes immediately when you rely on the Son. You don't have to labor for years for it—indeed, your labors can't rescue you. The Son's labor did.*Lk 19:1-9* Rescue was the reason the Son came.*Lk 19:10* This rescue came right out of the ancient writings.*Jn 3:22* All you need do is say you need him—and admit that the Father brought the Son right back to life.*Ro 10:9* A dead man can't rescue. Telling someone you need the Son confirms your rescue. Why, otherwise, should the Father accept it?*Ro 10:10-11* You can't hold back the good news.*Col 1:6-7* The Father wants everyone in, not just some.*1Ti 2:3-4* So just rely on the Son. You need it just as much as anyone else—maybe more.*1Ti 1:15* You've been breaking the rules a long time, but the Son never broke one. Relying on the Son gets you back on track.*1Jn 3:4-6* The Father then doesn't count anything against you. What relief!*Col 2:14* Walk with the Son. You'll get that great relief.*1Jn 1:7* When you admit you need the Son, the Father fills you, and you fill the Father.*1Jn 4:15* Just don't forget the Son. You need him.*1Co 15:1* Hold onto the Son. Listen to him, and do as he says.*1Co 15:2* The Son is listening to you and knows which way you've fallen, with him or against him. Oh, and no one succeeds standing against him.*Matt 3:12* Doesn't matter who you are or what you've done. The Son can rescue.*Matt 19:25-26* Just hang in there with him when things get rough.*Matt 24:9-13, Mk 13:13*

The next things that John saw for the future were of a spiritual rather than earthly future. When the Son opened the fifth seal, all those who died pursuing the Father asked how much longer they must wait for the Father to pay back those who had opposed them. The Father assured each that they had little longer to wait, now that the Son was returning.*Rev 6:9-11* When the Son opened the sixth seal, the great calamity began, the earth quaking, the sun turning black, the moon blood red, and meteors falling to earth. Every natural feature receded, disappeared.*Rev 6:12-14* Everyone left alive hid wherever they could, hoping to die. The Father and Son were judging every evil, unopposed.*Rev 6:15-17* A pause then came before the Son opened the writing's seventh and final seal, the one that would bring the final judgment. The Father's celestial beings had first to ensure that no one would harm those who initially relied on and served the Father, well over one-hundred thousand.*Rev 7:1-8*

Then John saw many more whom the Son had rescued, indeed so many that no one could count them. They were not just from one nation, race, or culture but from every people all over the world. They all stood before the Father and Son, crying out joyfully that the Father had rescued them through the Son.*Rev 7:9-10* All celestial beings fell facedown before the Father in his praise and honor.*Rev 7:11-12* This multitude of people had come out of the world's distracting clamor, drawn apart to the Son. The Son's sacrifice had made them perfect and brilliant like him.*Rev 7:13-14* The multitude was present to serve the Father while the Father protected them. These people would never again need a thing from anyone. They would always be comfortable, never hot or cold. They wouldn't even be hungry or thirsty. The Son would constantly supply them with special food and water. The Father would never let them be sad over anything. They were in paradise.*Rev 7:15-17* The Son had said that time would come when all in their graves would come out at his voice, those who have done good to rise to live but those who have done evil to face condemnation.*Jn 5:28-29*

The Father judges. The Son said that his glorious Father judges.*Jn 8:50* Dread falling on the wrong side of the Father.*Heb 10:31* The Father gets angry at self-seekers who reject the truth to do evil.*Ro 2:8* In the end, the Father will judge fast and final.*Ro 9:28* The Father is both kind and stern, kind to you while you do as he says but stern when you don't. Be careful.*Ro 11:22* The Father judges everyone, no exceptions.*Ro 14:11* You must each face the Father.*Ro 14:12* So don't get too comfortable. Stay cautious so that the Father judges you fit.*1Pe 1:17* Your judgment will go well for hearing the Father, but judgment won't go well for those who don't care for the Father.*1Pe 4:17-18* The Father judges all wrong.*Col 3:25* The Father especially condemns the lawless who indulge their flesh.*1Pe 2:10* The Father shows his anger for the immoral wicked who hide the truth.*Ro 1:18* The Father punishes all who do wrong. You've had your warning.*1Th 4:6* The Father will judge suddenly just when people think they're getting away with it. They'll not escape.*1Th 5:3* The Son brought both rescue and judgment.*Lk 12:49* The Father relies on the Son's judgment, so you'd better rely on the Son.*Jn 5:22-23* The Father gave judging to the Son.*Jn 5:27* The Son's sacrifice judged the world's evil, rescuing those who come to the Son.*Jn 12:30-32* You should tell others that the Father lets the Son judge so that they rely on the Son.*Acts 10:42-43*

Torment

Before the final judgment, though, the great oppressor will torment those who follow and rely on the Son. John received a vision of that torment. The great oppressor will enlist other oppressors and give them power to plague the Son's followers.*Rev 13:1-2* One of those other oppressors will mimic the Son's coming back to life, looking as if the oppressor had done the same so that people fear the oppressor's false power and honor the oppressor rather than the Son.*Rev 13:3-4* This other oppressor will have only short-term power to claim things that the oppressor is not and to slander the Father and Son and those who live with them.*Rev 13:5-6* This other oppressor will cast aside the Father's people so that everyone else honors the oppressor, just not the ones who rely on the Son. This other oppressor will kill or capture those followers of the Son, requiring them to endure and persevere.*Rev 13:7-8*

The torment will worsen when another great oppressor arises, sounding like the first oppressor and having the first oppressor's authority, like the second oppressor had. This third oppressor will make everyone who does not follow the Son honor the first oppressor.*Rev 13:11-12* The third oppressor will do things that look like great wonders but are not. Those false wonders will fool the earth's inhabitants, those who do not follow the Son, so that the inhabitants set up memorials to honor the first oppressor. The third oppressor will then kill all those who do not participate in the memorials, giving honor to the first oppressor.*Rev 13:13-15* The third oppressor will also force all people to receive a mark of the name or number of the oppressor on their hand or forehead. None will be able to do anything, whether buying or selling, without having the mark that they worship the oppressor. It will be an awful dictatorship.*Rev 13:16-18*

Many reject the Son. The religious leaders' rejection of the Son fulfilled the ancient writings' prediction. The rejection didn't interrupt the good news. The Son still came back to life for your relief and rescue, as many saw.*Acts 13:27-41* Religious traditionalists reject the Son out of jealousy.*Acts 13:44-45* Rejection by one group, though, just turns the good news on to another group, as the ancient writings predicted.*Acts 13:46-48* The good news inevitably spreads through the Father's Spirit, despite opposition.*Acts 13:49-52* Some will always accept and rely on the Son, while others won't. Be ready for division.*Acts 14:1-6* Reasoning from the ancient writings proves the good news to some but not others, especially jealous traditionalists who drive away those who share the good news.*Acts 17:1-14* When that happens, just move on to share the good news elsewhere.*Acts 18:5-8* Speak boldly and persuasively about the good news. If they don't accept it, then move on.*Acts 19:8-10* Some oppose the good news because it will cost them income they make from traditions.*Acts 19:23-41* Just work at it, from morning until evening if necessary. Some will accept it, even if not others.*Acts 28:22-23* Hard hearts reject the good news, causing it to go to soft hearts elsewhere.*Acts 28:25-28*

Judgment

When the Son opened the writing's seventh and final seal, silence fell for a short while in solemn anticipation. Then, seven celestial beings stood before the Father ready to give great fanfare. Another celestial being hurled the Father's judgment to earth with thunder and lightning, shaking the foundation of everything.*Rev 8:1-2* The seven beings prepared their fanfare.*Rev 8:6* When the first one sounded, marauding armies fought, destroying one third of earth, felling many of its dictator leaders, and destroying many of its people.*Rev 8:7* When the second one sounded, a great empire went to war, destroying many more people and also destroying much commerce and wealth.*Rev 8:8-9* When the third one sounded, these calamities accelerated, destroying the greatest seats of earthly power, subverting authority, and killing many more people.*Rev 8:10-11* When the fourth one sounded, the final light of earthly rule went out, so that humans were left without government of any kind, disorganized and hopeless.*Rev 8:12*

Don't anger the Father. Rejecting the Father only gives him good reason to show his power.*Ro 9:17-18* Those who reject the good news while opposing its teachers face the Father's anger.*1Th 2:16* The Father reserves the worst for the most corrupt.*1Pe 2:17* Those who don't do as the Father says face his anger.*Eph 5:6* The Father didn't spare his own celestial beings who disobeyed, so without the Son he won't spare you.*1Pe 2:4* The Father shows his anger over those who reject him to indulge their appetites.*Ro 1:18* Don't be stubborn. You'll just store up the Father's anger against you.*Ro 2:5* The self-seeking who reject the Son to follow the enemy face the Father's anger.*Ro 2:8* No exceptions.*Ro 2:9* The Father is fair but furious.*Ro 2:5-6* The Father won't spare the corrupt.*Col 3:6* Putting other things above the Father angers him.*Eph 5:6* The Father will show his anger.*Ro 1:18*

John then heard a messenger calling out final disasters on earth's inhabitants, a last tumbling of every corrupt thing that humans had imagined and built apart from the Father. Three remaining celestial beings had yet to sound their catastrophes.*Rev 8:13* When the fifth one sounded, the Father permitted the worst calamities to emerge from the abyss to torment the earth. Hell opened to release those torments.*Rev 9:1-3* Deceivers roamed the earth, fooling everyone who did not rely on the Son, so that all those destined for destruction writhed in agony, looking for a death that they could not find.*Rev 9:4-6* The hellish persecutors did effective battle, with the chief destroyer leading them.*Rev 9:9-11* A first period of great calamity ends here with two more to come.*Rev 9:12*

> **Rebels lose out.** Whoever rejects the Son dies forever. The Father's anger remains on them.*Jn 3:36* Once you know what to do, do it. If you keep doing wrong when you know it's wrong, no rescue comes from the Father's judgment.*Heb 10:27* Rejecting rules gets you nowhere.*Heb 10:28* Rejecting the rescuer Son is far worse. The Son gave you a chance. Don't blow it. Doing so would be an insult.*Heb 10:29* Be humble, not arrogant. Know your own faults, letting someone else toot your horn. And be careful. The Father can reject anyone, even someone whom you'd think would get special treatment. No one gets special treatment.*Ro 11:21* Everyone who goes bad gets the bad. Evil is in big trouble.*Ro 2:9* The Father of course judges unfaithful spouses and those who fool around when they shouldn't.*Heb 13:4*

When the sixth one sounded his blast, four warriors went out killing a third of humankind, with two-hundred-million troops.*Rev 9:13-16* Each soldier had a powerful mount that could destroy to front and rear.*Rev 9:17-19* Yet the rest of humankind that survived still did not turn from worshiping things that they made or from their murder, magic, and sexual immorality.*Rev 9:20-21* Then a great messenger came down in splendor, planting his feet on the sea and land, and giving a great roar, while holding a writing of the Son's good news.*Rev 10:1-4* The roar told that the seventh sounding blast should accomplish the Father's final mystery.*Rev 10:5-7* The voice also told John to diligently share the Son's good news as widely as possible.*Rev 10:9-11* John and those pursuing the Son with him were to administer the church to carry and spread the good news across the earth, against fearful opposition. Those who relied on the Son and spread his good news would die but live again, ending a second awful period of calamity.*Rev 11:1-14* Then the seventh one will sound the blast so that the world becomes the Son's place of rule forever.

The Father will receive continual thanks for the new rule, giving life to the dead who relied on the Son, destroying those who destroy the earth, and revealing his full promise and plan.*Rev 11:15-19*

> **The Father chooses, too.** When you accept someone whom the Son sends, you honor the Son. When you honor the Son, you honor the Father.*Jn 13:20* The Father gave you to the Son, and so you rely on the Son. The Son accepts whoever relies on him.*Jn 6:37* Even those from far away who were looking for something else will seek the Son.*Jn 12:20-22* The Father chooses you. It's not entirely up to you.*1Th 1:4* The Father chose you before you chose him. He has a say in it. He preserves you.*Ro 11:1-3* The Father chooses, although you should still go hard after him. He lets others go their own way.*Ro 11:7* Even today, the Father chooses.*Ro 11:5* You'll stumble but not beyond recovery. Just enough to keep rescue open to all.*Ro 11:11* The ones the Father chooses ahead of you keep you, too, set apart for him.*Ro 11:16* Don't think yourself better than those whom the Father chose ahead of you to keep you in line.*Ro 11:18* The Father rescues insiders, too, if they do as you do in relying on the Son.*Ro 11:23-24* The Father just gives insiders a hard time to ensure the rescue of outsiders.*Ro 11:25-26* So don't give insiders a hard time even when they give you a hard time. They're working for you. The Father still loves them.*Ro 11:28* The Father rejected his own insiders to rescue you, but he's bringing his insiders back to life, too.*Ro 11:15* When the Father brings the insiders in together with the outsiders, that will be truly special.*Ro 11:12* The Father wants you close to his Son.*1Co 1:9* The Father chose simple you so that he would be apparent in all things.*1Co 1:27* The Father chose the low and despised. He even made his own things to choose.*1Co 1:28-29* You once disobeyed the Father, but he took you anyway.*Ro 11:30* By taking you, the disobedient, the Father can take his insiders who also disobeyed.*Ro 11:31* The Father invites those who love him. He works in all things for their good.*Ro 8:28* The Father chose you before you earned anything, to show that his choice, not your effort, makes the difference.*Ro 9:10-12* The Father is still just. He's not unfair.*Ro 9:14-15* The Father invites both insiders and outsiders, choosing and loving those whom one would not expect and calling them his children.*Ro 9:24-26* Many are from the insiders, but few accept rescue.*Ro 9:27* Before he created everything, the Father chose you as if you were special.*Eph 1:4* When the Father invites you, go!*Gal 1:16* You are his first ones.*2Th 2:13* You are his choice whom he dearly loves.*Col 3:12*

The Son will stand with many who have his name and his Father's name on them, while they sing a roaring new song that only they could learn.*Rev 14:1-3* The best of the best will be among them for the Father and Son to especially celebrate, those who were blameless truthtellers.*Rev 14:4-5*

The Father's first messenger will bring the timeless good news to every nation, saying to honor the Father who made everything, because his judgment's hour had come.*Rev 14:6-7* A second messenger will follow, saying that the worldly ruler who made many corrupt had fallen.*Rev 14:8* A third messenger will follow, saying that those who took the oppressor's mark will face the Father's full-strength fury, with the Son and celestial beings looking on.*Rev 14:9-10* The Father's people who follow his rules while relying on the Son will endure patiently. The Father will protect those who die relying on the Son, so that they rest and receive reward from their fruitful labors.*Rev 14:12-13* A great one will then begin to harvest the earth of its wrongdoers.*Rev 14:14-16* Another one will join the harvest for the Father's fury.*Rev 14:17-20*

> **Some won't make it.** The words that the Son spoke at his Father's command will condemn some in the end. The Father will judge using those words, and some will fall short.*Jn 12:48* The Father has judged before, cleaning up the world in the great flood, and so he'll judge again in the end.*1Pe 2:5* The Father has burned cities to the ground before to show you what will happen to wrongdoers.*1Pe 2:6* The Father will destroy the lawless who put themselves in his place, as if they ruled everything.*2Th 2:3-4* Those who reject the Father don't even know what they're doing. Oh, but they'll catch it.*1Pe 2:12* Even the naturally corrupt places, where people just follow their old bad habits, will do better than those who know what to do but refuse to do it.*Matt 11:20-24* If you reject the Son, then the so-called bad folks, the know-nothings, will come teach you the right lesson.*Matt 12:41-42* The worldly think they can get away with it, but they can't because they rejected the Son. He was their only chance with the Father. The world's evil is now done for, condemned.*Jn 16:8-11* Yes, the Son rescues, but the Father will still destroy those who reject the Son and instead give themselves up to perversion. After all, the Father judged celestial beings who refused his authority, so he won't spare you.*Jude 5-7* The Father sent the disobedient ones to hell, chaining them for final judgment.*1Pe 2:4* In the end, the Son weeds everything out, destroying evil so that the good shine for the Father.*Matt 13:40-43* The Son's celestial workers will separate the evil for destruction.*Matt 13:47-50*

Fury

Rejecting the Father who created you is no small thing. Wouldn't you be angry if that which you made rejected you? Those who do don't just face judgment—they face fury. Then John saw another vision of seven celestial beings carrying seven last plagues with which the Father completes his judgment showing his anger.*Rev 15:1* Those followers of the Son who had beaten the oppressors stood beside a sea glowing with fire. They held the Father's musical instruments.*Rev 15:2* They sang a song of both the ancient and recent deliverers, Moses who led the people out of their first slavery and the Son who led all people out of all slavery. They sang of the greatest possible honor that the Son had brought the Father, causing everyone everywhere to respect and honor him.*Rev 15:2-4* Then out with the seven plagues came the seven celestial beings.*Rev 15:5-6* They also took with them seven golden bowls filled with the Father's fury.*Rev 15:7-8*

> **The Father doesn't play favorites.** The Father shows no favoritism.*Ro 2:11* The Father shows no favoritism when paying back for wrongs.*Col 3:25* The Father treats you each alike because all do wrong.*Ro 2:8-11* The Father has no insiders and outsiders because the same Father is Father of all, rescuing and richly rewarding all who pursue him.*Ro 10:12-13* So don't you show favoritism.*Jas 2:1* Give the poor person just as much attention as the rich person.*Jas 2:2-4* The Father chose the poor to love him and get their rich reward.*Jas 2:5* Why should you dishonor the poor when the rich are the ones exploiting you?*Jas 2:6-7* You do right to love your neighbor as yourself rather than show favoritism.*Jas 2:8-9* If you break one law, then you break them all.*Jas 2:10-11* Seek the Father's approval. Don't be a people-pleaser.*Gal 1:10* Just because others receive honor without helping you share the good news should make no difference to you. It'll all come out in the end.*Gal 2:6* Teach without partiality or favoritism. Father and Son are watching you.*1Ti 5:21*

The seven angels began to pour out the seven golden bowls of the Father's fury on the earth. The first left festering sores on the people who had taken the oppressor's mark and honored its image. The second poured out blood like that of a dead person killing everything in the sea. The third poured out just judgments on the waters until they became blood.*Rev 16:2-7* The fourth pour made the sun scorch and sear the people with intense heat as they cursed the Father, but they still would not honor him.*Rev 16:8-9* The fifth pour plunged the first great oppressor's rule into darkness so that the people were in agony and again cursed the Father, but they still refused to give up what they were doing.*Rev 16:10-11* The sixth pour dried up great rivers.*Rev 16:12* The oppressors, though, just poured out their own awful spirits, preparing for final battle.*Rev 16:13-16* Finally, the seventh pour brought a loud voice saying it was over.*Rev 16:17* A tremendous earthquake collapsed the earth's cities.*Rev 16:18-19* Every natural feature disappeared, while huge hailstones weighing one hundred pounds each fell on the people.*Rev 16:18-21*

> **Discern and hold to truth.** Learn from sound, not unsound, teaching.*2Ti 2:2* Hold to sound teaching, rejecting the unsound. The Spirit helps you distinguish.*2Ti 1:13-14* Remember teaching. Remember as taught.*1Co 11:2* Remember what you learned.*2Th 2:5* Don't let hard, weighty, and forceful teaching frighten you.*2Co 10:9-10* The Father shares special visions and revelations.*2Co 12:1* The Father shares some things that others cannot even express.*2Co 12:4* Do nothing against the truth but everything for the truth.*2Co 13:8* Stick entirely to the good news.*2Pe 1:19* Know the Father's will.*Eph 5:17* Forget corrupt, worldly teaching.*Eph 4:22* Let the good news correct your old thinking.*Eph 4:23-24* Study it carefully and earnestly.*Php 2:12-13* Listen to the Father's warnings.*Heb 12:25* Go beyond the simple stuff.*Heb 6:1-2* Reach maturity.*Heb 6:3* Stop thinking like children.*1Co 14:20* Grow up.*1Pe 2:2-3* Stick with truth.*1Ti 4:6* Accept hard teaching.*1Co 3:2* Don't just go for the easy stuff.*Heb 5:13* Train yourself to distinguish right from wrong.*Heb 5:14* Learn of spiritual things, not just material things.*Jn 3:10-12*

One of the seven celestial beings with the seven bowls then told John that he was seeing the destruction not only of the great oppressor released for a time from hell but also of false and wicked religion that aligns itself with the world rather than the Father.*Rev 17:1-2* This false religion glitters even while obviously carnal, obviously corrupt, mixed as it is with the world's broken ways, in which people too gladly take part.*Rev 17:3-4* This false religion had destroyed many of the Father's closest followers, those who had relied most heavily on the Son.*Rev 17:5-6* John hadn't expected this vision. But the celestial being explained that the first great oppressor would return briefly to rally the few remaining people who had not followed the Son.*Rev 17:7-8* The great oppressor had already lost most of the oppressor's leaders. The few still remaining would soon also fall.*Rev 17:9-11* The remaining leaders of the people will give the great oppressor one last shot for the briefest period, warring against the Son. But the Son will quickly win, and with the win will come his called, chosen, and faithful followers.*Rev 17:12-14* Multitudes will follow from every people, nation, and language.*Rev 17:15* The great oppressor will turn inward, devouring false religion, so that the Father accomplishes his full purpose.*Rev 17:16-17* That false religion will have ruled the earth's leaders.*Rev 17:18*

> ***Stay free like the Son made you free.*** Wrongdoing ties you down.*Jn 8:34* You lose your place when you do wrong.*Jn 8:35* Stay free, like the Father promised you. Don't make yourself a slave to wrongdoing, a slave to your desires.*Gal 4:22-23* If you slave to your desires, then law will lock you up. If instead you pursue the Son, then you stay free of the law.*Gal 4:24-28* Wrongdoers make it hard for those who rely on the Son.*Gal 4:29* To live forever, stay free.*Gal 4:30-31* The good news replaced enslaving principles.*Gal 4:8* Don't turn back to those miserable enslaving principles, like observing special days, seasons, and years.*Gal 4:9-10* Wrongdoers promise you freedom but slave to their wrongs.*1Pe 2:19* Get ahold of yourself. Don't let your body boss you around.*1Co 9:27* You get nothing from pursuing your desires, nothing but death.*Ro 6:21-22* The Son freed you. Stick with him rather than give up and give in again.*Gal 5:1* Death's fear enslaves those who don't rely on the Son.*Heb 2:15* You are free. But choose to help others become free.*1Co 9:19* You may have to let others go their own way until they come back free.*Phm 15-16* Submit to the Father, and he will free you for living forever.*Ro 6:21-22* When the Son died, your enslavement died with him. You are free now.*Ro 6:6-7*

Victory

Another celestial being with great authority then illuminated the earth with his splendor. The being said grandly that everything claiming to be true but that had mixed with falsehood had finally fallen into complete corruption.*Rev 18:1-2* Many had joined in that corruption, growing rich with excessive luxuries.*Rev 18:3* A messenger had warned them against doing so, but they had done it anyway, and now they had paid for it.*Rev 18:4-5* The Father was giving back double in torment what they had once consumed in ill-gained luxury.*Rev 18:6-7* Plagues, famine, and death had overtaken them, the Father judging them exactly as he should.*Rev 18:8* The earth's dictators would no longer be able to sell their luxury cargoes including slaves to make them rich while enslaving and destroying the people.*Rev 18:9-19* The Son's followers will rejoice because the Father judged with the judgment that the oppressor imposed on others.*Rev 18:20*

> ***Show gratitude.*** Thank the Father for his indescribable gift.*2Co 9:15* Thank the Father that you join him.*Heb 12:28-29* Thank the Father for happiness in the confidence of others.*1Th 3:9* Thank the Father for a clear conscience.*2Ti 1:3* Thank the Father for those who rely on the Son.*1Co 1:4* Thank the Father for the confidence of followers all over the world.*Ro 1:8* Thank the Father continually for

his word.*1Th 2:13* Always thank the Father for everything.*Eph 5:19-20* Thank the Father in all circumstances.*1Th 5:18* Thank the Father through the Son.*Col 3:17* Give joyful thanks to the Father for sharing his place.*Col 1:12* Sing to the Father in gratitude.*Col 3:16* Thank the Father for others who rely on the Son.*1Th 1:2* Always thank the Father for brothers and sisters.*2Th 2:13* Always thank the Father for growing confidence and love among the Son's followers.*2Th 1:3* Always thank the Father for others relying on the Son.*Col 1:3-4* Thank the Son that lets you teach.*1Ti 1:12* Give thanks for all people.*1Ti 2:1-2* Be thankful in place of coarse talk.*Eph 5:4* Receive everything with thanksgiving.*1Ti 4:4*

Then a mighty celestial being threw a boulder into the sea, washing away forever everything corrupt on earth.*Rev 18:21-24* The multitude of the Son's followers roared over the destruction, giving the Father full honor for his just judgment condemning the great oppressor and avenging the Son's followers.*Rev 19:1-3* Celestial beings and leaders rejoiced.*Rev 19:4* The multitude shouted for the Father's reign, rejoicing that the Son had finally joined his followers.*Rev 19:6-8* The celestial being told John to write and share this description to encourage the Son's followers.*Rev 19:9* John fell at the being's feet in honor, but the being told John not to do so because he was a fellow servant with John and the other brothers and sisters who follow the Son. John should instead honor the Spirit that showed him the Son's victory.*Rev 19:10*

Endure with the Son. No one and nothing can separate you from the Son's love, even the worst trials.*Ro 8:35-36* You can overcome anything with the Son's help.*Ro 8:37* Absolutely nothing can separate you from the Father's love shown in his Son.*Ro 8:38-39* Your suffering is so much less than what's coming for you.*Ro 8:18* Be happy to suffer with the Son.*1Pe 4:12* Offenses you take for the Son reward you.*1Pe 4:14* Don't suffer for wrongs. Suffer for the Son so that you can be glad that others know you rely on him.*1Pe 4:15-16* The Father will fix everything after you suffer a little bit.*1Pe 5:10* Others suffer for the good news, too. Be with them.*2Ti 1:8* Suffer with others who suffer for the Son.*2Ti 2:3* Endure it all, and the reward of the Son's rescue will be yours. You will live with him forever.*2Ti 2:10* Endure with the Son, reign with the Son. How about that?*2Ti 2:12* Stand with the Son, and you'll receive the Son's reward.*Lk 22:28-30*

John next saw the way to the Father's place standing open to a white horse on which the faithful and true Son rode.*Rev 19:11* The Son's eyes blazed like fire and his head bore many crowns. The Son had a name no one but he knows, although you know him as the Father's Word. He had dipped his robe in blood.*Rev 19:12-13* The Father's armies followed the Son, the soldiers also riding white horses and dressed in fine white linen.*Rev 19:14* The Son spoke words that would instantly strike down every resistance.*Rev 19:15* The Son's robe and thigh bore the words King of kings and Lord of lords.*Rev 19:16* A celestial being called out to scavenger birds to gather for the Father's great supper, the scavengers to eat the flesh of the dead world's awful dictators and all corrupt people.*Rev 19:17-18* The Son and his army then captured the great oppressor and his spokesperson, throwing them alive into a lake of burning sulphur and killing the rest of the oppressor's army with the words coming from the Son's mouth. Scavenger birds gorged themselves on the opposition's dead flesh.*Rev 19:19-21*

A celestial being then locked and chained the great oppressor in hell for a thousand years.*Rev 20:1-2* The oppressor would remain there so as not to deceive the earth's people again, although after the thousand years, the oppressor would be free again for a short time.*Rev 20:3* A first restoration then occurred in which those who had lost their lives for the Son came back to life to enjoy great prosperity on earth. The rest of the dead did not come back to life until after the thousand years.*Rev 20:4-6* When the thousand years ends, the great oppressor will go loose to once again deceive and gather opposition for battle. The opposition will surround the Father's people with a huge army.*Rev 20:7-9* But fire will descend to devour the opposition, throwing the great oppressor into the fiery lake where the other oppressors had already gone and where they suffer continuously forever.*Rev 20:10* Then the remaining dead will rise to face the Father who will judge them justly.*Rev 20:11-12* Everyone who died will face the Father's judgment.*Rev 20:13* Then death, hell, and anyone who did not follow the Son will get thrown into the fiery lake.*Rev 20:14-15*

> **Yes, you do get something out of it.** When you rely on the Son, you change for the better. You are more loving, completely loving. And no more judgment.*1Jn 4:17* When you love, you don't have to worry about the Father punishing you. No more guilt.*1Jn 4:18* Relying on the Son without having seen him makes you both loving *and* rescued.*1Pe 1:8-9* You're in, no longer a lonely, fearful outsider.*Eph 2:13* You start to live as you should.*Col 2:10* You also start to see what's right and what's wrong, no longer confused about it.*Ro 1:17* The Father knows your secrets, so why worry about it any longer?*Ro 2:16* You also get more influential. And you have conviction.*1Th 1:5* No one can beat you up anymore.*1Th 3:8* And you don't succumb to the mess going on around you.*Gal 1:4* No punishment for you, when everyone else is getting their due punishment.

> You get perfect peace, they get endless suffering.*2Th 1:8-10* You receive what the Son received, his Father's *everything*.*2Th 2:14* Most of all, you get to honor the Father, which is better than anything. Don't you want to root for once for a winner?*1Ti 1:11*

New

John then saw the Father's new place, both above and on the earth. The old had passed away.*Rev 21:1* The new capitol holy city descended to the earth, ready for the Son as a spectacular place for him to join his followers.*Rev 21:2* The Father said to look at his residence now among his people, where he will be with them and be theirs to honor and obey. The Father will let no tear fall, keeping all sadness away.*Rev 21:3-4* Death, mourning, crying, and pain will be absent, *gone*, all old things having passed away.*Rev 21:4* The Father said he is making everything new. He commanded his words recorded for you to read and rely on, for he has accomplished it already in his own command.*Rev 21:5-6* The Father said that he is the beginning and end, everything from start to finish. The Father satisfies you as your life spring. You have won, you who are his children.*Rev 21:6-7* The new place will be peaceful, trustworthy, and sound because the Father has destroyed the cowardly, vile, murderers, sexually immoral, liars, magicians, and those who refuse to honor him and his Son.*Rev 21:8*

> ***You'll receive rich reward.*** The Father has a permanent reward for you.*1Pe 1:4* Some have already received their reward for confidence in the Father.*Ro 4:13* Confidence in the Father invokes reward.*Ro 4:14-15* The poor who are rich for the Father receive his reward.*Jas 2:5* Children inherit. Employees do not.*Gal 4:30-31* Wrongdoing destroys your reward.*Gal 5:19-21* Wrongdoers receive no reward. The Father leaves them out in the cold.*1Co 6:9-10* Get your reward by repaying evil with good.*1Pe 3:9* Imitate those who through confidence and patience get the reward.*Heb 6:12* Do not give away your inheritance for nothing.*Heb 12:17* Thank the Father for your reward.*Col 1:12* You'll get a reward for the least service that you do for someone who relies on the Son.*Mk 9:41* The Father's words build you up for a reward.*Acts 20:32* You receive your rich reward because of the Son's complete sacrifice.*Heb 9:23* Suffer with the Son, reward with the Son.*Ro 8:16-17* The Son makes your reward possible.*Heb 9:15* The Father sends ministering spirits to help you if you rely on the Son.*Heb 1:14* Do-gooders receive their reward.*Eph 5:5* Those who put other things before the Father get no reward.*Eph 5:5* You'll get

Spiritspeak

your reward if you work hard._{2Ti 2:6} You'll get a reward for sound earthly work, as working for the Son._{Col 3:24} The Son will ensure your reward when he returns._{Matt 25:34}

One of the seven messengers told John to come see the Son's new residence. John could see the new capitol holy city descending._{Rev 21:9-10} The Son had said that his new residence would appear in just that way._{Rev 3:12} The city shone with the Father's honor, clear as crystal. The city had a great wall with gates and a celestial keeper at each gate. The foundations had the Son's leading student's names on them._{Rev 21:11-14} The messenger showed John how huge the city was, about 1,400 miles long, wide, and high. Its jasper wall was 200 feet thick, and everything else was glass-pure gold._{Rev 21:15-18} The foundations were each of a different precious stone, the gates each a single enormous pearl, and the streets of transparent gold._{Rev 21:19-21} The city didn't need a place of honor because the presence of Father and Son was constant, all around._{Rev 21:22} The city also needed no lights because the presence of Father and Son lit the city, with everyone relying on their light._{Rev 21:23-24} The city's gates never shut because no night exists._{Rev 21:25} The city contained everything of any true honor._{Rev 21:24, 26} Only those with the Son's approval entered._{Rev 21:27} Life water flowed from the place where Father and Son ruled, down the city's great street. Fruit trees grew along the river, feeding and healing everyone._{Rev 22:1-2} Father and Son rule from the city, everyone serving them, while looking on the Son._{Rev 22:3}

Hold on to the good news. All you need do is hold on to the good news. The Father's not taking it away from you._{Heb 10:23} The Father has kept every promise. No one has any argument._{Heb 6:13-16} The Father's not going to change the terms. He has one thing in mind, which is your rescue._{Heb 6:17} The Father keeps promises to show that you can rely on him._{Heb 6:18} You were not born with it. You, too, like everyone else, had to come to the good news. But now you've got it, really *got* it._{Eph 2:12} The Father had the good news ready from the start: he was bringing his Son back to life._{Heb 13:20} No secrets anymore: you're in this good news together with everyone else, old-timers and newcomers. You've all got the same promise._{Eph 3:6} Yes, the Son started with the old-timers. He had to do so to keep his Father's promise to them. But you're still in if you want to be, old-timer or not._{Ro 15:8-9} Knowing the Father's keeping his word, maybe you should keep yours? Stop fooling around, and get on track._{2Co 7:1} Don't go through the motions. Mean it when you say you want to live in perfect peace forever._{Heb 4:1}

Eternity

That is how things will remain forever. The Son said that you would live forever with him but die without him, in his Father's anger.*Jn 3:36* The Son said that whoever does what he says will never die.*Jn 8:51* When an expert questioned the Son about how to live forever, the Son pointed him to the command to love the Father with all your heart, soul, strength, and mind, and to love your neighbor like yourself.*Lk 10:25-28* The Son said that doing what the Son says to do, as the Father commands, lets you live forever.*Jn 12:50* For once, believe what you see: the Son showed you immortality.*2Ti 1:10* The Father has honor and glory forever.*1Ti 1:17* You'd be like withered grass or fallen flowers without the Father's word, which lasts forever. Now you've heard it.*1Pe 1:24-25* When the Father brought the Son right back to life, he made you a promise that will never change.*Heb 13:20* Corruption leads to certain death. But when the Son died and came back to life, he wiped away corruption and replaced it with perfection, a perfection that lets you live forever, uncorrupted.*Ro 5:21*

> **Immortality is here.** You've now seen it's true: the Father gives life back after death.*Ro 4:17* Because the Father gave life right back to the Son, the Son cannot die again. Death has no effect on him.*Ro 6:9* The Son died once for all. He now lives forever with the Father.*Ro 6:10* The Son died for you so that you may live with him.*1Th 3:10* When you die relying on him, you live again with him.*2Ti 2:11* The Son died and returned to life so that he would have power over both the dead and living.*Ro 14:9* The Son destroyed death and brought immortality.*2Ti 1:10* The perishable put on the imperishable. The mortal became immortal. And the ancient writings had predicted it.*1Co 15:54* Death loses. Death doesn't hurt. All the corruption is gone, powerless to bring death.*1Co 15:55-56* The Father can take you even before you die, if he wishes.*Heb 11:5* People have long trusted that the Father can raise the dead.*Heb 11:19* Even long ago, confidence in the Father enabled some to die without fear and others to face death for talking up the Father.*Heb 11:37*

So use your mind. Look behind what you see because what you see is temporary. It keeps changing. But what you don't see lasts forever.*2Co 4:18* The Son's rule will last forever.*Heb 1:8* Everything will disappear, but Father and Son will remain.*Heb 1:11* The Father will change everything, but he will remain the same forever.*Heb 1:12* The rich who want to live forever won't do so from their earthly possessions or even from keeping all the rules. They need to pursue the Son, just like everyone else.*Matt 19:16-22, Mk 10:17-21, Lk 18:18-22* The Son separates those who will live with him forever from those who will not, who get nothing but punishment.*Matt 25:46* Everyone who relies on the Son will live forever.*Jn 3:14-15* The Father loved you so much that he let his own Son die so that you could rely on his Son, escape death, and live forever.*Jn 3:16* You cross over from death to living forever when you rely on the Son.*Jn 5:24* You won't find a magic potion by study. You'll live forever when you rely on the Son.*Jn 5:39-40* You have no other place to turn. The Son's words let you live forever.*Jn 6:67-69* Just rely on the Son, and he'll bring you back from death to life.*Jn 10:27-29* That was the whole plan. That's why his Father put him where he did, to give you life forever.*Jn 17:2* You live forever when you know Father and Son.*Jn 17:3*

> **The Son is truth—personified.** The Son came to show truth.*Jn 18:37* The wonders the Son did showed that what he said was true.*Jn 5:36* The Father said that the Son was exactly who and what he said he was.*Jn 5:37-38* The Father's Spirit carries truth, especially about the Son.*Jn 15:26* You, too, may as well speak truthfully about the Son.*Jn 15:27* What the Son says is true because the Father supports the Son. They both say it together, making it true.*Jn 8:13-18* You can rely on the good news as true. Eyewitnesses saw it and said so.*Jn 19:35* The records record only a few of the endless wonders that the Son did but enough for you to know that his good news is true.*Jn 20:30* No one could write down everything that the Son did. The writings would fill the universe.*Jn 21:24-25* The Spirit repeats what the Father and Son both said about what the Son would do and did, confirming its truth.*1Jn 5:6-9* You choose, but whoever relies on the Son accepts truth, while whoever does not rely on the Son makes his Father out to be a liar.*1Jn 5:10* The truth is that the Father gave us eternal life in his Son and only in his Son.*1Jn 5:11-13*

Destiny

You want to talk about your destiny? The Father wants everyone who relies on the Son to live forever. That's it. The Son will keep you alive.*Jn. 6:40* Just rely, and you'll have it.*Jn 6:47* Everyone who eats normal food dies. Anyone who eats from the Son's hand lives forever.*Jn 6:50-51* Loving what you have loses it. Seeking what you don't have gains it.*Jn 12:25* Your relying on the Son rather than yourself lets you live forever.*Tit 3:7* You get what the Father promised you, which is freedom from your corrupt state, now that the Son set you free.*Heb 9:15* The Son lets you live joyfully, knowing that you will live forever.*2Th 2:16-17* You live forever relying on the Son.*1Ti 1:16* What the Father told you through the Son let you have a new life that never dies.*1Pe 1:23* The Son took care of everything for you, making you good as new—forever.*Heb 10:14* So stick with it. Keep close to the Father. Trust the Son to keep you alive forever.*Jude 20-21* Fight the Son's good fight, and you'll get it, this living forever.*1Ti 6:12* He's grabbed hold of you. Grab hold of him, and you'll be with him forever.*2Ti 2:10* Just stick with it. Keep doing the right things, truly relying on the Son, and you'll live forever.*Ro 2:7*

> **Emulate your heroes.** Your spiritual heroes were still waiting for it and trusting when they died. The earth remained foreign and strange to them.*Heb 11:13* The world has not been worthy of your heroes.*Heb 11:38* Your heroes died before receiving what the Father promised because the Father planned something better. The Father makes them perfect together with you.*Heb 11:39-40* Heroes offered the Father better things.*Heb 11:4* One's offer pleased the Father so much that the Father didn't let him die.*Heb 11:5* The Father commends your heroes for their confidence.*Heb 11:2* One's trust led him to build an ark to save his family when warned.*Heb 11:7* Another's trust led him to assure good things for his children's future.*Heb 11:20* Another's confidence led him, when dying, to assure his grandsons while honoring the Father.*Heb 11:21* Another's trust led him to predict a great liberation from slavery.*Heb 11:22* Walls fell by another's confidence.*Heb 11:30* Another's confidence led her to welcome spies, saving her life.*Heb 11:31* Other heroes conquered lands, administered justice, gained the promise, avoided certain death, quenched flames, and escaped the sword, all through confident reliance on the Father. Their weakness became strength, routing enemies.*Heb 11:32-34* Show the confidence of your heroes. They were right.*Heb 13:7*

Shortcuts gain you nothing, only death. You get to live forever under the Son when you do what the Father says.*Ro 6:21-22* Competitors train to win. You should, too, and to win not just once but forever.*1Co 9:25* Living forever is worth this little trouble now.*2Co 4:17* Ask the Son, and he'll give you what you need to live forever.*Jn 4:4-10* It may not look like it to you now, but the Son can absolutely do it for you, fixing it all.*Jn 4:11-14* The little that you give up now gains you a fortune later, plus living forever with it.*Matt 19:27-29, Mk 10:28-30, Lk 18:28-30* So don't just go through the motions. Work at it as if your life depends on it because it *does*. The Son will see your work and give you the life you need.*Jn 6:26-27* Those who stick with it to the end will win a paradise life forever. You'll have your way then.*Rev 2:7, 11, 17, 26-28* You'll walk with the Son, who'll talk you up to everyone important.*Rev 3:4-5* You'll have it all when you have Father and Son.*Rev 3:12* To the Father, you'll be just like his Son.*Rev 3:21*

It's good news. Share it. Everyone will eventually hear the good news. Be a part of sharing it.*Mk13:10* When the Son does something great for you, let folks know, *please*? They'll appreciate it.*Mk 5:18-20* When people share the good news, others get excited about it.*Lk 16:16* Serve the good news, will you please?*Col 1:23* You should be happy to do so.*1Th 2:7-8* Tell the good news to those who don't hear it much. They need it.*1Th 2:16* Work at sharing the good news, really *work* at it.*1Th 3:2* You know that you're with the Son and he's with you when you're sharing the good news.*1Jn 4:13-14* The Father may be calling you to lead in sharing the good news.*Ro 1:1* Why have any shame over the good news when all it does is rescue people?*Ro 1:16* Just go tell it. Do it.*Ro 15:19* Better yet, tell the good news where others haven't. Do your own good work rather than rely on the good work of others. That way, you'll be part of more rescues.*Ro 15:20-21* The good news comes from very long ago, way before the ancient writings announced it. The Father always had it.*Ro 16:25-26* Look, it's simple: the Son died but came right back to life, not as some magic act but *for your rescue*.*1Co 15:3* Your one duty you owe the Father who made you is to tell the good news so that others may join in your rescue.*Ro 15:16* Don't add to it or take away from it. Just tell the good news as it is.*Rev 22:18-19*

Conclusion

The good news is more than that. It's the *best* news. Thank you for sharing it with me in fresh organization and form. The above interpretation intentionally omits some very significant words including Jesus, Christ, Lord, Savior, Messiah, and God, I hope without omitting those concepts. I didn't use other significant words like faith, grace, mercy, forgiveness, holy, righteousness, sanctification, baptism, redemption, and salvation, again I hope without missing those critically important meanings. The above interpretation omits the words disciple and apostle, and omits the names of many. Indeed, it omits the names and titles of kings, caesars, and other rulers, and high priests, priests, and council members, among others, I hope without unduly reducing their significance. I didn't even use national or religious identifiers like Israel, the Jews, the Gentiles, Syria, Babylon, and Egypt, I hope without unduly confusing their roles.

Wherever I found a term or phrase that we who are saturated in the faith take for granted, loaded with spiritual meaning, I tried to find roughly equivalent words that would make you think again of what the good news tells us. I have read the good news so often that I needed a freshening. Perhaps you have, too. Or you may not have read the good news much at all but may just have wished to avoid some of the words with which committed readers grow so comfortable—the same words that make the uncommitted reader grow so uncomfortable. May the Father show his usual willingness to look the other way at any offense my interpretation gives you or him. I trust the Son and Spirit to ask the Father to do so. I hope that you, too, trust the Son. He brought us very, very good news.

Abbreviations

Matthew	*Matt*	1 Timothy	*1Ti*
Mark	*Mk*	2 Timothy	*2Ti*
Luke	*Lk*	Titus	*Tit*
John	*Jn*	Philemon	*Phm*
Acts	*Acts*	Hebrews	*Heb*
Romans	*Ro*	James	*Jas*
1 Corinthians	*1Co*	1 Peter	*1Pe*
2 Corinthians	*2Co*	2 Peter	*2Pe*
Galatians	*Gal*	1 John	*1Jn*
Ephesians	*Eph*	2 John	*2Jn*
Philippians	*Php*	3 John	*3Jn*
Colossians	*Col*	Jude	*Jude*
1 Thessalonians	*1Th*	Revelation	*Rev*
2 Thessalonians	*2Th*		

Other Faith Books by Nelson Miller

Gospelspeak: The New Testament

Biblespeak: The Epistles

Following Jesus

Looking to Jesus

Answered Prayers

Secret Devotion

The Faithful Lawyer

Facing Death

Gospel Stories

www.ingramcontent.com/pod-product-compliance
Lightning Source LLC
Chambersburg PA
CBHW052210090526
44584CB00016BA/1891